LEADERING VISUALS TWO

LEADERING VISUALS TWO

Paradigm Shift to Peak Legacy

Lauren Holmes

Naturality.Net, LLC

Toronto

Copyright © 2010 by Lauren Holmes.

All rights reserved.

This publication may not be reproduced, stored in a retrieval system, or transmitted in whole or in part, in any form or by any means, electronic, mechanical, photocopying, recording, or otherwise, without the prior written permission of the copyright owner. For private use only.

Reproduction or translation of any part of this work beyond that permitted by Section 107 or 108 of the 1976 United States Copyright Act without the permission of the copyright owner is unlawful. Brief quotations embodied in critical articles and reviews are permitted.

LEADERING and FRONTIERING are trademarks owned by Lauren Holmes. All rights reserved.

Requests for permission or further information should be addressed to Permissions, Leadering, 123 Queen Street West, Box 164, Toronto, ON, Canada or emailed to info@leadering.com.

Leadering Education:
    Leadering.com   Leadering™ Expertise Development

Leadering Application:
    Frontiering.com   Leadering™ Legacy-Making Services and Products

FIRST EDITION

Cover Image © iLexx

Library of Congress in Publication Data

Holmes, Lauren
    Leadering Visuals One

1. Success   2. Personal Development   3. Professional Development   4. Leadership   5. Performance   6. Entrepreneurial Development   7. Self-Help   I. Holmes, Lauren   II. Title

ISBN: 978-0-9711981-3-5

Manufactured in the United States of America by Naturality.Net, LLC

Dedicated to those who commit their unique creative expression to advancing our world

The person who knows one thing and does it better than anyone else, even if it only be the art of raising lentils, receives the crown he merits. If he raises all his energy to that end, he is a benefactor of mankind and is rewarded as such. — Og Mandino

It is those who concentrate on but one thing at a time who advance in this world. The great man or woman is the one who never steps outside his or her specialty or foolishly dissipates his or her individuality. — Og Mandino

I am here for a purpose and that purpose is to grow into a mountain, not to shrink to a grain of sand. Henceforth will I apply ALL my efforts to become the highest mountain of all and I will strain my potential until it cries for mercy. — Og Mandino

LEADERING VISUALS TWO
Paradigm Shift to Peak Legacy

LEADERING SUPPORT   info@leadering.com

EDUCATION: **Leadering.com**   Leadering™ Expertise Development

Educational support for such things as speeding and integrating the paradigm shift, Leadering's paradigm personalization exercises, identifying client strategies for peak legacy, growth, and re-centring to core strength, action-learning experimentation, and breaking through frontiering™ and adaptivity challenges.

APPLICATION: **Frontiering.com**   Leadering Legacy-Making Services and Products

On your behalf, multi-disciplinary experts will design, launch, and accelerate companies, philanthropic organizations, careers, and fields of study or invention personalized in Leadering terms for your peak legacy until you feel you comfortable taking over. Alternatively, we can support you in launching your own structure(s) through which to achieve your peak legacy.

RECRUITMENT: **Become a Leadering Services Provider**

If you wish to provide products and services through either Leadering.com or Frontiering.com you are invited to email the following to info@leadering.com: your proposed offerings, your credentials, and a brief summary of your personal peak legacy findings from Leadering's flow maximization exercises (*Leadering Visuals Two*, recordings 10-18).

Leadering™ instills an integrated system of meta-skills, dynamics, drives, reflexes, instincts, identities, ways of operating, and evolved states of being and consciousness shared by adept leaders, entrepreneurs, innovators, and achievers. This system has been formulated into a powerful paradigm so that it can be assimilated through a single paradigm shift. The shift spans 25 recordings and a multitude of original visuals and exercises. The magnitude and speed of transformation is unprecedented.

Nature has a plethora of mechanisms and forces dedicated to *maximizing* and *synchronizing human systems* that are already advancing our world. Leadering™ empowers one to adapt to and harness these existing powers and processes inside and outside of us to achieve one's greatest legacy, one's greatest contribution to that advance.

As such, leaving your most impactful lifetime footprint - your peak legacy - requires *frontiering*™ *to* penetrate new territory, and *creation* to bring 'the new' into existence. All of these elements define the essence and dynamics of leadership, even if leading is not your goal. Hence the name, '*Leadering*™'.

LEADERING™ CULTIVATES NEW FUNCTIONALITY IN HUMAN SYSTEMS:
individuals - companies - countries - civilizations

- **Mental agility and thinking modes** such as systems, conceptual, abstract, deductive, inductive, relational, and big-picture thinking
  (expanded and unity consciousness)

- **Frontiering**™ **new territory**: leading, entrepreneuring, pioneering, innovating, creating, adapting, resolving ambiguity, learning agility, model development / application, pattern / trend recognition, environmental scanning, problem reframing, and a propensity for unfounded knowing, AHA! experiences, creative inspirations, and coincidences

- **Collaboration and cooperativeness:**
  - multi-system mode of operation
  - mass maximization, mass transformation, mass synchronization
  - co-evolving, co-creating, integrating, adapting, synergizing, partnering, and clustering
  - the thinking modes listed above, especially systems, relational, conceptual, and big-picture thinking
  - contributions to humanity's evolutionary goals as a byproduct of meeting one's own goals.

- **Performance:** as a result of the above. As well, Leadering™ maximizes us in our peak-performing, peak-growth, talent-based, *flow* state

LEADERING VISUALS TWO
Paradigm Shift to Peak Legacy

LEADERING BOOK INDEX

1. GETTING STARTED

2. PRE- AND POST-PROGRAM ASSESSMENT

3. THE PROGRAM

4. THE PARADIGM

5. THE PARADIGM SHIFT PROCESS

6. FIFTEEN PARADIGM LEADER DRIVES
   to maximize human systems for goal achievement

7. PERSONALIZING THE PARADIGM - EXERCISES I
   I FLOW maximization exercises

8. PERSONALIZING THE PARADIGM - EXERCISES II
   II BELIEF maximization exercises

9. COMPLETING THE PARADIGM SHIFT

10. OPERATIONALIZING THE PARADIGM

11. LEADERING: A POWER TOOL FOR LEADERS or SYSTEM MAXIMIZERS

12. THE USER'S GUIDE

13. THE DEVELOPMENT OF LEADERING

LEADERING VISUALS INDEX

LEADERING RECORDING TITLE and DESCRIPTION	MINUTES	FIGURES	PAGE NO.
1 GETTING STARTED			Visuals One
2 PRE- AND POST-PROGRAM ASSESSMENT			Visuals One
3 THE LEADERING™ PROGRAM			
1. Leadering™ Program Overview	17	3	
THE MULTI-RECORDING PARADIGM SHIFT NOW BEGINS			Visuals One
4 THE LEADERING™ PARADIGM			
2. Leadering™ Paradigm Overview	43	1	
3. *Leadering frequency workout gym™*	5		
4. Leadering™ Paradigm Components	38	6	
5 THE PARADIGM SHIFT PROCESS			Visuals One
5. Leadering™ Paradigm Shift	19	1	
6. Leadering™ Quantum Leap Overview	16	4	
7. Leadering™ Quantum Leap Process	50	10	
8. The Quantum Leap to Quantum Leap Expert	74	6	
6 FIFTEEN PARADIGM LEADER DRIVES **to maximize human systems for goal achievement** Adept leaders and system maximizers operate as extensions of nature's system's maximization process The 15 dynamics of the Leadering™ systems maximization toolkit are presented in 1 presentation that has been broken into 8 parts. The same 21 figures are shared by each of these 8 recordings:			Visuals One
9. 15 Leader Drives			
9.1 Introduction	23	Same 21	
9.2 Systems mindset: congruence, systems-based expanded consciousness	22	Same 21	Visuals One
9.3 Advancement mechanics: quantum leap templating, self-organizing, emergence	22	Same 21	
9.4 Advancement directions: knowledge-pursuit	16	Same 21	
9.5 Advancement directions: adaptation, evolution	17	Same 21	
9.6 Leader drives quantum leap preparation and initiation, plus the part that the frontier-pursuit drive, creation / creativity-pursuit drives play in all the dynamics	22	Same 21	Visuals One
9.7 Co-evolution, talent-based flow, flow-to-flow plus additional information for the frontier-pursuit drive and the creation / creativity-pursuit drives	55	Same 21	Visuals One
9.8 Quantum leap to operating with the 15 leader drives as a way of life. Repeated post-paradigm-shift as recording 24: Driving a Multi-System Paradigm	57	Same 21	Visuals One

LEADERING RECORDING TITLE and DESCRIPTION	MINUTES	FIGURES	PAGE NO.

7 PERSONALIZING THE LEADERING™ PARADIGM
INSTRUCTIONS:
I FLOW MAXIMIZATION EXERCISES
II BELIEF MAXIMIZATION EXERCISES
   Completing the Paradigm Shift
   Operationalizing the Paradigm

I FLOW MAXIMIZATION EXERCISES

These exercises may be started any time after the Paradigm Shift Launch but cannot be completed before completing 6. The *Fifteen Paradigm Leader Drives*. Take advantage of your altered state of more expanded functionality resulting from each audio to aerial view your system and your life as a system to more accurately complete the *Paradigm Personalization Exercises* (Sections 7 and 8).
(a) This will increase your precision and power when driving the Leadering™ paradigm.
(b) Improving your accuracy with these core determination exercises for your own system will train you to more accurately apply the same insights to other human systems such as individuals, organizations, families, communities, countries, and all of human civilization in order to maximize them for goal achievement.

	MINUTES	FIGURES	PAGE NO.

10. Big-Picture positioning for developing your 5 maximizing formulas
ADVANCING YOUR SYSTEM
    Formula 1: Talent-based lifetime development formula
    Formula 2: Greatest lifetime level of talent-based operation as an individual
ADVANCING YOUR SYSTEM BY ADVANCING OTHER HUMAN SYSTEMS
    Formula 3: Talent-based leadership formula
    Formula 4: Talent-based leadership development formula
    Formula 5: Greatest life-time level of talent-based operation as a leader or *systems maximizer*
	22	15	3

11. Introduction to the 5 Leadering™ Maximizing formulas	18	12	19
12. Advice for the core determination exercises for identifying one's 5 maximizing formulas for the Leadering™ paradigm	11	4	33
13. Life Themes Exercises	48	5	39
14. Key-Talent System-Application Exercise	36	28	45
15. Growth built into the Leadering™ paradigm	23	19	75
16. Key Talents Exercises	21	17	95
17. 5-Formula Exercise Preparation	51	18	115

LEADERING VISUALS INDEX

LEADERING RECORDING TITLE and DESCRIPTION	MINUTES	FIGURES	PAGE NO.
18. Determining your 5 Formulas for maximizing in the Leadering™ paradigm	34	18	135
Exercises, notes, and questions to assist you in determining each of your 5 formulas for maximizing within the Leadering™ paradigm:			
Formula 1: 14 figures	0	14	155
Formula 2: 8 figures	0	8	171
Formula 3: 17 figures	0	17	181
Formula 4: 18 figures	0	18	199
Formula 5: 13 figures	0	13	219

8 PERSONALIZING THE PARADIGM

II BELIEF MAXIMIZATION EXERCISES to promote Flow Maximization

These exercises may be started any time after the Paradigm Shift Launch but cannot be completed before completing the Paradigm-Based Leadership segment			Visuals One
19. Belief Maximization Introduction: Identity Quantum leaps:	108	41	Visuals One

9 COMPLETING THE PARADIGM SHIFT

20. Natural Identity quantum leaps (immutable beliefs):	50	39	
Subset: Growth or expansion identity quantum leaps			
Completing the Paradigm Shift:			
Natural identity quantum leaps (immutable beliefs)			Visuals One
Operationalizing the Paradigm:			
Growth or expansion identity quantum leaps			
The transition from completing the paradigm shift to operating in the paradigm is made within this recording			

10 OPERATIONALIZING THE PARADIGM

21. Goal-driven Identity quantum leaps (changeable beliefs):	35	20	Visuals One
Subset: Flow-driven identity quantum leaps			
Subset: Corporate identity quantum Leaps			
22. Belief Clearing with Identity quantum leaps	18	9	
23. Multi-System Identity quantum leaps	41	23	
Leadering™ toolkit identity quantum leaps			
Subset: Leadering™ meta-competency identity quantum leaps			Visuals One
Quantum leaps to goal 'states of being' rather than goal 'states':			
Subset: Assimilated Expert Identity quantum leaps			
Subset: Projected Expert Identity quantum leaps			

LEADERING VISUALS INDEX

LEADERING RECORDING TITLE and DESCRIPTION	MINUTES	FIGURES	PAGE NO.
24. Driving a Multi-System Paradigm (Repeat of 9h post-shift)	57	1	
OPERATING THE LEADERING™ PARADIGM: Action-Learning Experimentation Action-learning experimentation with the Leadering™ paradigm is encouraged for the rest of your life to accelerate the advancement of your functionality and achievement.			Visuals One
11 Leadering - A POWER TOOL FOR LEADERS or SYSTEM MAXIMIZERS			Visuals One
25. Capitalizing on human systems for goal achievement	24	10	
12 THE LEADERING™ USERS GUIDE			
1. Powering your paradigm shift	14	0	
2. Only need to be a paradigm driver not a mechanic	8	0	
3. Timing for progressing through the program	5	0	
4. Overwhelm is a Leadering™ tool for stretching you to new meta-competencies	3	0	Visuals One
5. Falling asleep during the recordings: What is really going on?	4	0	
6. Visuals: their importance	3	0	
7. Personalization Exercises Tips	1	0	
8. Leadering™ Program Support	4	0	
9. Arguments for beliefs create reality concept	8	0	
10. Examples of cascading quantum leaps incited by a quantum leap to a belief-created reality. The strengthening of the beliefs and belief engineering capabilities to create and develop leaders.	13	0	Visuals One
11. How Leadering™ Works	5	0	
12. The Leadering™ frequency workout gym	5	0	

We would value your feedback

Send comments, experiences, or suggestions to info@leadering.com

RECORDINGS 10-18

LEADERING™ VISUALS TWO
Paradigm Shift to Peak Legacy

7 PERSONALIZING THE LEADERING™ PARADIGM

    I FLOW MAXIMIZATION EXERCISES
   II BELIEF MAXIMIZATION EXERCISES
       Completing the Paradigm Shift
       Operationalizing the Paradigm

Instructions:

The paradigm personalization exercises may be started any time after the quantum leap to quantum leap expert, the first quantum leap in the program. Within the progression of the recordings to progressively catalyze the paradigm shift, these audios have actually been recorded to follow the 8 paradigm-based leadership audios above. However, using the Leadering™ frequency workout gym™ built into each recording will put you into a better frequency and expansion of perspective for doing the exercises than trying to do them in your normal consciousness. Therefore, doing these exercises while going through the paradigm-based leadership audios above could create a good partnership for some.

You will need to have completed the exercise under FLOW MAXIMIZATION before proceeding to the BELIEF MAXIMIZATION segment since belief maximization is designed to support flow maximization which relates to capitalizing on forces attempting to maximize your system.

RECORDINGS 10-18

Leadering's breakthrough exercises provide personalized lifetime strategies which capitalize on your strengths, and the natural growth mechanisms and directions pre-wired into your system.

7 PERSONALIZING THE LEADERING™ PARADIGM

I FLOW MAXIMIZATION EXERCISES: Capitalizing on the flow

These exercises may be started any time after the Paradigm Shift Launch but cannot be completed before completing the Paradigm-Based Leadership segment

The first 3 recordings are really one presentation that has been split out for ease of use. All 3 prepare you for doing the core determination and strategy development exercises that follow

10. Big-Picture positioning for developing your 5 maximizing formulas
    22 minutes   15 figures
    ADVANCING YOUR SYSTEM
       Formula 1: Talent-based lifetime development formula
       Formula 2: Greatest lifetime level of talent-based operation as an individual
    ADVANCING YOUR SYSTEM BY ADVANCING OTHER HUMAN SYSTEMS
       Formula 3: Talent-based leadership formula
       Formula 4: Talent-based leadership development formula
       Formula 5: Greatest life-time level of talent-based operation as a leader or systems maximizer
11. Introduction to the 5 Leadering™ maximizing formulas
    18 minutes   12 figures
12. Advice for the core determination exercises for identifying one's 5 operating formulas for the Leadering™ paradigm   11 minutes   4 figures
13. Life Themes Exercises   48 minutes   5 figures
14. System Categories Exercises   36 minutes   28 figures
15. Growth built into the Leadering™ paradigm   23 minutes   19 figures
16. Key Talents Exercises   21 minutes   17 figures
17. Your 5 personalized Formulas for operating in the Leadering™ paradigm: intro   51 minutes   19 figures
18. 5 Formulas Specifics - Exercises for determining each of your 5 formulas for maximizing within the Leadering™ paradigm   34 minutes   18 figures

       Formula 1: 14 figures   Formula 3: 17 figures   Formula 5: 13 figures
       Formula 2:   8 figures   Formula 4: 18 figures

RECORDING 10

Leadering merges man's machinery with nature's to paradigm shift people to the extraordinary

7 PERSONALIZING THE LEADERING™ PARADIGM

I FLOW MAXIMIZATION EXERCISES

10. **Big-Picture positioning for developing your 5 talent-based operating formulas or strategies for the Leadering™ paradigm:**   22 minutes   15 figures
    This review is especially useful for those starting the exercises before or while listening to the paradigm-based leadership recordings when all of this material has been presented.

    This recording is a high-level look at the Leadering™ paradigm shift and operating in the Leadering™ paradigm in order to ready participants for developing their personalized formulas and strategies for operating in the paradigm.

    This recording continues the technique in Leadering™ for looking big picture, then at some detailed aspect of the paradigm, and then looking big picture again to understand where it fits into the totality.

    Also this is part of the process of bringing all of the paradigm elements contributing to the new information, in this case the 5 formulas, to the fore-front of your thinking so you can not only understand the new concept better but integrate all sides relevant to the issue.

    In addition, as the paradigm shift progresses, you are not the same person with the same belief template who first looked at this information. This is an opportunity to recombine information and consolidate it with the current state of advancement of your belief template, your core, and your assimilation of the Leadering™ paradigm.

    Leadering™ is a transformative experience not course merely providing information. It is not the consumption of information that can cause the paradigm shift. Adding information to your existing machinery will not achieve a paradigm shift of this magnitude.

    Rather, the paradigm shift is achieved by the integration of that information into the information structure of your system in order for a synergy to create a whole which is greater than the sum of its parts. In this way, Leadering™ uses natural levers to install new replacement machinery and then add new information to maximize it.

COMPONENTS OF THE INTEGRATED TARGET PARADIGM - 1

System Organization:
a congruence dynamic
a self-organizing dynamic
a systems-based dynamic
a templating dynamic
an emergence dynamic
 	
Multi-System Organization:
an adaptation dynamic
a co-evolution dynamic
an expanding
    consciousness dynamic
a flow-within-flow dynamic
    (subsystems achieve
    congruence with their
    contextual system
 	
Improved Performance and Functionality:
a quantum leap dynamic
a frontier-pursuit dynamic
a creation/creativity dynamic
a flow dynamic
an evolution dynamic
a knowledge-pursuit dynamic
	Drives to
	   internal congruence
	   external congruence
	
	flow state
	   (our peak-performance
	   / peak-evolution state
	   of int/ext congruence)
	naturality
	   (internal congruence)
	expanded natural core
	   (growth congruence)
	resonance
	   (frequency congruence)
	meaning
	positive emotions
	adapt
	learn
	new knowledge
	emergence
	co-evolve
	frontiering™
	creativity/creation
	achievement
	self-expression
		Systems-Based Approach
		systems thinking, systems-based operation, systems-based emotional intelligence, belief system management, quantum leaping, expanded consciousness, conceptual skills, templating
		
		Continuous Development
		accelerating growth, co-evolution, re-optimization, agility, fluidity, expanding self-expression, learning/adaptation agility, belief upgrading, expanding consciousness
		
		Cognitive Capabilities
		learning agility, knowing, conceptual skills, abstract thinking, expanding consciousness, internally referenced, expanding self-expression and self-awareness, emotional intelligence, deductive reasoning, pattern recognition
		
		Mastering the Unknown
		frontiering™, creating, innovating, systems thinking, informationless decision-making, abstract thinking, conceptual skills, expanded consciousness
		
		Performance Improvement
		talent-based flow and other peak performance states, accelerated implementation, advancement by nonlinear quantum leaps, systems thinking, systems-based operation, expanding self-expression, learning/adaptation agility

© 2006 Lauren Holmes

COMPONENTS OF THE INTEGRATED TARGET PARADIGM - 2

KEY THEMES TRACKED FOR HARNESSING THE FLOW OF SYSTEMS TO CONGRUENCE

unpaid work theme, knowledge-pursuit theme, frontier-pursuit theme, creativity-pursuit theme, learning-pursuit theme, meaning-pursuit theme, talent-based flow state events theme, resonance events theme, positive emotion events theme, spontaneous knowledge events theme, creative invention events theme, spontaneous creativity events theme, theme of talent-based projects which had many coincidences and flow events.

HIGHLIGHTS OF THE TARGET PARADIGM

Advancing by wholes: Promotes: systems-based thinking and operation; a quantum leap process; template-based change management; coincidences; spontaneous knowledge; spontaneous creativity; spontaneous self-organization. Used to adapt and enhance human systems such as a leader, a follower, an organizational system, a market system, or leadership development.

Re-optimization, adaptation, co-evolution: All paradigm dynamics and drives serve these never-ending goals synergistically and opportunistically.

Flow-within-flow: Paradigm is powered by the flow of systems to congruence internally and externally.

Talent-based flow: The peak-performing/peak-evolving goal state of being which capitalizes on natural mechanisms built in to support a system's natural talents and passions.

Evolution direction: Human systems intensify around their natural core through an endless series of expansion quantum leaps rather than advance linearly.

Belief Engineering: Each human system and its reality are a single system defined by a single belief template. Change beliefs to change both the system and its reality. Beliefs can be known from reality patterns. Leadering conditioned reflexes triggered by problem events internally and externally activate an automatic belief template upgrade process. Reality is used as a self-correcting feedback system.

15 LEADERING™ PARADIGM DYNAMICS

FLOW to GENERATIVE CONGRUENCE DRIVE

FLOW to FLOW DRIVE – THE FLOW ENGINE

Nature pressures all human systems into generative congruence internally and externally. Successful leaders do the same thing.

The 14 paradigm dynamics or leader drives below promote the 15th drive: the flow of systems to generative congruence internally and externally. Congruence is the driving force of the target paradigm of Leadering™.

SYSTEMS MINDSET

A systems-based drive
Everything in the paradigm is a system, including individuals, organizations, and processes.

An expanding consciousness drive to oneness. Consciousness expands due to operating in the flow to congruence and stretching to view interacting systems.

ADVANCEMENT MECHANICS

A quantum leap drive
A templating drive
A self-organizing drive
An emergence drive
Leaders orchestrate abrupt nonlinear system advancements, adaptations, co-evolutions, and re-optimizations using mechanisms available in the flow to congruence. They operate as belief engineers, cultural engineers, reality architects, quantum leap leaders, and emergence leaders: NONLINEAR UPGRADE MECHANISMS

ADVANCEMENT DIRECTIONS

A knowledge-pursuit drive*
Leaders harness a system's innate drives for advancing its talent-based expression in order to achieve multi-system goals and maximization: EVOLUTIONARY PATH DETERMINANT

An adaptation drive*
Externally driven adjustment to advances in the shared contextual system caused by the adaptation / evolution of other subsystems: CHAIN REACTION: THE DANCE

An evolution drive*
'*Growth*' and '*Learning*' help human systems achieve their existing potential. '*Evolution*' advances that potential. Human systems advance by (1) quantum-leap intensifications of their natural core and (2) belief template upgrades: UPGRADED POTENTIAL / FUNCTIONALITY

A co-evolution drive*
Internally driven system upgrade achieved by capitalizing on external upgrading systems: OPPORTUNISTIC SYNERGY + LOCKSTEP ADVANCEMENT

A talent-based flow drive* (internal)
A flow-within-flow drive* (hierarchical)
The flow to internal/external congruence: PEAK-PERFORMING / PEAK-EVOLVING STATE

DRIVES FOR THE UNKNOWN:

the essence of leadership, entrepreneurship, innovation, and career creation

1. **A frontier-pursuit drive*:** Penetrate unknown systems.
2. **A creation / creativity-pursuit drive*:** Bring unknown into existence.

NATURE IS ENDLESS MULTI-SYSTEM CREATIVITY - LEADERSHIP IS AN EXTENSION

These dynamics form the toolkit for maximizing any human system in the paradigm whether the system is an individual, organization, market, civilization, or process such as leadership development, career management, or organizational change.

10-2 upgraded © 2006 Lauren Holmes * addicting talent-based drives

EVENT PATTERNS TRACKED FOR THEMES
These patterns are indicative of the flow-to-flow

In the target paradigm, the life-long patterns of the following 'talent-based' or 'work' events are analyzed for themes indicating the flow to generative congruence or flow internally or externally:

- **an unpaid work theme** based on patterns of events in which you freely give away "work" that others would charge for or that you are so passionate about that you would pay for the opportunity to do.
- **a talent-based knowledge-pursuit or learning-pursuit theme** based on patterns of events of seeking knowledge passionately and willingly for the application of key talents (learning-pursuit theme)
- **a talent-based spontaneous knowledge theme** based on patterns of events in which spontaneous knowledge emerged to support the application of key talents
- **a talent-based frontier-pursuit theme** based on patterns of events of new territories of growth, learning and achievement the system was drawn to pursue for the application of key talents
- **a talent-based creativity-pursuit theme** based on patterns of events of preferred creative expression or creative expression which you or system was drawn to pursue for the application of key talents along with events in which creativity or creative invention or innovation spontaneously emerged for the application of key talents
- **a talent-based creative expression theme** based on patterns of events of creative expression in which your passion and enthusiasm were inflamed
- **a talent-based meaning-pursuit theme** based on patterns of events of work or achievements or contributions considered a meaningful application of key talents
- **the theme(s) of talent-based flow states** indicated by patterns of events whereby you went into flow state during the application of key talents
- **a talent-based flow-to-flow theme, theme(s) of projects** requiring the application of key talents which were supported by lots of coincidences, flows, spontaneous knowledge / creativity (figure 9-5N)
- **talent-based naturality expansion theme** (figure 9-5G) indicated by patterns of expansions or intensifications of your system around its core to greater impact on reality - the key direction of growth and advancement of any system in the Leadering™ paradigm.
- **a talent-based resonance theme** based on patterns of subjects or activities for the application of key talents with which you resonated
- **a talent-based positive emotion theme** based on patterns of events in which passion, excitement, and enthusiasm emerged during the application of key talents

The above themes are consistent with each other in indicating when a system is integrated into the flow to congruence.

THE LEADERING™ PARADIGM SHIFT

Quantum leaps to internalize subsets of an integrated paradigm belief system result in an integrated system of leader drives, reflexes and meta-competencies

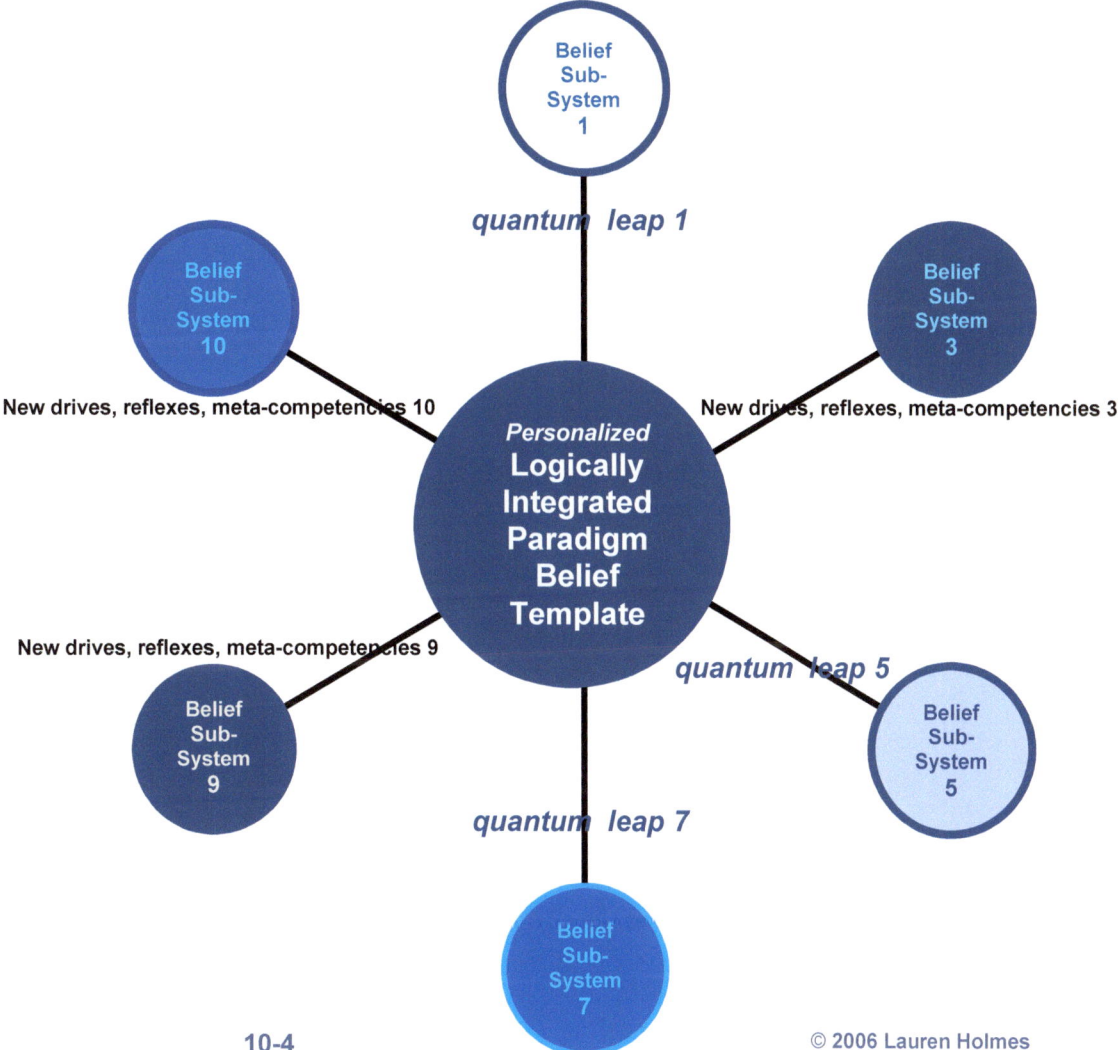

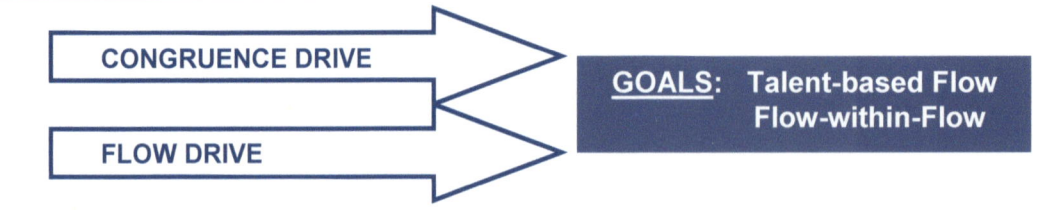

THE FLOW DRIVE = THE CONGRUENCE DRIVE

The **flow to congruence** or **the congruence-pursuit drive**
is identical to **the talent-based, flow-pursuit drive.**

Therefore all of the 15 dynamics contributing to the flow to congruence identified
in Figure 2 are also contributing to the achievement of talent-based flow
- the peak-performance / peak-evolution state of any human system.

**100% talent-based flow state is Leadering's goal state
for you and for any systems you choose to lead.**

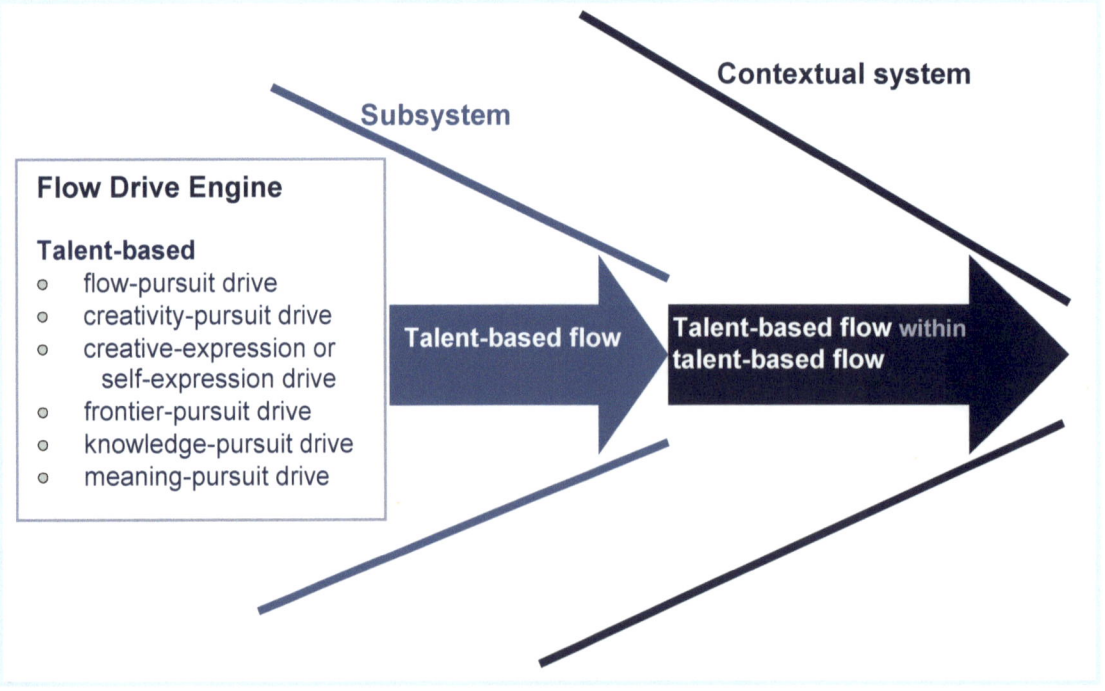

THE NATURE – HUMAN DRIVE CONTINUUM

All successful human systems must have links into the flow to congruence and their maximization in flow state. These links are human drives.

The drives in humans are the same as nature's drives.
These are the same dynamics found in nature and our Leadering paradigm.

The drives in humans and the dynamics in nature compose a single systems management continuum

TALENT-BASED FLOW STATE
(Internal Generative Congruence)

The flow state which occurs while doing activities using the talents one is most passionate about using and improving

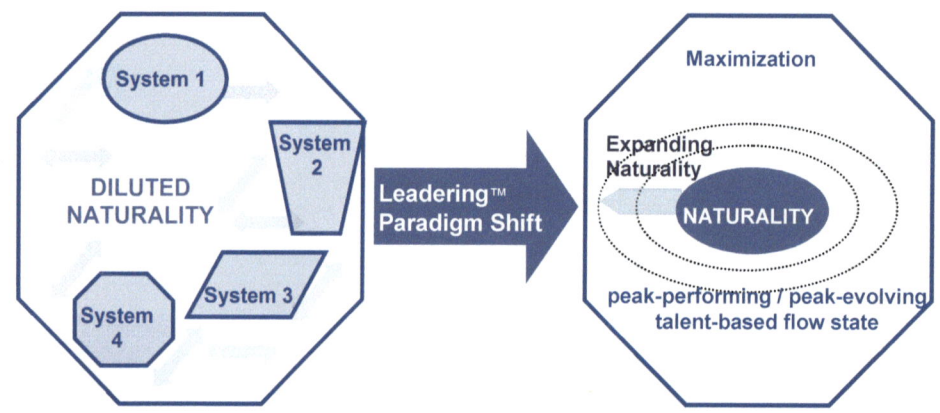

Fragmented and competing systems. No integration, internal cohesiveness or congruence.

Fully integrated around one's naturality, natural talents, and creative expression (one's 'art').

A pre-flow system

A system in talent-based flow or internal congruence

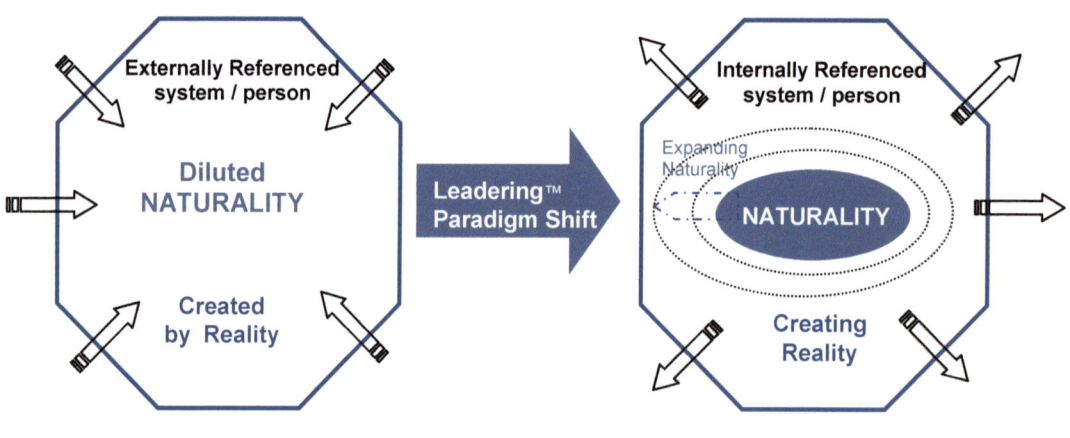

© 2006 Lauren Holmes

TWO EVOLUTIONARY DIRECTIONS

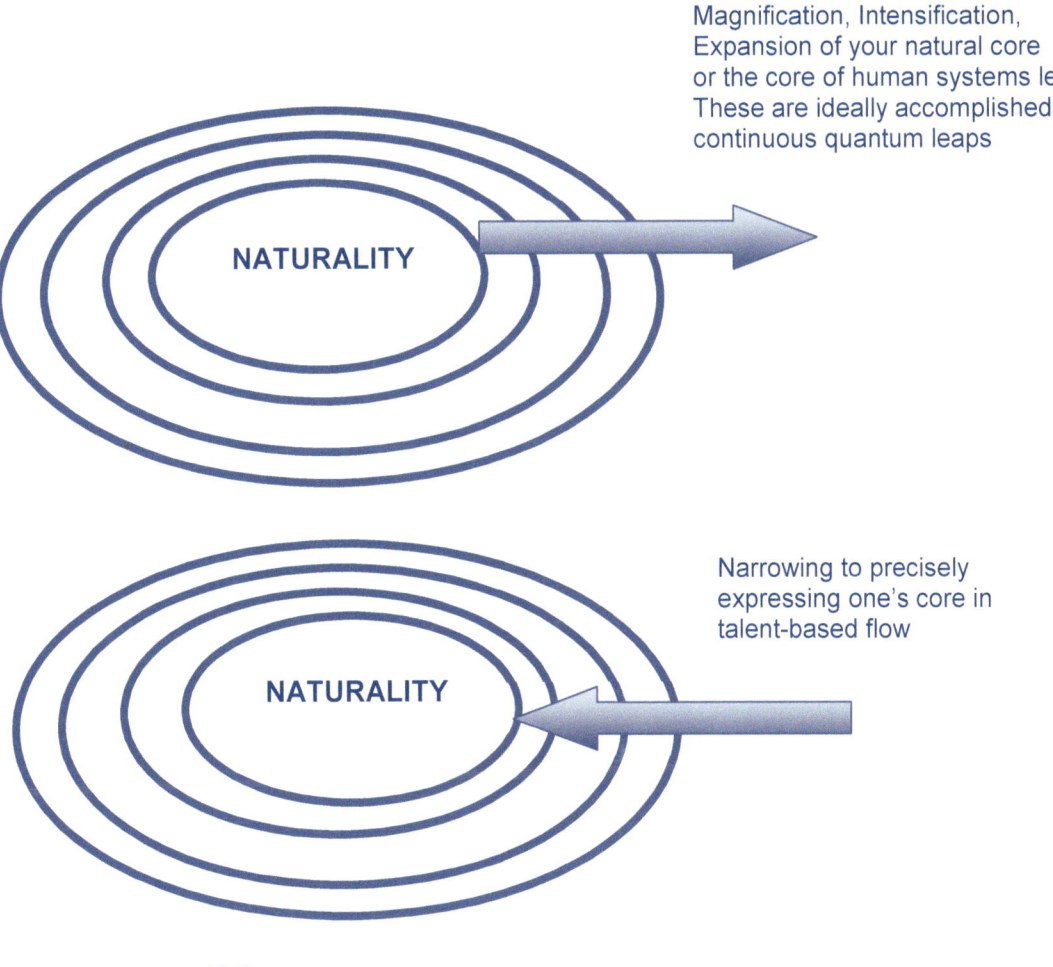

NATURAL QUANTUM LEAPS CLUSTER IN THE FLOW

The advantage of operating in talent-based flow within the talent-based flow of the contextual system

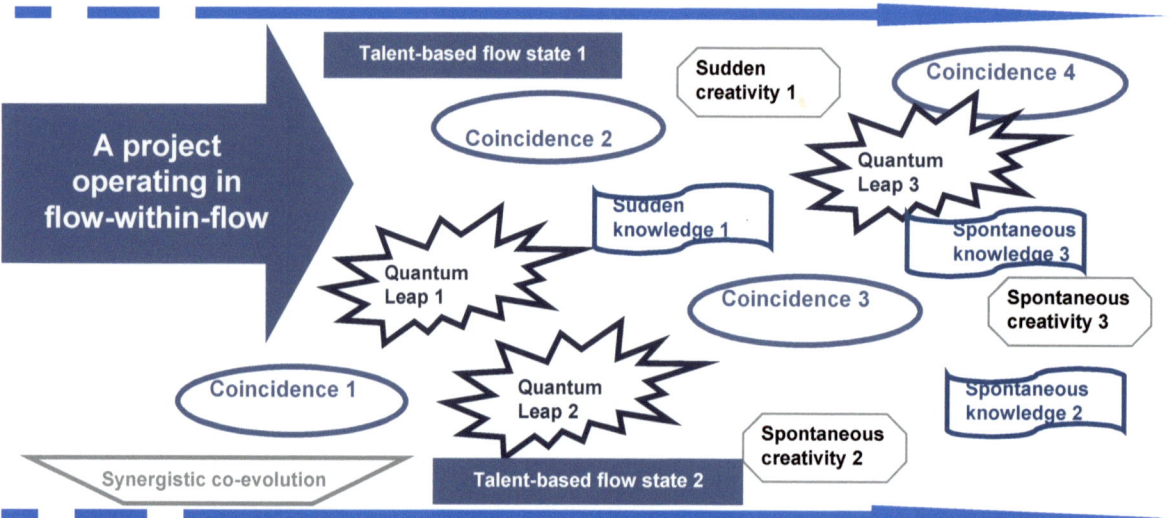

**Flow to Congruence   or   Flow-to-Flow   or   Flow to Fusion
or   projection of your talent-based life themes into the future**

Increasing functionality with each flow experience:
- expanding consciousness and conceptual capacity
- peak performance
- peak evolution
- increasing creative capability
- expansion / intensification / enlargement of the system's natural creative expression

Proof of the Leadering™ paradigm – Proof of the accuracy of your 5 formulas
If you are operating in talent-based flow and the clustering of natural quantum leaps above emerge in your reality, then you have proof that the Leadering paradigm™ and nature's machinery inside and outside of you do indeed operate in the way Leadering™ describes.

We are all born with the drives that energize natural leaders

Drives for
creativity, innovation, frontiering™, advancement, learning, achievement, adaptation, self-expression, and talent-based flow

Our drives hook us to nature's endless evolutionary flow to which all successful living systems are linked.

All are drives for penetrating the unknown or bringing the unknown into existence — the essence of leadership —

A NASA test for hiring innovative engineers and scientists was given to 1,600 children as they aged:

Leader drives at age 5:	98%
Leader drives at age 10:	30%
Leader drives at age 15:	12%
Leader drives of 280,000 adults:	2%

Leader drives are culturally deterred.

The Leadering™ paradigm shift *reactivates* the natural drives of leadership

If the drives associated with leaders, entrepreneurs, and innovators can be reactivated through a natural addiction for your system to use the key talents forming its dynamic core, then they are available to improve your performance in every aspect of your life.

For example, if you learn to learn, and are drawn to frontier new territory and create new realities through your natural addiction to learning new and better ways to change your reality with your key talents, then these addictive drives become your normal modus operandi. Every time you use these drives increases one's desire to use them. That is what causes the addiction. Therefore, they will energize every part of your life.

This is how Leadering™ cultivates the meta-competencies of leaders, entrepreneurs, innovators and high achievers. These meta-competencies and drives provide the dynamic foundation on which the skills of traditional leadership development and performance improvement programs can more easily be assimilated into your system, sustained, and applied.

WHAT ARE THE LEADING™ FORMULAS ?

The 5 formulas link your drives, nature's drives, and your key talents

These 5 interlinked formulas all capitalize on a system of forces internal and external to us which promote the use of our greatest talents for creation.

Creativity is at the foundation of all 15 of the dynamics of the Leadering™ systems management toolkit. Like all successful systems, human beings rely on creativity, creation and creative expression for the perpetuation of the species. We are therefore benevolently addicted to creation.

We have evolved addictive drives for using and improving the creative expression of our system of key talents. These include our drive for operating in our peak-performing and peak-evolving flow state while using our system of key talents. This is designed to ensure the maximum health, performance, adaptation, evolution, and survival of the human species.

The 5 formulas are strategies which take advantage of evolutionary addictions, drives, and forces to achieve dramatic and continuous improvements to your performance and functionality.

© 2006 Lauren Holmes

Recording 10: Big Picture – 5 Maximizing Formulas   16

OUR FLOW ENGINE

OUR CORE FLOW DRIVE COMPLEX:

Your flow engine consists of addictive drives associated with your key talents

Flow is addicting because each of its component drives are addicting: the more you use them the more you want to use them

Our key talent-based drives:
                our flow engine

    flow-pursuit drive
    creativity-pursuit drive
    creative-expression or
        self-expression drive
    frontier-pursuit drive
    knowledge-pursuit drive
    meaning-pursuit drive

Our secondary talent-based drives:
    quantum leap drive
    evolution drive
    co-evolution drive
    self-organization drive

These addictive drives form a unique synergistic thrust within each of us:
                our flow engine

Your 5 talent-based operating formulas or strategies for top performance in the Leadering™ paradigm

→ Talent-based lifetime development formula

→ Greatest talent-based individual performance

→ Talent-based leader formula

→ Talent-based leader development formula

→ Greatest talent-based leader performance

The 5 formulas are the best guess at the strategies which will allow one to capitalize on the flow-to-flow and all of the accompanying 15 dynamics in the Leadering™ paradigm to achieve peak performance and peak development.

10-13 © 2006 Lauren Holmes

EVENT PATTERNS TRACKED FOR THEMES
These patterns are indicative of the flow to internal and external congruence or the flow to flow

In the target paradigm, the life-long patterns of the following 'talent-based' or 'work' events are analyzed for themes indicating the flow to generative congruence or flow internally or externally:

- **an unpaid work theme** based on patterns of events in which you freely give away "work" that others would charge for or that you are so passionate about that you would pay for the opportunity to do.
- **a knowledge-pursuit theme** based on patterns of events of seeking knowledge passionately and willingly for the application of key talents (learning-pursuit theme)
- **a spontaneous knowledge theme** based on patterns of events in which spontaneous knowledge emerged to support the application of key talents
- **a frontier-pursuit theme** based on patterns of events of new territories of growth, learning and achievement the system was drawn to pursue for the application of key talents
- **a creativity-pursuit theme** based on patterns of events of preferred creative expression or creative expression which you or system was drawn to pursue for the application of key talents along with events in which creativity or creative invention or innovation spontaneously emerged for the application of key talents
- **a talent-based creative expression theme** based on patterns of events of creative expression in which your passion and enthusiasm were inflamed
- **a meaning-pursuit theme** based on patterns of events of work or achievements or contributions considered a meaningful application of key talents
- **the theme(s) of talent-based flow states** indicated by patterns of events whereby you went into flow state during the application of key talents
- **a naturality expansion theme** indicated by patterns of expansions or intensifications of your system around its core to greater impact on reality - the key direction of growth and advancement of any system in the Leading™ paradigm.
- **a flow-to-flow theme, theme(s) of projects** requiring the application of key talents which were supported by lots of coincidences, flows, spontaneous knowledge / creativity
- **a resonance theme** based on patterns of subjects or activities for the application of key talents with which you resonated
- **a positive emotion theme** based on patterns of events in which passion, excitement, and enthusiasm emerged during the application of key talents

The above themes synchronously arise when a system is integrated into the flow to congruence – the magic that happens in the Leadering paradigm

FIVE PERSONAL FORMULAS
for operating in the target Leadering™ paradigm

Based on the themes of the event patterns tracked in the paradigm, the following 5 formulas will emerge to help participants determine how to capitalize on the flow to flow of all human systems.

Your key talents are a system of your strongest capabilities which you are passionate about using and improving which advance reality in some way. This system is what is being acted upon by the flow to flow and your addictive drives.

ADVANCING YOUR SYSTEM

1. **Talent-based lifetime development formula** or personal evolution formula

2. **Greatest lifetime level of talent-based operation**: the culmination of living one's lifetime development formula.

ADVANCING OTHER SYSTEMS TO ADVANCE YOUR SYSTEM

3. **Talent-based leadership formula**: leadership as an expression of one's lifetime development formula

4. **Talent-based leadership development formula**: merging one's lifetime development formula with one's talent-based leadership formula.

5. **Greatest lifetime talent-based operating level as a leader**: based on the previous 4 formulas.

© 2006 Lauren Holmes

YOUR FIVE PERSONALIZED OPERATING FORMULAS
for maximizing in the Leadering™ paradigm

Key talents being acted on by the flow-to-flow
Your key talents are a system of your strongest capabilities which you are addicted to using and improving. When used, they advance reality in some way. All 5 formulas are operating strategies for capitalizing on your key talents. Therefore they are interlinked. Your key talents are also interlinked into a system of addictive drives which form your flow engine. The flow engine promotes operating in a peak performance flow state in which you are using your key talents. The key talents being acted on by the flow engine need to be known in order to determine one's 5 operating formulas for the Leadering™ paradigm.

1. Your talent-based lifetime development formula: Advancing your system
If natural forces continuously pressure you to expand or intensify your ability to use your key talents for creation - to advance reality - what will be the development path or theme of that intensification process underpinning your life?

2. Your greatest talent-based performance as an individual:
If you were to pursue the continuous expansion of your key talents over a lifetime and at top speeds, what is the highest level of creative impact or reality creation that you would likely achieve. What is the highest possible culmination of living your lifetime development formula? What is your maximum attainment based on a lifetime of accelerating development of your key talents?

Advancing other systems to advance your system
3. Your talent-based leadership formula
If you complied with the addictive drives pulling you to the continuous expansion of your key talents, what would be the territory and form of your leadership? How would formulas 1 and 2 define you as a leader by logical extension? What would your leadership formula look like if it was 100% based on your greatest performance with your key talents and their continuous expansion?

4. Your talent-based leadership development formula:
Your leadership development formula just allows you a more specialized lens with which to examine and strategize your personal development. The continuous expansion of the intensity and impact of your key talents define both your development as an individual and a leader. Therefore, leadership development and lifetime development form the same single continuum. The advancement of your key talents increases your strength, impact, and creativity as a leader. How would the previous 3 formulas define a leadership development formula? For those on the Leadering™ program who assume they will never be a leader, it is built in.

5. Your greatest talent-based performance as a leader:
Based on your 4 previous formulas, determine your greatest lifetime level of performance as a leader. Given your advancement as an individual and a leader based on the continuous intensification of your key talents, and given the formula for your greatest performance as an individual, what would be the dimensions of your ultimate performance level as a leader: generically, what will be your greatest levels of capability for causing reality advances?

RECORDINGS 11

Leadering™ harnesses natural levers within you which are always pressuring you to reposition your system to its natural core and natural mode of operation, and then to expand and intensify around that core. Core-based is the only foundation upon which to attain and sustain your greatest levels of performance and lifetime achievement.

7 PERSONALIZING THE LEADERING™ PARADIGM

I FLOW MAXIMIZATION EXERCISES continued

11. **Introduction to the 5 Leadering™ Maximizing Formulas**   18 minutes   12 figures
    Advancing your system
    Formula 1: Talent-based lifetime development formula
    Formula 2: Greatest lifetime level of talent-based operation as an individual
    Advancing your system by advancing other human systems
    Formula 3: Talent-based leadership formula
    Formula 4: Talent-based leadership development formula
    Formula 5: Greatest life-time level of talent-based operation as a leader or systems maximizer

This recording overviews the process and many exercises that will be used to develop 5 strategies customized to your system which will permit the lifetime maximization of your system by capitalizing on the Leadering™ machinery.

All 5 formulas are refinements of a single integrated lifetime maximization strategy for your system that has been segmented to allow more effective application. The remaining 4 formulas split off from the first one to allow you to see the dimensions of the overarching strategy and to put it into more practical terms whereby progress is achievable and measurable.

Once you learn how to maximize your system, it will be easier to extrapolate what you have learned to maximize other systems using the same Leadering™ toolkit. You will eventually be able to advance your system by advancing and capitalizing other human systems. Extended by the capabilities of other systems, you are in a position to operate beyond the potential and capabilities of your system to accelerate your growth and to increase your achievements.

YOUR FIVE PERSONALIZED OPERATING FORMULAS
for maximizing in the Leadering™ paradigm

Key talents being acted on by the flow-to-flow
Your key talents are a system of your strongest capabilities which you are addicted to using and improving. When used, they advance reality in some way. All 5 formulas are operating strategies for capitalizing on your key talents. Therefore they are interlinked. Your key talents are also interlinked into a system of addictive drives which form your flow engine. The flow engine promotes operating in a peak performance flow state in which you are using your key talents. The key talents being acted on by the flow engine need to be known in order to determine one's 5 operating formulas for the Leadering™ paradigm.

1. Your talent-based lifetime development formula: **advancing your system**
If natural forces continuously pressure you to expand or intensify your ability to use your key talents for creation - to advance reality - what will be the development path or theme of that intensification process underpinning your life?

2. Your greatest talent-based performance as an individual:
If you were to pursue the continuous expansion of your key talents over a lifetime and at top speeds, what is the highest level of creative impact or reality creation that you would likely achieve. What is the highest possible culmination of living your lifetime development formula? What is your maximum attainment based on a lifetime of accelerating development of your key talents?

3. Your talent-based leadership formula: **advancing other systems**
If you complied with the addictive drives pulling you to the continuous expansion of your key talents, what would be the territory and form of your leadership? How would formulas 1 and 2 define you as a leader by logical extension? What would your leadership formula look like if it was 100% based on your greatest performance with your key talents and their continuous expansion?

4. Your talent-based leadership development formula:
Your leadership development formula just allows you a more specialized lens with which to examine and strategize your personal development. The continuous expansion of the intensity and impact of your key talents define both your development as an individual and a leader. Therefore, leadership development and lifetime development form the same single continuum. The advancement of your key talents increases your strength, impact, and creativity as a leader. How would the previous 3 formulas define a leadership development formula? For those on the Leadering™ program who assume they will never be a leader, it is built in.

5. Your greatest talent-based performance as a leader:
Based on your 4 previous formulas, determine your greatest lifetime level of performance as a leader. Given your advancement as an individual and a leader based on the continuous intensification of your key talents, and given the formula for your greatest performance as an individual, what would be the dimensions of your ultimate performance level as a leader: generically, what will be your greatest levels of capability for causing reality advances?

11-13B (unmentioned)

PROCESS TO DETERMINE YOUR 5 PERSONAL FORMULAS
for complying with the flow-to-flow in the target Leading™ paradigm

1. **Determine your key talents:**
   Do any or all of the following as required:
   - Recording 13: Analyze the patterns of historical events in your life for themes (figure 11-3)
     Use the same findings to determine the flow to congruence or flow-to-flow in your life
     NOTE: The flow-to-flow pressures operating in talent-based flow, a flow state that emerges while using your core system of talents. Therefore, determining the flow-to-flow will always reveal your key talents and vice versa.

   - Recording 16: Do these additional key talent determination exercises if required

   - Recording 14: Determine how your key talents and highest creative expression are 'biased to' or 'drawn to' or 'addicted to' benefitting human systems: system creation, system advancement, system relationships, or system maintenance.
     NOTE: Formulas 3, 4, and 5 are the means to advance your personal system by advancing and maximizing other systems.

   - Figure 11-17: Use additional support as required.

2. **Develop hypotheses for each of the 5 formulas as an integrated set of strategies based on the continual expansion of your key talents.**
   Ensure they are consistent with the pressures of natural forces inside and outside of us such as the flow to peak performance and peak advancement flow state in which your key talents are central.

3. **Do quantum leaps to lock in the new information and beliefs of each of the formulas**

4. **Develop and implement strategies for action learning experimentation to test for the accuracy of your formulas**
   The criteria for determining accuracy of your 5 formulas are identified in figures 11-18 through 11-19

5. **Develop and implement strategies for integrating the formulas into your life, work, and career**

6. **Revisit the themes of the historical patterns of events exercise as proof of the accuracy of the Leading™ paradigm** (figure 10-3). If the flow-to-flow has been operating this way in the past, one can assume that it will continue this way in the future. **Develop strategies to capitalize on the themes and flow-to-flow going forward.**
   Your time in talent-based flow state should increase dramatically.

7. **Begin operating consistent with the historical themes and the flow-to-flow as a way of life.**

Recording 11: Intro – 5 Maximizing Formulas 22

THE LEADERING™ CORE CONGRUENCE EXERCISES

These exercises are designed to identify the core of your system which is being acted upon by natural forces inside and outside of you so you can comply with and capitalize on them and avoid operating contrary to them.

FLOW MAXIMIZATION EXERCISES
for maximum performance and advancement

Life Theme exercises
- key talent determination
- flow to flow determination

Key talent Determination exercises
- system-based key talent exercise
- various other exercises

5 Talent-Based Operating Formulas exercises
1: your lifetime development formula
2: your greatest lifetime achievement formula
3: your natural leader formula
4: your leadership development formula
5: your greatest leader performance formula

BELIEF MAXIMIZATION EXERCISES
for Core Congruence

Belief Template Analysis and Upgrade:
- beneficial belief determination:
   ideal talent-based and flow-based beliefs
   identity beliefs, reality creation beliefs
- problem belief determination:
   fear beliefs, toxic beliefs, conflicting beliefs
- event-driven template upgrade process
- quantum leap template exchange process:
   goal-packaging identities, reincarnation

Action Learning Experimentation
- proving beliefs create reality
- improving belief engineering in your own and other systems
- improving template determination / design
- quantum leap experimentation

YOUR FLOW ENGINE:

Natural forces inside and outside of you act on your core

YOUR BELIEF TEMPLATE

Your belief template governs both you and your reality as a single system

Beliefs are information storage units like genes

YOUR CORE CONSISTS OF:

1. **KEY TALENTS**

2. **ADDICTIVE DRIVES**
   pulling you to use your key talents

   *Note: Your key talents and associated drives are the immutable beliefs below. They continuously
   - create your reality and
   - are being acted upon by the flow-to-flow and Leadering's built-in growth continuums which amplify core impact.

3. **IMMUTABLE BELIEFS**
   (innate gene-based beliefs)
   These define the essence of your system and why it came together in the first place. These beliefs are genetically based and inherent to the built-in creative expression of your system. See *Note above.

4. **CHANGEABLE BELIEFS**
   ideally designed to support the key talents, addictive drives, and immutable beliefs to maximize your performance, development, and survival in biological terms. The goal is core congruence.

11- 14B (unmentioned)

© 2006 Lauren Holmes

im·mu·ta·ble: unchanging or unchangeable: not changing or not able to be changed

EXERCISES FOR DETERMINING YOUR KEY TALENTS

TALENTS YOU ARE ADDICTED TO USING AND IMPROVING

Total gratification exercise: What work would you do to creatively express your natural talents and passion for learning within a specific territory associated with those talents if you had 100% security of having revenues of millions of dollars every year for the rest of your life.

The amnesia exercise: If you had no memory of your past, what work would choose to do to creatively express your natural talents and passion for learning within a specific territory associated with those talents if you already had a lot of money and it wasn't a factor.

Childhood talents exercise: When you felt totally free as a child, what were the childhood talents you chose to improve, pursue, cultivate, or express as a child.

Preferred activities exercise: Determine the common theme to your preferred activities or preferred creative expression. It is important to think generically and look for the common thread. This will be a recurring theme that exists in all of the things that you love to do. What is the common pattern among all of the things that you love to do

Dream or fantasy exercise: Is there a common theme that emerges spontaneously in any dreams or daydreams that you have with respect to work that you are doing.

The Enthusiasm and Resonance Exercise: Of the list of possible learning/creative expression themes that could be the foundation of your natural evolutionary path, which ones cause your resonance or enthusiasm to go up when you think of spending a lifetime pursuing them.

Meaningful Work Exercise: What work using your natural talents and knowledge-pursuit themes and creativity-pursuit and frontiering-pursuit themes would, if you spend a lifetime pursuing them, give your life the greatest meaning and give you the most pride in your achievements.

11-15A Overview © 2006 Lauren Holmes

Figure 11-15B provides more instruction on the 11-15A exercises and can be found with the recording and figures for the key talents exercises.

To what kinds of systems do you apply your key talents to?

SYSTEM MAINTENANCE Single / Multi-System	SYSTEM ADVANCEMENT Single / Multi-System	SYSTEM CREATION Single / Multi-System	SYSTEM RELATIONSHIPS Each relationship creates a new system
manager: very little new creation is required. **Creativity and creation increase with each column to the right.** **Since beliefs create reality, this means that the need for belief changes increase as your move to the right.**	strategy development people development organization development multi-organization synergy process development knowledge development technology development **change leadership** • transitional • transformational • facilitative **frontier leadership** **creational leadership** **flow leadership**	**creational leadership** **frontier leadership** **quantum leap leadership** **template leadership** **emergence leadership** system creation strategy system creation implementation entrepreneur company creation intrapreneur project creation new product creation new technology creation new infrastructure creation new process creation new science creation new knowledge creation new skill creation new frontier creation creation research merger-created system acquisition-created system innovation / creativity	System relationships: • to maintain systems • to advance systems • to create systems **co-evolutionary leadership** **co-adaptation leadership** collaboration and synergy business web development CRM: customer relationship management customer development customer chain development supplier chain development network development relationship building team building market development unifying and integrating problem solving conflict resolution peace keeping negotiation mergers and acquisitions relationship strategy/vision relationship-related implementation

→

- **Increasing belief and information changes**
- **Increasing impact on reality**

- In the Leadering™ paradigm, leadership extends nature's systems management.
- This exercise demonstrates Leadering's single systems maximization toolkit

Which System Types do your key talents advance?

SYSTEM TYPES
- **individual system**
- **multi-individual system**
- **organizational system**
- **multi-organizational system**
- **knowledge system**
- **process system**

- you, a person, a follower, your child
- individuals *en masse*: a consumer market, a university
- a group of people: an organization or company
- a business web or community
- a science, a field, a discipline
- leadership development, business process, reengineering

11-16B

© 2006 Lauren Holmes

NOTE:

Figures 11-16A-F charts can be found with the recording and figures for the Systems Application Categories exercise.

Figures 11-16A and 11-16B below are summaries for the 11-16A-F charts for selecting the categories of systems one will apply one's key talents to now and in the future as one advances with the built-in growth processes in the Leading™ paradigm.

Additional Support for Determining your 5 Talent-Based Operating Formulas

for capitalizing on the flow-to-flow in the target Leadering™ paradigm

ADDITIONAL SUPPORT FOR DEVELOPING YOUR 5 FORMULAS

Telegroup or in-person brainstorming with peers or advisors :

1. **Leadering™ professionals:** Have a Leadering™ professional take a pass at your information though interviews and building on what you have developed.

2. **Brainstorming Groups: Pair Leadering™ participants up or have brainstorming groups of 3 to 10 participants either in person or by teleconference to brainstorm and refine these formulas for each person.**

3. **Systems and Conceptual Skills:** Consult individuals and leaders with well developed systems thinking and conceptual skills to assist you with synthesizing your historical patterns into viable hypotheses for your formulas. They may have the skills to assimilate the historical patterns of events you develop during the personalization exercise to tell you the themes in your life. From the themes they can help you determine:
   - your key talents
   - your 5 formulas based on those themes
   - where the flow-to-flow has been in your life and therefore project where it will be in the future
   - how to interpret the signposts indicating the flow-to-flow in any immediate situations which you are trying to master.

4. **Individuals in talent-based flow:** It would be ideal to choose someone whose key talents and flow engine are precisely expressed in doing this support work for you so they actually move to talent-based flow state in the service of supporting you. Then you know they will not only be supporting you with from peak performance but will also have their capabilities extended by nature's capabilities. Spontaneous knowledge, spontaneous creativity, coincidences and facilitating events will be supporting them in supporting you.

5. **Action learning experiments** will give you feedback as to whether your proposed formulas have put you in the flow-to-flow or not (figures 10-10, 11-18 through 11-19, and suggested action learning experiments)

6. **Action learning experimentation and paradigm implementation support:** Project managers, brainstorming groups with meeting facilitators, strategists and idea people, would all contribute one's ability to maximize performance and advancement in the Leadering™ paradigm.

7. **Documentation of sample Leadering™ formulas** is available from which to either find or extrapolate hypotheses as to what your formulas are.

INDICATORS OF THE ACCURACY OF THE FORMULAS

What happens when you identify your right talent-based formulas?

Examples:

1. When right, the very idea of the formula invokes immediate emotional highs, elation, enthusiasm, passion, an 'aha!' experience, and /or a feeling of nourishment and of finally being home.

2. All of the historical event patterns and life themes confirm the accuracy: all of the dots logically connect up. In the future, the patterns continue and are surrounded by signals of the flow-to-flow as you operate with the formula.

3. Action learning experimentation by operating as if the formulas are correct will validate them by yielding clusters of the indicators of alignment with the flow-to-flow. Figures 10-6, 10-7, and 10-10 are achieved. Clusters of natural quantum leaps will abound: increased coincidences, talent-based flow states, spontaneous knowledge, spontaneous creativity, inspiration, emotional highs, and other facilitating events all of which accelerate your progress.

4. Uncharacteristic fearlessness in the face of the unknown when scaling new frontiers of using and improving your key talents as a result of operating with the talent-based formulas. Addictive drives pull you along this natural learning continuum. Improved proficiency with change, or even a passion for change.

5. The foundational dynamic of your life becomes knowledge-pursuit and creation-pursuit around applying and improving your key talents.

6. Increased time in talent-based flow state which enables maximum advancement of your key talents and maximum performance in advancing reality. Your functionality continuously increases founding your life on a natural learning theme.

7. Growth continuums built into the Leadering™ paradigm are launched: See figures 11-18B, 11-18C and/or recording 15 which is dedicated to Leadering's built-in growth.

8. More precise, more profound, more impactful, and speedier reality creation.

HOW GROWTH IS BUILT INTO LEADERING™

The Key Leadering™ Paradigm Growth Players

System Core:
   System Flow engine:
- flow pursuit of the system
- key talents
- core addictive drives

   System Template:
- immutable beliefs
- changeable beliefs: event-driven template upgrade process

System Meta-Competencies

Conditioned Reflexes

Leadering™ System Management Toolkit: The 15 Dynamics
   Systems Mindset
      systems-based dynamic
      expanding consciousness
   Advancement Mechanics
      quantum leap dynamic
      templating dynamic
      self-organizing dynamic
      emergence dynamic
   Advancement Directions
      knowledge-pursuit drive
      adaptation drive
      evolution drive
      co-evolution drive
      talent-based flow drive
      flow-within-flow drive
   Drives for the Unknown:
      frontier-pursuit drive
      creation / creativity-pursuit drive

Five Talent-based Operating Formulas
lifetime development, greatest lifetime performance, leadership, leadership development, greatest leader lifetime performance

Self- or System-Initiated Quantum Leaps

Nature-Initiated Quantum Leaps imbedded in the flow-to-flow
- coincidences (multi-system synergy, co-evolution, co-adaptation)
- spontaneous knowledge
- spontaneous creativity
- facilitating events
- flow states

for opportunistic synergy, co-evolution, co-adaptation, creative problem-solving, and flow-within-flow

Talent-Based Themes of your 'Life System'
   an unpaid work theme
   a knowledge-pursuit theme
   a spontaneous knowledge theme
   a frontier-pursuit theme
   a creativity-pursuit theme
   a talent-based creative expression theme
   a meaning-pursuit theme
   the theme(s) of talent-based flow states
   a flow-to-flow theme,
   theme(s) of talent-based projects
   a naturality expansion theme
   a resonance theme
   a positive emotion theme

© 2006 Lauren Holmes

SAMPLE CATEGORIES OF LEADERING'S BUILT-IN GROWTH

CONTINUOUSLY IMPROVING PERFORMANCE
1. Increasing time operating in peak performance and peak advancement flow states
2. Depth of your talent-based flow states increases with each experience thus increasing performance further
3. Event-driven belief upgrade process continually improves performance through more supportive beliefs

CONTINUOUSLY INCREASING IMPACT
1. Increasing impact of creations, magnitude of advancement of reality, and reality creation precision
2. Reality creation precision
3. Increasing creativity and innovation
4. An increase in the level of complexity handled: from single system to multiple systems impact; from transactions to process; from process to quantum leaps; from linear to nonlinear; more impactful quantum leaps impacting more systems more quickly

CONTINUOUS DEVELOPMENT
Addiction to continuous development:
- the continuous increase in drives which addict you to using and improving your system of core talents
- these addictive drives cause the continuous improvement of your system of core talents becomes the founding dynamic of your life to which the other segments of your life are integrated.
- an accelerating increase in speed of development of your system of core talents
- the continuous increase in the development of drives associated with meta-competencies such as frontiering™, creativity, learning to learn, and learning agility which promote continuous development
- addiction to flow states which continuously improve your key talents, functionality, and performance

CONTINUOUSLY INCREASING FUNCTIONALITY
1. Continuous increase in the specialization of your system of core talents
2. Accelerating improvement of abilities to use your core talents
3. Increasing ability to penetrate the unknown or bring the unknown into existence and a craving for both: frontiering™ and creativity.
4. Continuous improvement in your facility for nonlinear quantum leaps to speed advancement of your system and other systems
5. Systems-based modus operandi: single toolkit for advancing systems, continuous increase in your ability to advance systems and to create new systems
6. Continuous acquisition and improvement of meta-competencies associated with successful leaders, entrepreneurs, innovators and high achievers. (Meta-competencies improve the ability to assimilate and use competencies): continuous development, improved cognitive capabilities, improved performance. These allow you to move more quickly easily and safely into unknown territory and frontiers, increase your creativity and innovation, increase your knowledge-acquisition capabilities, and increase your ability to court coincidences and facilitating events which will improve your performance of your art.
7. Continuous improvement to cognitive skills:
- concept formation, conceptualization of complex ideas, abstract thinking, deductive and inductive logic, problem reframing, dealing with multiple perspectives and ambiguity, skillful formulation of ends, ways, means
- frame of reference development: systems understanding, environmental scanning, pattern recognition
- proactive thinking using critical, creative, and reflective thinking
- analysis of complicated events, trend perception, change detection, creative and opportunistic problem-solving
- deployment of models, theories and inferences
- visualization, addressing, and capitalization of complex interrelationships: see the interaction of more systems and the opportunities for synergy and co-evolution; impact more systems, impact more complex systems, impact larger systems
- big-picture thinking and seeing more patterns to have more information for decision-making and strategic and tactical planning

WHAT HAPPENS WHEN YOUR FORMULA HYPOTHESES ARE WRONG

When the working hypothesis for a talent-based formula is wrong:

If there are tons of blocks, or fears, toxic emotions, and traumatic events with respect to operating in the Leadering™ paradigm with the formula, these indicate that you need to revise your hypothesis. You are not on the talent-based flow-to-flow or the 'river' to your peak-performing and peak-advancing talent-based flow state.

When the formula is wrong, the historical patterns or events that you have experienced in the past, are no longer evident or logically integrated in the future.

LIFE-LONG FORMULA REFINEMENT

Refinements to these 5 formulas are a life-long process based on action-learning experimentation.

Refinements are required as one continuously intensifies and expands around one's dynamic core:

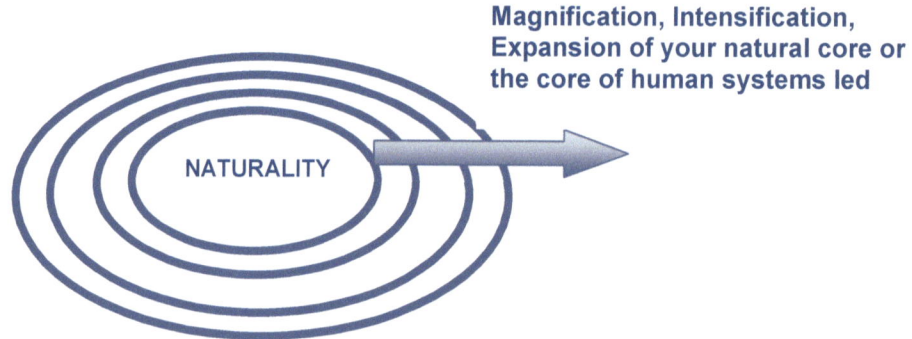

Refinements are required as one's use of one's key talents narrows to specialization.

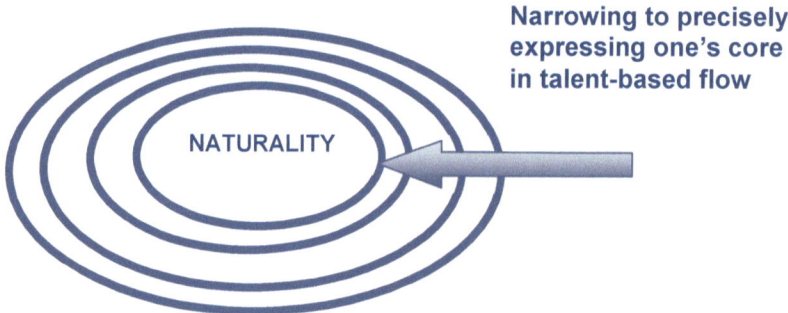

Refinements will also be necessary as the flow-to-flow changes direction and/or brings different co-evolving systems into your context.

RECORDING 12

Leadering's penetrating exercises provide
- extreme self-knowledge
- personalized strategies for maximizing lifetime achievement
- one's historical growth themes and how to capitalize on them for faster, more effective, more meaningful, future achievement

7 PERSONALIZING THE LEADERING™ PARADIGM

I FLOW MAXIMIZATION EXERCISES continued

12. **Advice for the core determination exercises for identifying one's 5 maximizing formulas**
    11 minutes 4 figures
    - Advice is provided for the core determination exercises. It includes addressing the issue of side ventures which might disguise your true key talents. It is important to assume you have all of the resources and freedom required to maximize your system over your lifetime for all exercises.
    - Advice for the final formulation of your 5 operating formulas is provided
    - Specific pre-exercise advice is provided for the following:
      for leaders, for non-leaders, for those pursuing entrepreneuring, innovation, recareering™ and peak performance

Three categories of quantum leaps are recommended to lock your findings from the exercises and process into your system as permanent template changes:
- core upgrade quantum leaps
- core expansion quantum leaps
- realignment quantum leaps

FIND THE THEME IN YOUR TALENT-DEVELOPING SIDE VENTURES
to determine your true system of key talents

SIDE VENTURES: ANOTHER EVOLUTIONARY DIRECTION
Developing the component skills of your 'art'

Since the flow engine often causes component skill development to progress sequentially, it can appear as if any one of these component skill development phases is actually your evolutionary formula   -   especially since, at the time you investigate them, you are very passionate about learning them and using them.   However, keep focused on what binds them all together to determine your evolutionary formula.

© 2006 Lauren Holmes

SIDE VENTURES: ANOTHER EVOLUTIONARY DIRECTION

Developing the component skills of your 'art'

FIND THE THEME IN YOUR TALENT-DEVELOPING SIDE VENTURES
to determine your true system of key talents

To sustain talent-based flow state, one must always be pushing beyond one's previous capabilities into new frontiers of doing one's art. These frontiers are not always linear advancements or expansions of a known state. They include increases in complexity, span of impact, and penetration into the various skills and knowledge associated with every aspect of using your key talents.

The flow to flow will take you into these areas of specialization with the same flow of natural quantum leaps, coincidences and spontaneous knowledge and creativity. They will feel every bit as right as when you are moving ahead with your total system of key talents.

As you review patterns of historical events, it is important not to be misled by these side ventures which bring you specialized capabilities for better using your system of key talents when you are trying to determine what those key talents are. You will want to see through these side investigations to the central theme that links them all together when trying to figure out your key talents and your 5 formulas.

By the same token, you will also want to comply with these side ventures pressured by the flow to flow as the means to advance your system as a whole more proficiently.

© 2006 Lauren Holmes

ADVICE FOR DEVELOPING YOUR 5 LEADING™ OPERATING FORMULAS

1. **For Leaders:** For those taking Leadering™ with the intention of becoming visible leaders in positions of authority and commanding others, you should attempt to include in formulas 3, 4, and 5, a specific theme for your leadership which is based on the expansion of your key talents over your lifetime as prescribed by formula 1.

2. **For Non-Leaders:** For those who do not plan to become visible leaders with followers reporting, please use this exercise to identify a strategy for developing your ability to advance human systems for goal achievement using your key talents in the Leadering™ paradigm.

3. **For those pursuing entrepreneuring, innovation, recareering™ and peak performance:** For those taking Leadering™ for recareering™, for peak performance, and for maximum lifetime achievement, you should translate all 5 formulas in terms of your career and being paid for continuously scaling new frontiers of application of your talents. The pursuit of p*aid peak evolution* should be the determinant for your career choices. You want to be paid for pursuing your lifetime maximum.

4. **The 5 formulas are logically interlinked:**
   All 5 formulas should be logically integrated into a single cohesive whole based on the advancement of your core.
   Each formula is based on the intensification of your key talents.
   Each formula is about how those key talents will advance reality.
   Each formula must agree with the evidence you uncovered in the patterns of historical events in the talent-based life themes exercise. The themes indicate where the flow to flow internally and externally has been pressuring the expansion of your key talents. Formula 1 has already been operating throughout your life. You are now going to proactively support its strategy.
   Formulas 3 to 5 should agree with your findings in the systems-based key talents exercise.

5. **Quantum leaps** should be used to lock new information uncovered by the process into your system as permanent template changes.

6. Assume you have all of the resources and freedom required to maximize your system over your lifetime.

Leadering™ Quantum Leap Categories for All 5 Formulas

Examples

CORE UPGRADE QUANTUM LEAPS
1. Quantum leaps to new functionality such as increased cognitive skills, leader meta-competencies, and an increasingly supportive belief template.
2. Paid peak evolution quantum leap to a life founded on your knowledge-pursuit, creativity-pursuit, meaning-pursuit, and frontiering-pursuit themes so that you are
   - earning revenues doing only the work you are most passionately drawn to do,
   - using your talents to their maximum, and
   - being paid to learn the information and skills you would pursue anyway to improve your key talent capabilities if you had total freedom and all the resources you needed.

CORE EXPANSION QUANTUM LEAPS
The Leadering™ paradigm honours a pressure of internal and external drives to expand your system around its core with its system of key talents.
1. Quantum leaps to the next wider expansion of power and impact of your system. These. These expansion quantum leaps should be supported by natural forces and therefore should be incorporated into your modus operandi for the rest of your life.
2. A series of quantum leaps through frontier after frontier to expand the art and science behind the use of your system of key and your prowess in using both.
3. Your 10-Year Maximum Quantum Leap: a quantum leap to full life-time expansion as if you have been operating at your maximum for 10 years.

REALIGNMENT QUANTUM LEAPS
1. Quantum leaps to re-boot your system onto its natural core in compliance with natural forces continuously pressuring this re-centering.
2. Quantum leaps to re-position your system merged into the-flow-to-flow

12-24 (not mentioned) © 2006 Lauren Holmes

RECORDING 13

> Because Leadering™ copies and capitalizes on nature's systems maximization process, powerful natural forces, capabilities, and mechanisms are available to extend the functionality of any human system so that it can perform beyond its potential.

7 PERSONALIZING THE LEADERING™ PARADIGM

I FLOW MAXIMIZATION EXERCISES continued

13. **Life Themes Exercises**   48 minutes   5 figures

This is the first core determination exercise. Your findings will help you identify the core that is being acted on by natural forces so that you can develop strategies for capitalizing on them going forward.

Event patterns over your lifetime are tracked for themes. These themes are indicative of both your key talents and the flow-to-flow operating on those key talents. These event patterns and themes will continue in the future. You can capitalize on them to harness the flow-to-flow and all of the dynamics and growth continuums built into the Leadering™ paradigm. Your 5 formulas identify the strategies for accomplishing this.

These life-long 'talent-based' or 'work' event patterns are analyzed for themes in order to discover the commonality which will define one's key talents:
- an unpaid work theme
- a knowledge-pursuit theme or learning-pursuit theme
- a spontaneous knowledge theme
- a frontier-pursuit theme
- a creativity-pursuit theme
- a talent-based creative expression theme
- a meaning-pursuit theme
- the theme(s) of talent-based flow states
- a flow-to-flow theme, theme(s) of projects
- a naturality expansion theme
- a resonance theme
- a positive emotion theme

EVENT PATTERNS TRACKED FOR THEMES	FIVE PERSONAL FORMULAS for operating in the target Leadering™ paradigm
These patterns are indicative of the flow to internal and external congruence or the flow-to-flow	

In the target paradigm, the life-long patterns of the following 'talent-based' or 'work' events are analyzed for themes indicating the flow to generative congruence or flow internally or externally:

- **an unpaid work theme**
- **a knowledge-pursuit theme or learning-pursuit theme**
- **a spontaneous knowledge theme**
- **a frontier-pursuit theme**
- **a creativity-pursuit theme**
- **a talent-based creative expression theme**
- **a meaning-pursuit theme**
- **the theme(s) of talent-based flow states**
- **a flow-to-flow theme, theme(s) of projects**
- **a naturality expansion theme**
- **a resonance theme**
- **a positive emotion theme**

All of the above themes indicate when a system is integrated into the flow to congruence.

Based on the themes of the event patterns tracked in the paradigm, the following 5 formulas will emerge to help participants determine how to capitalize on the flow to flow of all human systems.

Your key talents are a system of your strongest capabilities which you are passionate about using and improving which advance reality in some way. This system is what is being acted upon by the flow to flow and your addictive drives.

ADVANCING YOUR SYSTEM

1. **Talent-based lifetime development formula** or personal evolution formula

2. **Greatest lifetime level of talent-based operation**: the culmination of living one's lifetime development formula.

ADVANCING OTHER SYSTEMS TO ADVANCE YOUR SYSTEM

3. **Talent-based leadership formula**: leadership as an expression of one's lifetime development formula

4. **Talent-based leadership development formula**: merging one's lifetime development formula with one's talent-based leadership formula.

5. **Greatest lifetime talent-based operating level as a leader**: based on the previous 4 formulas.

Caution: If you have lived your life directed by external elements (externally referenced) rather than complying with your natural drives internally (internally referenced) you will have less consistent patterns or fewer of them.

TALENT-BASED FLOW STATE
(Internal Generative Congruence)

The flow state which occurs while doing activities using the talents one is most passionate about using and improving

Fragmented and competing systems. No integration, internal cohesiveness or congruence.

Fully integrated around one's naturality, natural talents, and creative expression (one's 'art').

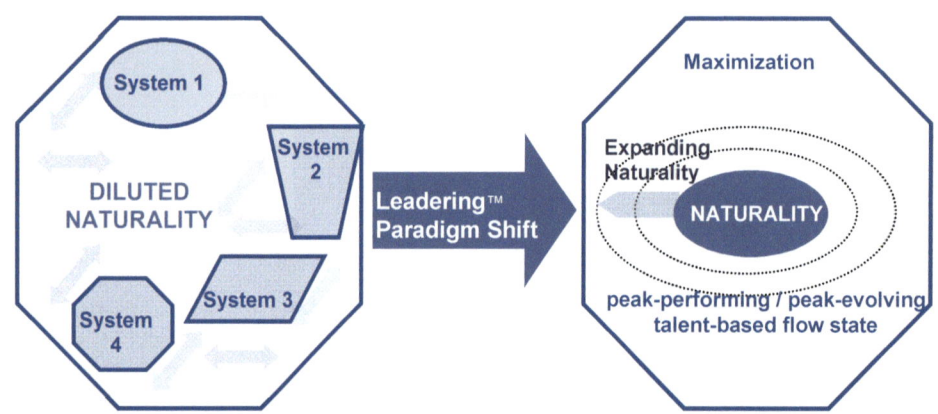

A pre-flow system | A system in talent-based flow or internal congruence

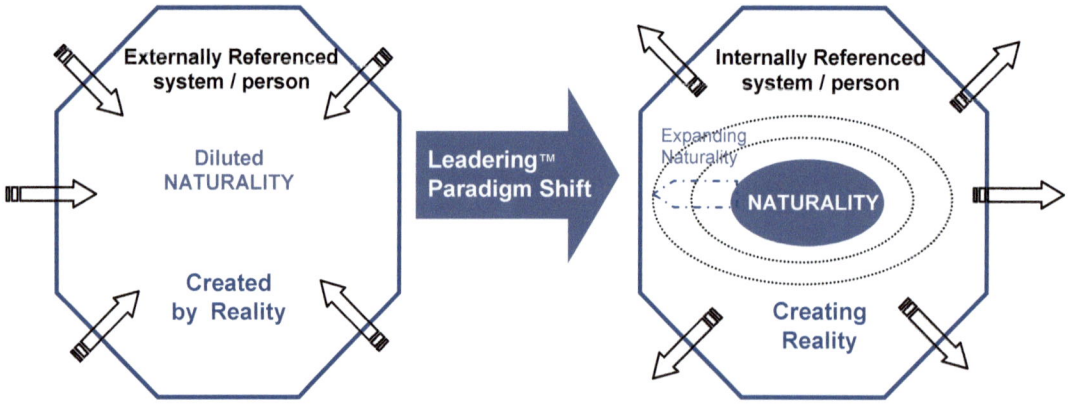

In the Leadering™ paradigm, you and your reality are a single system created and run by a single belief template. Therefore, the quantum leap from externally referenced to internally referenced is critical to leadership, entrepreneurship, innovation, reality creation, and thus, *peak legacy*

© 2006 Lauren Holmes

TWO EVOLUTIONARY DIRECTIONS

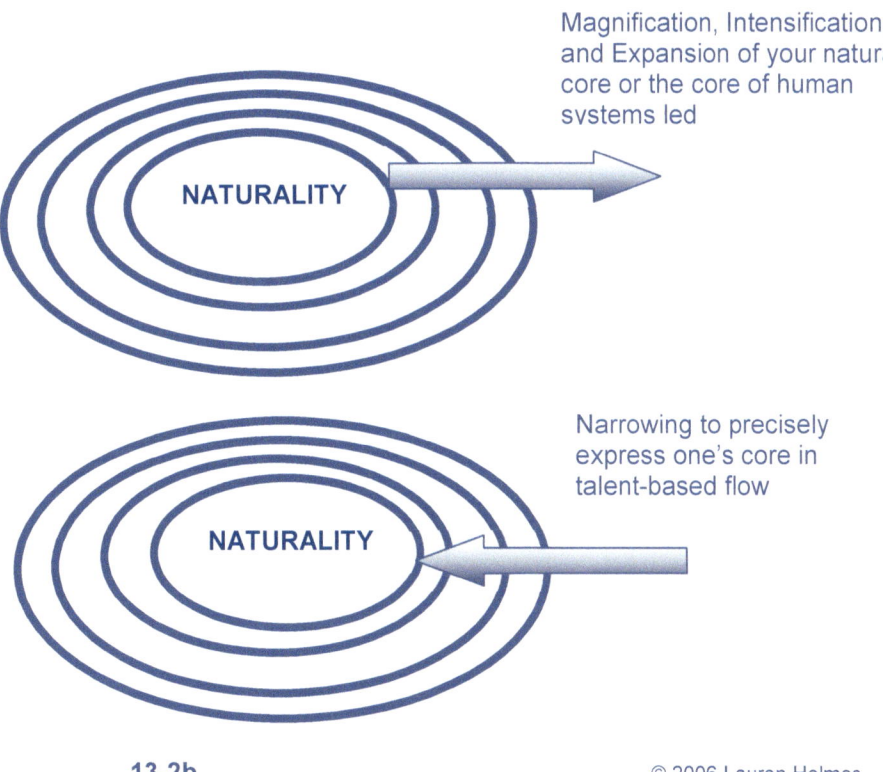

13-2b

EVENT PATTERNS TRACKED FOR THEMES
These patterns are indicative of the flow to flow

In the target paradigm, the life-long patterns of the following 'talent-based' or 'work' events are analyzed for themes indicating the flow to generative congruence or flow internally or externally:

- **an unpaid work theme** based on patterns of events in which you freely give away "work" that others would charge for or that you are so passionate about that you would pay for the opportunity to do.

- **a talent-based knowledge-pursuit or learning-pursuit theme** based on patterns of events of seeking knowledge passionately and willingly for the application of key talents (learning-pursuit theme)

- **a talent-based spontaneous knowledge theme** based on patterns of events in which spontaneous knowledge emerged to support the application of key talents

- **a talent-based frontier-pursuit theme** based on patterns of events of new territories of growth, learning and achievement the system was drawn to pursue for the application of key talents

- **a talent-based creativity-pursuit theme** based on patterns of events of preferred creative expression or creative expression which you or system was drawn to pursue for the application of key talents along with events in which creativity or creative invention or innovation spontaneously emerged for the application of key talents

- **a talent-based creative expression theme** based on patterns of events of creative expression in which your passion and enthusiasm were inflamed

- **a talent-based meaning-pursuit theme** based on patterns of events of work or achievements or contributions considered a meaningful application of key talents

- **the theme(s) of talent-based flow states** indicated by patterns of events whereby you went into flow state during the application of key talents

- **a talent-based flow-to-flow theme, theme(s) of projects** requiring the application of key talents which were supported by lots of coincidences, flows, spontaneous knowledge / creativity (fig13- 4)

- **talent-based naturality expansion theme** (figures 13-2 and 13-2b) indicated by patterns of expansions or intensifications of your system around its core to greater impact on reality - the key direction of growth and advancement of any system in the Leading™ paradigm.

- **a talent-based resonance theme** based on patterns of subjects or activities for the application of key talents with which you resonated

- **a talent-based positive emotion theme** based on patterns of events in which passion, excitement, and enthusiasm emerged during the application of key talents

The above themes emerge synchronously when a system is integrated into the flow to congruence – the outcome of operating in the Leading paradigm. Choose the pattern(s) that works best for you for directing your system to peak legacy

NATURAL QUANTUM LEAPS CLUSTER IN THE FLOW

The advantage of operating in talent-based flow within the talent-based flow of the contextual system

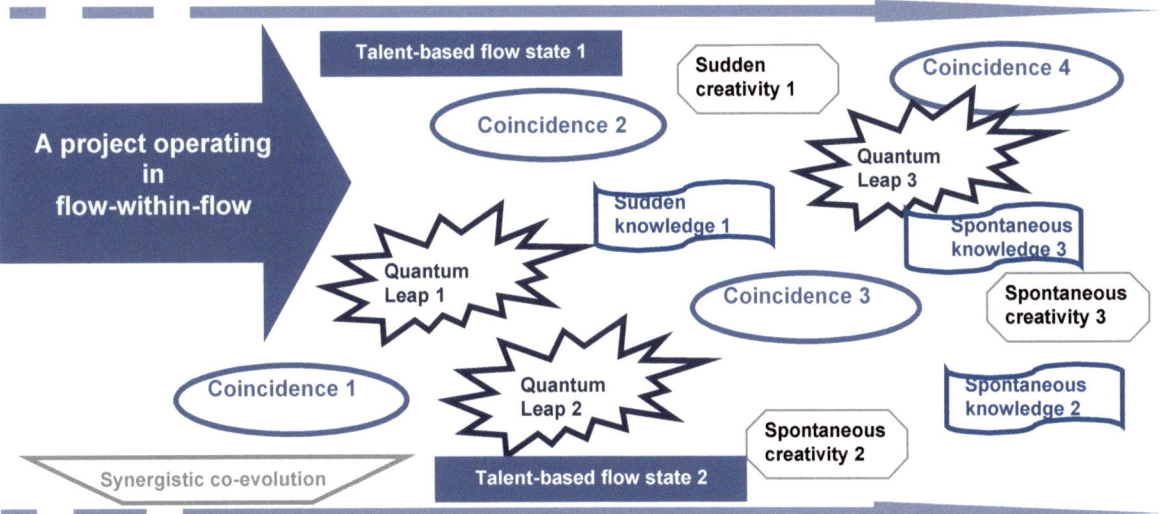

Flow to Congruence   or   Flow-to-Flow   or   Flow to Fusion
or   projection of your talent-based life themes into the future

---

Increasing functionality with each flow experience:
- expanding consciousness and conceptual capacity
- peak performance
- peak evolution
- increasing creative capability
- expansion / intensification / enlargement of the system's natural creative expression

Proof of the Leadering™ paradigm – Proof of the accuracy of your 5 formulas
If you are operating in talent-based flow and the clustering of natural quantum leaps above emerge in your reality, then you have proof that the Leadering paradigm™ and nature's machinery inside and outside of you do indeed operate in the way Leadering™ describes.

RECORDING 14

The Leadering™ program and paradigm will induce evolved states. These will raise your baseline of operation and commensurately increase the magnitude of your lifetime achievement and legacy

7 PERSONALIZING THE LEADERING™ PARADIGM

I FLOW MAXIMIZATION EXERCISES continued

14. Key-talent System-Application Exercise 36 minutes   28 figures

This exercise determines the types of human systems your key talents can be ideally applied to in order to benefit your achievement and advancement and theirs. The Leadering™ machinery is a multi-system environment. Therefore, it is important to think in terms of what types of systems your key talents will ideally impact, advance, and capitalize on for your growth and creative expression. This information is especially important to your development of formulas 3, 4, and 5 since these are strategies for advancing your systems through advancing other systems.

The agenda for the rest of the core determination exercises or exercises for personalizing the paradigm is reviewed. An introduction to Leadering's view of the core is provided leading to a comparison of traditional leadership to Leadering's integrated, core-based, system-based leadership is presented.

To centre your system onto its natural core

The Goals of Leadering's Core Determination Exercises:

- To determine the dynamic core of your system which is being acted on by natural forces inside and outside of you so as to not only comply with them but to capitalize on them.
- To re-boot your system onto this core foundation for peak performance. This is the only foundation for sustained greatness.
- To enable you to sustain your system centred on that core
- To continuously expand that core to intensify your impact and legacy

To plug the core of your centered system into the flow-to-flow - the flow that is centring the core of the larger human system of which you are a part. Harnessing all of the mechanisms and forces centring your system inside and your contextual system outside allows you to achieve beyond your potential.
Peak Legacy. Unprecedented legacy.

THE LEADERING™ CORE CONGRUENCE EXERCISES

These exercises are designed to identify the core of your system which is being acted upon by natural forces inside and outside of you so you can comply with and capitalize on them and avoid operating contrary to them.

FLOW EXPLOITATION EXERCISES
for maximum performance and advancement

Life Theme exercises
- key talent determination
- flow to flow determination

Key talent Determination exercises
- system-based key talent exercise
- various other exercises

5 Talent-Based Operating Formulas exercises
1: your lifetime development formula
2: your greatest lifetime achievement formula
3: your natural leader formula
4: your leadership development formula
5: your greatest leader performance formula

YOUR FLOW ENGINE:

Natural forces inside and outside of you act on your core

YOUR CORE CONSISTS OF:

1. **KEY TALENTS**

2. **ADDICTIVE DRIVES**
   pulling you to use your key talents

*Note: Your key talents and associated drives are the immutable beliefs below. They continuously
- create your reality and
- are being acted upon by the flow to flow and Leadering's built-in growth continuums which amplify core impact.

BELIEF MAXIMIZATION EXERCISES
for Core Congruence

Belief Template Analysis and Upgrade:
- beneficial belief determination:
  ideal talent-based and flow-based beliefs
  identity beliefs, reality creation beliefs
- problem belief determination:
  fear beliefs, toxic beliefs, conflicting beliefs
- event-driven template upgrade process
- quantum leap template exchange process:
  goal-packaging identities, reincarnation

Action Learning Experimentation
- proving beliefs create reality
- improving belief engineering in your own and other systems
- improving template determination / design
- quantum leap experimentation

YOUR BELIEF TEMPLATE

Your belief template governs both you and your reality as a single system

Beliefs are information storage units like genes

---

3. **IMMUTABLE BELIEFS**
   (innate gene-based beliefs)
   These define the essence of your system and why it came together in the first place. These beliefs are genetically based and inherent to the built-in creative expression of your system. See *Note above.

4. **CHANGEABLE BELIEFS**
   ideally designed to support the key talents, addictive drives, and immutable beliefs to maximize your performance, development, and survival in biological terms. The goal is core congruence.

14-1B   © 2006 Lauren Holmes

im·mu·ta·ble: unchanging or unchangeable: not changing or not able to be changed

OUR FLOW ENGINE

OUR CORE FLOW DRIVE COMPLEX:

Your flow engine consists of addictive drives associated with your key talents

Flow is addicting because each of its component drives are addicting: the more you use them the more you want to use them

Our key talent-based drives: our flow engine
- flow-pursuit drive
- creativity-pursuit drive
- creative-expression or self-expression drive
- frontier-pursuit drive
- knowledge-pursuit drive
- meaning-pursuit drive

Our secondary talent-based drives:
- quantum leap drive
- evolution drive
- co-evolution drive
- self-organization drive

These addictive drives form a unique synergistic thrust within each of us: our flow engine

Your 5 talent-based operating formulas or strategies for top performance in the Leadering™ paradigm

→ Talent-based lifetime development formula

→ Greatest talent-based individual performance

→ Talent-based leader formula

→ Talent-based leader development formula

→ Greatest talent-based leader performance

The 5 formulas are the best guess at the strategies which will allow one to capitalize on the flow-to-flow and all of the accompanying 15 dynamics in the Leadering™ paradigm to achieve peak performance and peak development.

YOUR FIVE PERSONALIZED OPERATING FORMULAS
for maximizing in the Leadering™ paradigm

Key talents being acted on by the flow to flow

Your key talents are a system of your strongest capabilities which you are addicted to using and improving. When used, they advance reality in some way. All 5 formulas are operating strategies for capitalizing on your key talents. Therefore they are interlinked. Your key talents are also interlinked into a system of addictive drives which form your flow engine. The flow engine promotes operating in a peak performance flow state in which you are using your key talents. The key talents being acted on by the flow engine need to be known in order to determine one's 5 operating formulas for the Leadering™ paradigm.

1. Your talent-based lifetime development formula: advancing your system

If natural forces continuously pressure you to expand or intensify your ability to use your key talents for creation - to advance reality - what will be the development path or theme of that intensification process underpinning your life?

2. Your greatest talent-based performance as an individual:

If you were to pursue the continuous expansion of your key talents over a lifetime and at top speeds, what is the highest level of creative impact or reality creation that you would likely achieve. What is the highest possible culmination of living your lifetime development formula? What is your maximum attainment based on a lifetime of accelerating development of your key talents?

3. Your talent-based leadership formula: advancing other systems

If you complied with the addictive drives pulling you to the continuous expansion of your key talents, what would be the territory and form of your leadership? How would formulas 1 and 2 define you as a leader by logical extension? What would your leadership formula look like if it was 100% based on your greatest performance with your key talents and their continuous expansion?

4. Your talent-based leadership development formula:

Your leadership development formula just allows you a more specialized lens with which to examine and strategize your personal development. The continuous expansion of the intensity and impact of your key talents define both your development as an individual and a leader. Therefore, leadership development and lifetime development form the same single continuum. The advancement of your key talents increases your strength, impact, and creativity as a leader. How would the previous 3 formulas define a leadership development formula? For those on the Leadering™ program who assume they will never be a leader, it is built in. (figure 14-6E)

5. Your greatest talent-based performance as a leader:

Based on your 4 previous formulas, determine your greatest lifetime level of performance as a leader. Given your advancement as an individual and a leader based on the continuous intensification of your key talents, and given the formula for your greatest performance as an individual, what would be the dimensions of your ultimate performance level as a leader: generically, what will be your greatest levels of capability for causing reality advances?

NUCLEUS: the Core of the Atom

- The smallest unit of matter having all the characteristics of that element.
- Consisting of a dense, central, positively charged nucleus surrounded by a system of electrons.

Leadering re-centres you onto your core system of greatest strengths, talents, passions, and immutable beliefs - your nucleus. This is the only foundation for peak performance and thus your *peak legacy*

A recurring theme in nature and thus in Leadering is that a blueprint or template or DNA or nucleus or core system of information defines a system's expression in reality. Clarity of your template will define the magnitude of your *peak legacy* expressed in reality.

14-3A © 2006 Lauren Holmes

- **NUCLEUS:** the core of every Human Cell
- **DNA:** the core of every Cell Nucleus

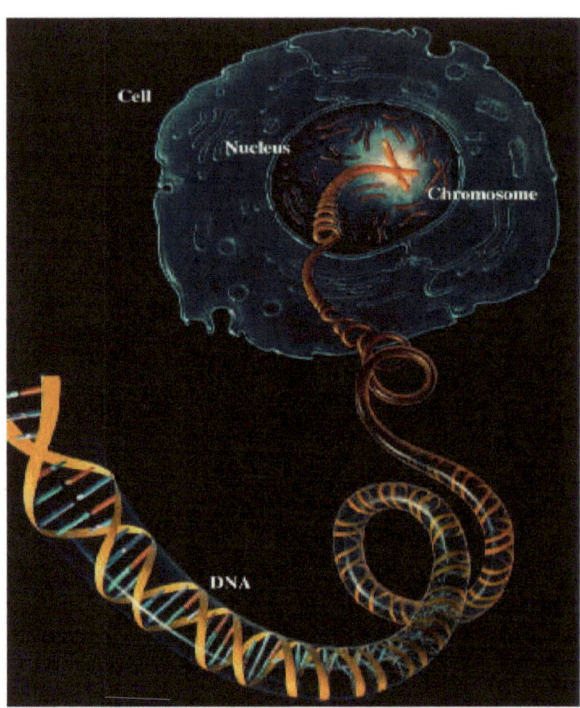

© The National Human Genome Research Institute

This is a diagram of a typical cell from the human body. In this picture you can get a sense of where the DNA resides in the cell as well as how it is organized in the nucleus. Double-stranded DNA is organized into chromosomes. Chromosomes are situated in the nucleus and the membrane bound nucleus is found in the cell.

If every cell in your body has a nucleus or natural core, it makes sense that you too have a natural core or template for you and your reality.

"The part contains the information for the whole" is a recurring theme throughout the universe. As the part, you would therefore contain the template for your whole system which includes you and your reality. This repetitious recurrence is at the foundation of **Leadering's single systems maximization toolkit for all human systems.**

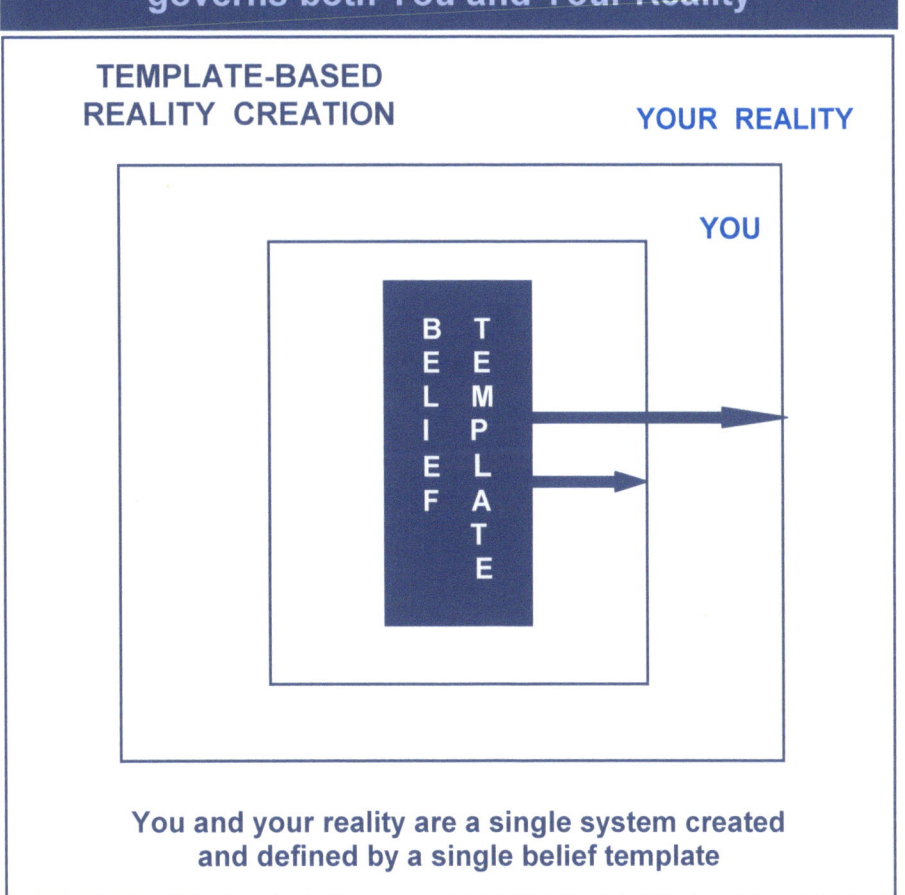

Elements in reality are replicated from beliefs using the same transcription process metaphorically as DNA uses to replicate itself, instruct RNA and protein synthesis. The result is a belief-created reality. It is instructed by your *immutable beliefs* which are linked to your genes plus your *changeable beliefs* which you can choose to support natural processes working on your system internally and externally.

Leadering™ Simplifies Leadership to its Dynamics

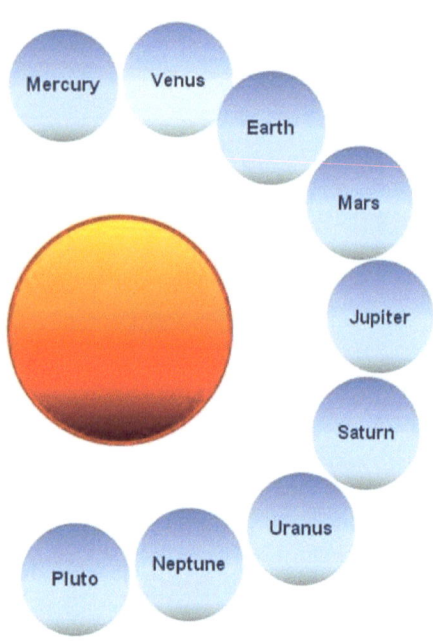

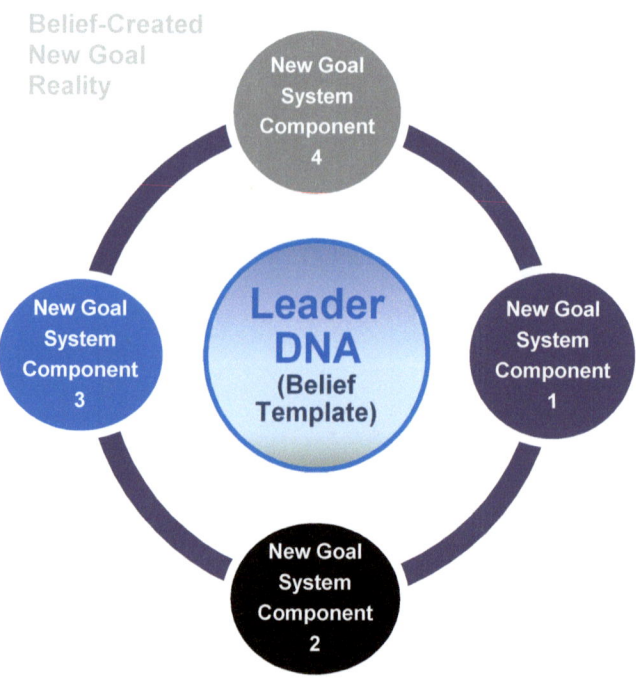

Traditional Leadership
Metaphor: Sun-Planet Relationship

The sun locks the planets in by force. It directs planet movement. However, the cores of the planets are unchanged by the sun and the core of the sun is unchanged by the planets. Neither the sun nor the planets benefit from each other. There is no synergy whereby the whole is greater than the sum of the parts.

Leadering's Core-Based Leadership
Metaphor: DNA or genes defining a human cell

In the Leadering Paradigm, a leader's beliefs and decision-making systems are replicated in individual or organizational systems so that their natural operation will result in achieving a goal in the same way the leader would accomplish it personally.

Rather than a leader acting on others, leaders with their follower individuals and systems operate as a single integrated system with a shared belief template for creating the goal reality. It is about multi-system reality creation.

The leader's belief template must be strong enough and clear enough to define this new multi-component system and its goal reality. A non-leader can use the same approach to capitalize on relevant human systems. By extending one's capabilities with those of other systems one can achieve beyond one's potential.

Beliefs create reality in the Leadering paradigm. Just as in nature, there must always be a blueprint or information structure defining the expression. Human cells and the human body are examples. Beliefs (not thoughts) are how we lock in the new blueprint or, metaphorically, the new DNA. If the information structure does not change inside, nothing will express differently outside . . . . no matter how much action is taken. This is why passionate entrepreneurs can succeed where brilliant experts fail.

HIERARCHICAL LEADERSHIP

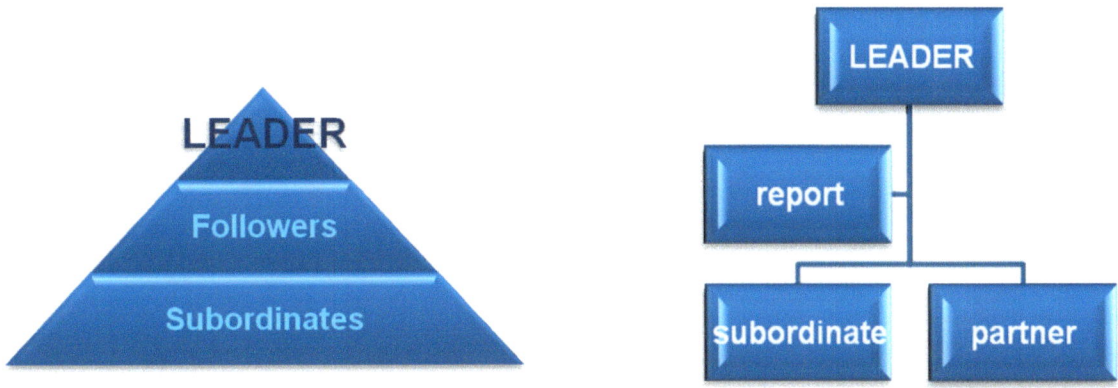

TRADITIONAL LEADER-AT-THE-TOP MODEL
one leader acting on one or more individuals

LEADING, CREATING and ACHIEVING in the PARADIGM

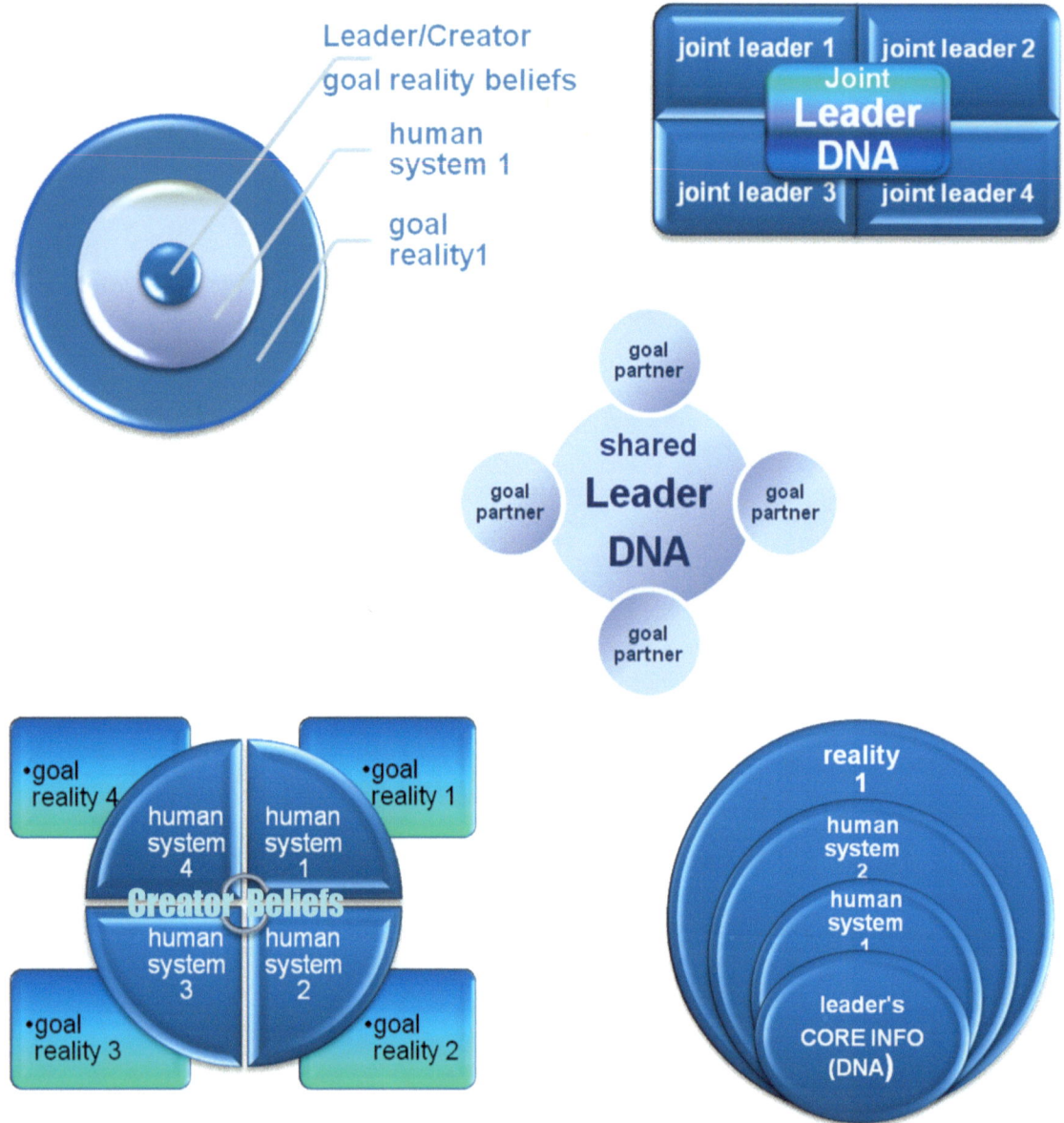

SYSTEMS-BASED or CORE-BASED LEADING, CREATING and ACHIEVING in the LEADERING™ PARADIGM

Reality creation is accomplished by one or more leaders or system maximizers creating the core 'DNA' for defining the new goal reality system based on a belief template shared by multiple systems. **You and your reality are a system.**
Merge yourself and relevant systems to a single system for *peak legacy*.

System-Based Key Talents Exercise
INSTRUCTIONS - 1

This system-based key talents exercise provides examples of key talents categorized by the systems they impact. Everything in the Leading™ paradigm is a system. Therefore, natural forces will pressure your key talents to act on systems.

In the Life Themes exercise, you had a chance to view yourself and your life as a system. With this exercise, you can begin applying your systems thinking capabilities to maximizing your own system by creating, improving and advancing other systems. Your key talents may be used in an infinite number of contexts and jobs which you might choose for your career.

Your determinations in the Life Themes exercise and this one are designed to assist you with the development of the 5 operating strategies or formulas in the next exercises which will help you to capitalize on natural forces acting on your system from the inside and outside.

1. This exercise should be done with the intention of viewing yourself and your life in terms of systems and with developing the 5 talent-based operating formulas in mind.

2. Review figures 5C and 5D to see an overview of the exercise selection charts which will follow. This allows you to get a feel for the categories at a glance in order to begin assessing where you would prefer to apply your key talents.
    - When you are applying your key talents - doing your art - are you maintaining or advancing existing systems, creating new systems from existing systems or creating entirely new standalone systems? (Formulas 1, 2, 3 and 5)
    - Evaluate each of the columns in Figure 5D to determine what kind of systems you will be leading in Formulas 3 and 5
    - What are the most complex systems you will be impacting at the height of your personal (Formula 2) or leadership strength (Formula 5): maximizing individual systems? maximizing multiple systems? . . .

14-5A

System-Based Key Talents Exercise
INSTRUCTIONS - 2

3. **CURRENT**: Review the exercise charts (Figure 5E-5H) under the headings of
   - System Maintenance — Figure 5E
   - System Advancement — Figure 5F
   - System Creation and/or — Figure 5G
   - System Relationships — Figure 5H

   Assume you have the freedom, resources, and opportunities to use your greatest talents to the maximum. Choose the box(es) for the intersection of the horizontal and vertical categories which generically describe(s) the territories where:
   - there is work you love to do
   - you love to change reality (creation and creativity)
   - you love to learn more or develop new skills or knowledge (frontiering™)
   - you would love to be paid to learn and create: your ideal territory of paid peak evolution
   - you would like to make your greatest contribution to the world
   - you could leave your greatest legacy because your perform so well
   - the activities to be done would be work to others but are compelling play to you
   - given total freedom and resources, you would feel compelled to create and learn

   Capture what you learn from this segment of the exercise in the key talents exercise and Formulas 1 and 2.

4. **FUTURE**: Assume you have had the freedom, the resources, and opportunities to use your greatest talents to the maximum year after year over your lifetime. Repeat step 2 taking into consideration all of the built-in growth directions inherent in the Leading™ paradigm and launched by the Leading™ paradigm shift to determine which box(es) most reflect the person you will become and the advancement of your key talents when you operate in flow to flow day after day. Some of the built-in growth directions inherent in the Leading™ paradigm have been identified in Figures 6A to 6G. Capture what you learn from this segment of the exercise in Formulas 2, 4, and 5.

The system-based key talent exercise not only identifies where you are now but how you could advance based on your art: What if year after year you simply pushed through new frontiers of the art and science of using your key talents? Where would you end up? Who would you become? What would you be capable of? Identify which boxes would most represent your lifetime maximum performance and achievement resulting from using your key talents.

Take another pass at determining this 'future you' after the key talents and 5 key-talent-based formula exercises after the current exercise to follow.

> ## System-Based Key Talents Exercise
> # INSTRUCTIONS - 3

5. **System maintenance is unlikely the creative expression of your key talents:**

   Let me speak to those who think their art in the future will be system maintenance. Leadering™ unleashes meta-competencies associated with frontiering™, creativity, creation, penetrating the unknown. Since there is no creation or change in reality with system maintenance, this may not be an accurate reading of the application of your key talents after Leadering™.

   Given all of the creative, evolutionary, and adaptive forces within the flow to flow, and the addictive nature of the drives around your key talents, it is unlikely that systems maintenance will be how your key talents are applied in the future. Please think twice about making it future.

   Consider all of the built-in growth elements of Leadering™ listed in figures 14-6A to 14-6E and assume you have experienced them all for decades. Pay particular attention to the progression demonstrated in the Leadership Development Continuum in figure 14-6C. Notice that the first box is the manager or systems maintenance box. Imagine yourself in one of the other boxes. How are you applying your key talents? How are you changing reality? For those systems maintenance individuals who choose to shift over to the Leadering™ paradigm, your addictive drives around your key talents along with nature's flow to flow drives will be pulling you through this progression

   As the addictive drives increase around using your key talents, they will be influencing how you operate in every aspect of your life. Creativity and its subset, frontiering™, will become the norm for you, so I encourage you to choose a box in the creation and advancement of individual systems or groups of systems as in system relationships

6. Quantum leap to lock in the changes of the future you to reinforce your natural core. (See figure 14-7 for a reminder on the steps of a quantum leap)

7. Begin operating with these formulas

8. As you are comfortable, begin applying core determination to other systems you wish to lead or advance.

System-Based Key Talent Categories

SYSTEM MAINTENANCE Single / Multi-System	SYSTEM ADVANCEMENT Single / Multi-System	SYSTEM CREATION Single / Multi-System	SYSTEM RELATIONSHIPS Each relationship creates a new system
manager: very little new creation is required. **Creativity and creation increase with each column to the right.** **Since beliefs create reality, this means that the need for belief changes increase as your move to the right.**	strategy development people development organization development multi-organization synergy process development knowledge development technology development **change leadership** • transitional • transformational • facilitative **frontier leadership** **creational leadership** **flow leadership**	**creational leadership** **frontier leadership** **quantum leap leadership** **template leadership** **emergence leadership** system creation strategy system creation implementation entrepreneur company creation intrapreneur project creation new product creation new technology creation new infrastructure creation new process creation new science creation new knowledge creation new skill creation new frontier creation creation research merger-created system acquisition-created system innovation / creativity	System relationships: • to maintain systems • to advance systems • to create systems **co-evolutionary leadership** **co-adaptation leadership** collaboration and synergy business web development CRM: customer relationship management customer development customer chain development supplier chain development network development relationship building team building market development unifying and integrating problem solving conflict resolution peace keeping negotiation mergers and acquisitions relationship strategy/vision relationship-related implementation

→

- Increasing belief and information changes
- Increasing impact on reality

- In the Leadering™ paradigm, leadership extends nature's systems management.
- This exercise demonstrates Leadering's single systems maximization toolkit

EXAMPLES OF AREAS OF ONE'S ADDICTIVE KEY TALENTS	INDIV'L SYSTEM	MULTI-INDIV'L SYSTEM	ORG'L SYSTEM	MULTI-ORG'L SYSTEM	KNOW-LEDGE SYSTEM	PROCESS SYSTEM
Description and/or Examples	*You *a person *a follower *your child	Individuals en masse: a consumer market, a university	A group of people: an organization or company	A business web or community	A science, field, discipline	*Leadership development * Business process reengineering

14-5E

SYSTEM MAINTENANCE

Your key talents are addicted to running existing systems

EXAMPLES OF AREAS OF ONE'S ADDICTIVE KEY TALENTS	INDIV'L SYSTEM	MULTI-INDIV'L SYSTEM	ORG'L SYSTEM	MULTI-ORG'L SYSTEM	KNOW-LEDGE SYSTEM	PROCESS SYSTEM
Description and/or Examples	you a person a follower your child	Individuals en masse: a consumer market, a university	A group of people: an organization or company	A business web or community	A science, field, discipline	*Leadership development * Business process reengineering
recordkeeping						
manufacturing						
accounting						
repetitive sales						

14-5F

SYSTEM ADVANCEMENT

Your key talents are addicted to advancing existing systems by capitalizing on other systems through synergy, adaptation, symbiosis, and co-evolution.

EXAMPLES OF AREAS OF ONE'S ADDICTIVE KEY TALENTS	INDIV'L SYSTEM	MULTI-INDIV'L SYSTEM	ORG'L SYSTEM	MULTI-ORG'L SYSTEM	KNOW-LEDGE SYSTEM	PROCESS SYSTEM
Description and/or Examples	*You *a person *a follower *your child	Individuals en masse: a consumer market, a university	A group of people: an organization or company	A business web or community	A science, field, discipline	*Leadership development * Business process reengineering
STRATEGY DEVELOPMENT						
vision dev't						
vision implementation						
strategy implementation						
strategy formulations						
strategy buy-in						
PEOPLE DEVELOPMENT						
recruiting						
skill dev't						
training						
teaching						
course / program development						
succession planning						
integration						
leadership dev't						
parenting						
performance improvement						
ORGANIZATION DEVELOPMENT						
change leadership						
change facilitation						
reengineering						
performance improvements						
problem solving						
conflict resolution						

quantum leaps						
infrastructure dev't						
org. dev't strategy						
O.D. implementation						
cultural dev't						
integration						
MULTI-ORGANIZATION SYNERGY	**see Systems Relationships below**					
partnerships						
business webs						
PROCESS DEVELOPMENT						
process reconceptualization						
implementation strategy						
reengineering						
innovation						
performance improvements						
experimentation						
KNOWLEDGE DEVELOPMENT						
teaching						
research						
creativity						
problem solving						
technology development						
experimentation						
data base dev't						
IT						
conceptualization						
idea-generation						
knowledge management strategy						
TECHNOLOGY DEVELOPMENT						

CHANGE LEADERSHIP						
transitional						
transformational						
facilitative						
FRONTIER LEADERSHIP						
FLOW LEADERSHIP						

14-5G © 2006 Lauren Holmes

SYSTEM CREATION

Your key talents are addicted to creating new systems or new systems from existing systems

EXAMPLES OF AREAS OF ONE'S ADDICTIVE KEY TALENTS	INDIV'L SYSTEM	MULTI-INDIV'L SYSTEM	ORG'L SYSTEM	MULTI-ORG'L SYSTEM	KNOW-LEDGE SYSTEM	PROCESS SYSTEM
Description and/or Examples	* You * a person * a follower * your child	Individuals en masse: a consumer market, a university	* A group of people: an organization or company	A company, business web or community	A science, field, discipline, or skill	*Leadership development * Business process reengineering
system creation strategy						
system creation implementation						
entrepreneur company creation						
intrapreneur project creation						
new product creation						
new technology creation						
new infrastructure creation						
new process creation						
new science creation						
new knowledge creation						
new skill creation						
new frontier creation						
creation research						
merger-created system						
acquisition-created system						
innovation / creativity						

14-5H © 2006 Lauren Holmes

SYSTEM RELATIONSHIPS

Your key talents are addicted to the creation of multi-individual and multi-organizational systems to support system creation and system advancement and system maintenance

EXAMPLES OF AREAS OF ONE'S ADDICTIVE KEY TALENTS	INDIV'L SYSTEM	MULTI-INDIV'L SYSTEM	ORG'L SYSTEM	MULTI-ORG'L SYSTEM	KNOW-LEDGE SYSTEM	PROCESS SYSTEM
Description and/or Examples	*You a person a follower your child*	*Individuals en masse: a consumer market, a university*	*A group of people: an organization or company*	*A business web or community*	*A science, field, discipline*	**Leadership development * Business process reengineering*
collaboration						
synergy						
customer development						
customer chain dev't						
supplier chain dev't						
network dev't						
relationship building						
team building						
market dev't						
co-evolution						
adaptation						
system unification						
advancement						
problem solving						
conflict resolution						
negotiation						
mergers						
acquisitions						
relationship strategy and vision						
relationship-related implementation						
unifying/ integrating						
peace keeping						

14-5I

© 2006 Lauren Holmes

Note: Figures 14-6A to 14-6H are dealt with in more detail in the next presentation devoted to the growth launched and built into the Leadering™ paradigm and process

LEADERING'S BUILT-IN KEY TALENT DEVELOPMENT - 1

Use these to surmise the lifetime maximum possible impact of your key talents - your *peak legacy* - as an individual, a leader, an entrepreneur, and/or an innovator

Consider the following talent development processes built into the Leadering paradigm and this program when doing the core determination exercises to identify your key talents and 5 ideal operating formulas:

If the below assumptions are true,
1. **How would the art and science behind the use of your system of key talents develop over your lifetime?**
2. **What could be the maximum possible impact of your key talents on reality?**
3. **What would your five operating formulas or strategies be in the Leadering paradigm?**

- Assume you have all of the money and resources and freedom to pursue the use of your key talents to the maximum.
- Assume your system operates day after day in talent-based flow state within the talent-based flow state of the larger contextual system of which you are a part.
- Assume your capabilities are extended by nature's capabilities.
- Assume your drives merge with nature's drives to shift you into overdrive.

- Assume you will be constantly breaking through new frontiers of the art and science behind applying your key talents.

- Assume a constant increase in the impact on reality of your key talent system as you constantly expand or intensify around your core. (Figure 14-6Dtop)

- Assume the depth of your talent-based flow states increases with each experience thus
    - speeding the increase of your functionality and performance
    - speeding the advancement of your art,
    - speeding the increase of your levels of peak performance
    - increasing the speed of your development exponentially.
    - allowing you to advance reality continuously in your peak performance state

- Assume the addictive drives associated with using your key talents get stronger with each use and pull you to accomplish more without "work" or discipline. Assume the more you use them the more you want to use them.

- Assume these addictive drives and the growth built into talent-based flow states pull you along the development continuum in Figure 14-6F.

© 2006 Lauren Holmes

LEADERING'S BUILT-IN KEY TALENT DEVELOPMENT - 2

Use these to surmise the lifetime maximum possible impact of your key talents - your *peak legacy* - as an individual, a leader, an entrepreneur, and/or an innovator

- assume a narrowing of your work to using your key talents more precisely and accurately with less baggage and encumbrances around them. You eliminate from your life the things you think you need to do in order to do your art or to be able to do your art but are not your art. (Figure 14-6D bottom)

- assume that Leadering™ increases the meta-competencies of leaders, entrepreneurs, innovators, and high achievers (figure 14-6E) which will allow you
  - to move more quickly easily and safely into unknown territory and frontiers,
  - to increase your creativity and innovation,
  - to increase your knowledge,
  - to increase your coincidences and facilitating events which will improve your performance of your art.

- assume years of side ventures which have increased your specialization in various aspects of your art

- assume an increase in the level of complexity that you are able to deal with and apply your key talents to (figure 14-6H):
  - from single system to multiple system impact
  - from transactions to process. from process to quantum leaps
  - from linear to nonlinear

- assume your consciousness, big picture thinking, and conceptual skills continue to increase and expand so that you can
  - see more patterns
  - see the flow of systems to congruence or the flow to flow
  - see the interaction of more systems and the opportunities for synergy and co-evolution
  - have more information
  - impact more systems
  - impact more complex systems
  - impact larger systems

14-6B

© 2006 Lauren Holmes

LEADERING'S BUILT-IN KEY TALENT DEVELOPMENT - 3

Use these to surmise the lifetime maximum possible impact of your key talents - your *peak legacy* - as an individual, a leader, an entrepreneur, and/or an innovator

Note: Conceptual competencies consist of the appropriate paradigms, mindsets, and conceptual skills necessary to:
- assess the environment
- see the long-range needs and implications of a situation and to build a plan for meeting these needs and
- visualize, address, and capitalize on the complex interrelationships that exist in a workplace in order to set priorities, make decisions, anticipate the future, and formulate strategies and tactics, and
- comprehend the culture of historically developed values, beliefs, and norms in order to visualize its future.

Note: Conceptual skills include:
- concept formation which is the capacity to analyze relationships between objects
- abstraction or the ability to think symbolically
- deductive logic which is the application of general rules or concepts in making a decision for a specific set of stimuli and/or
- inductive logic which is the analysis of feedback or identification of relevant details in formulating a concept to use in decision making,
- problem reframing to enhance creativity
- dealing with multiple perspectives and ambiguity
- frame of reference development including systems understanding, environmental scanning, pattern recognition
- idea and concept development and use to solve complex problems
- envisioning to anticipate the future
- proactive thinking using critical, creative, reflective thinking
- skillful formulation of ends, ways, means
- analysis of complicated events
- trend perception
- change detection
- creative and opportunistic problem-solving
- ability to conceptualize complex ideas
- deployment of models, theories and inferences, and
- pattern recognition.

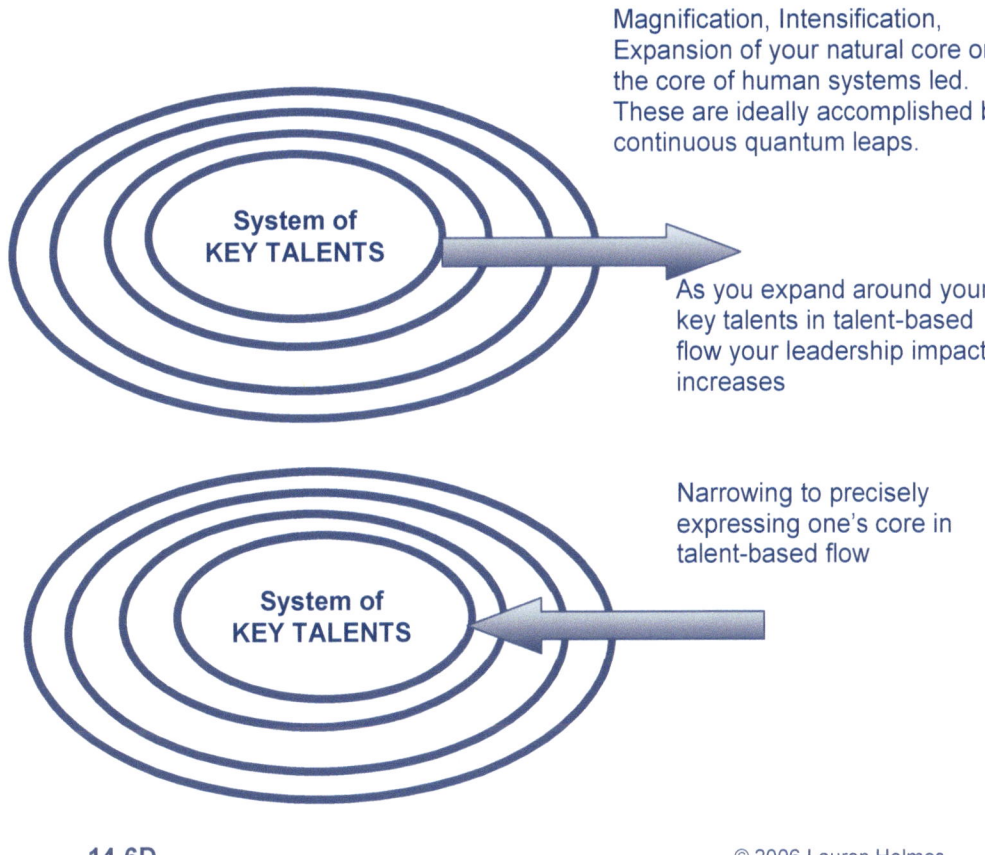

THE META-COMPETENCIES
of Leaders, Entrepreneurs, Innovators, and High Achievers
unleashed by the Leading™ Paradigm shift

Systems-Based Approach
systems thinking, systems-based operation, systems-based emotional intelligence, belief system management, quantum leaping, expanded consciousness, conceptual skills, templating

Continuous Development
accelerating growth, co-evolution, re-optimization, agility, fluidity, expanding self-expression, learning/adaptation agility, belief upgrading, expanding consciousness

Cognitive Capabilities
learning agility, knowing, conceptual skills, abstract thinking, expanding consciousness, internally referenced, expanding self-expression and self-awareness, emotional intelligence, deductive reasoning, pattern recognition

Mastering the Unknown
frontiering™, creating, innovating, systems thinking, informationless decision-making, abstract thinking, conceptual skills, expanded consciousness

Performance
talent-based flow and other peak performance states, accelerated implementation, advancement by nonlinear quantum leaps, systems thinking, systems-based operation, expanding self-expression, learning/adaptation agility

© 2006 Lauren Holmes

A New Paradigm-based Leadership Development Continuum

LEADERING™ AMPLIFIES LEADER DRIVES

Manager	Transitional Change Leader	Transformational Change Leader	Creational Leader / Frontiering Leader
Run an existing business as is	**Linearly advance an existing business** • Incremental upgrades • Harvest	**Nonlinearly advance an existing business** • Turnarounds • Explosive Growth • Merge 2 existing businesses	**Create the unknown or Penetrate the unknown** • Business startups • Pioneering / Frontiering • Re-engineering • New ventures / Innovation

As leader drives strengthen, leader impact increases:
INCREASED DRIVES TO change – creativity/creation – frontiering™
risk – learning – belief changes – adaptation – growth – congruence ➡

Leader drive subset

Managers manage what exists ➡ Leaders bring *the new* into existence
Many skills taught in leadership development programs emerge naturally as Leadering™ stimulates an increase in the leader drives and dynamics observed in great leaders.

As individuals advance along the leadership development continuum,
their ability to advance reality increases.
If there is no change in beliefs, there is no change in reality.
If there is no change in reality, leadership has not occurred.
The magnitude of change achieved in reality is the measure of leadership strength.

14-6F © 1995 Lauren Holmes

CREATING WORLD LEADERS

YOUR REALITY · ORGANIZATION · INDUSTRY · BUSINESS ECOSYSTEM · CIVILIZATION

POWER MUST INCREASE TO:

> Imprint **Beliefs** → Unify **Identities** → Increase **Creations**

14-6G

© 1995 Lauren Holmes

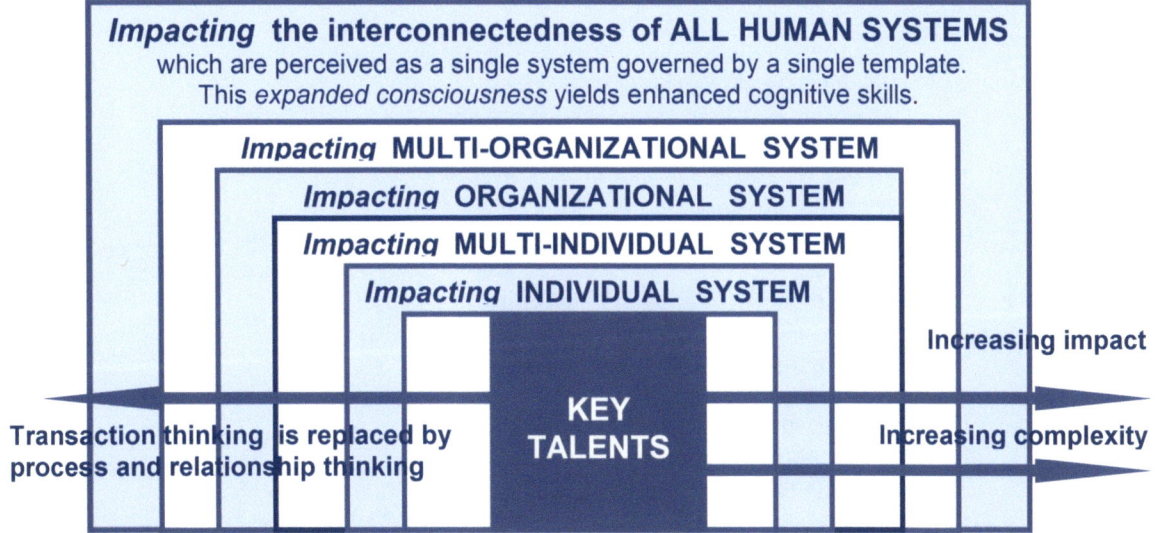

THE LEADING™ QUANTUM LEAP PROCESS

Design it!   Feel it!   Be it!

PRE-LEAP
1. Choose the right quantum leap or post-leap state
2. Define the post-leap state with clarity
3. Define the post-leap state without previous limitations or toxicity
4. Emotionally template the post-leap state
5. Add the information to fuel emergence
6. Expect the unexpected post-leap

LEAP
1. Release the linear connection to the past
2. Feel yourself 100% fluid
3. Feel the post-leap state
4. Feel who the "post-leap you" will be
5. Commit to the quantum leap
6. Make an abrupt, no-return, reincarnation
7. Trigger spontaneous self-organization by intent

POST-LEAP
1. Operate as if the quantum leap was successful
2. Walk around as the person with the post-leap reality
3. Hold this new identity until reality restructures
4. Ignore evidence of events created by the old template
5. Trigger cascading quantum leaps by intent
6. Establish quantum leaping as a way of life
7. Consolidate your new quantum leap expert beliefs

© 1998 Lauren Holmes

RECORDING 15

> Leadering™ maximizes human systems whether those systems are individuals, companies, countries or families. Once you learn how to maximize your own system you can use the same model to maximize any human system to help you to achieve your goals.

7 PERSONALIZING THE LEADERING™ PARADIGM

I   FLOW MAXIMIZATION EXERCISES   continued

15. Growth built into the Leadering™ paradigm   23 minutes   19 figures

It is important to take a brief break here from the exercises to review the many ways in which growth is built into the Leadering™ paradigm. With this information fresh in your mind, you can re-visit the maximum application of your key talent to systems in the previous exercise. In addition, this information will be critical to determining your lifetime maximums as both an individual and a leader as required by your Leadering™ operating formulas 2 and 5.

Many of the ways in which growth is launched, sustained and accelerated over one's lifetime through the Leadering™ paradigm shift and operating in the Leadering™ paradigm are identified. This helps you to better project the advancement of your system to determine lifetime maximums and continuums to those maximums as required by the paradigm personalization or core determination exercises.

In the process of describing all of the built-in growth mechanisms, many Leadering™ concepts presented to this point are reviewed and organized in new ways for easier assimilation.

HOW GROWTH IS BUILT INTO LEADERING™

The Key Leadering™ Paradigm Growth Players

System Core:
System Flow engine (Figure 15-3A):
- flow pursuit of the system
- key talents
- core addictive drives (15-3A)

System Template:
- immutable beliefs
- changeable beliefs: event-driven template upgrade process

System Meta-Competencies (15-5D)

Conditioned Reflexes (Figures 15-4A-C)

Leadering System Management Toolkit:

The 15 Dynamics (Figure 15-2):
  Systems Mindset
    systems-based dynamic
    expanding consciousness
  Advancement Mechanics
    quantum leap dynamic
    templating dynamic
    self-organizing dynamic
    emergence dynamic
  Advancement Directions
    knowledge-pursuit drive
    adaptation drive
    evolution drive
    co-evolution drive
    talent-based flow drive
    flow-within-flow drive
  Drives for the Unknown:
    frontier-pursuit drive
    creation / creativity-pursuit drive

Five Talent-based Operating Formulas
(Figures 15-3A-B)
lifetime development, greatest lifetime performance, leadership, leadership development, greatest leader lifetime performance

Self- or **System-Initiated Quantum Leaps**

Nature-Initiated Quantum Leaps imbedded in the flow to flow
- coincidences (multi-system synergy, co-evolution, co-adaptation)
- spontaneous knowledge
- spontaneous creativity
- facilitating events
- flow states

for opportunistic synergy, co-evolution, co-adaptation, creative problem-solving, and flow-within-flow

Talent-Based Themes of your 'Life System' (Figure 15-3B)
  an unpaid work theme
  a knowledge-pursuit theme
  a spontaneous knowledge theme
  a frontier-pursuit theme
  a creativity-pursuit theme
  a talent-based creative expression theme
  a meaning-pursuit theme
  the theme(s) of talent-based flow states
  a flow-to-flow theme,
  theme(s) of talent-based projects
  a naturality expansion theme
  a resonance theme
  a positive emotion theme

15-1A   © 2006 Lauren Holmes

HOW GROWTH IS BUILT INTO LEADERING™

Leadering™ launches a series of growth continuums so its effect does not end when the paradigm shift is completed. The following are a few examples.

1. **FLOW TO FLOW**
   Merging with natural forces which are advancing systems means your system will advance. Your system becomes part of a dance of creativity in response to the continuous change of its context as other systems use creativity to co-adapt and co-evolve.

2. **TALENT-BASED FLOW STATE**
   - One must be stretched beyond one's existing capabilities to enter flow state.
   - One leaves each talent-based flow state more advanced.
   - Each flow state cultivates expanded consciousness and conceptual capabilities. Flow state can be called "active meditation" since many of the same benefits documented for meditation emerge as a result of experiencing flow state.
   - One operates at peak performance in flow. Operating at peak performance around your key talents means that, over time, your accomplishments are greater. This lays the foundation for operating at even higher levels of performance in future flow states. More impactful and novel changes to reality result and new frontiers are scaled.
   - Since one cannot experience toxic emotions and the beliefs behind them in flow state, they atrophy from disuse.
   - Flow state is an addictive drive - the more you experience, the more you want to experience it - until you are operating 100% of your day in talent-based flow state or at least flow state and growing continuously as a result.

3. **15 DYNAMICS and ADDICTIVE DRIVES**
   which advance your system are cultivated
   - the 15 dynamics underpinning the Leadering paradigm which are listed in 1A all advance human systems as a way of life.
   - the 15 dynamics include the key talent-based drives of our flow engine: flow-pursuit drive, creativity-pursuit drive, creative-expression or self-expression drive, frontier-pursuit drive, knowledge-pursuit drive, meaning-pursuit drive. The more you use these drives, the more you will want to use them. Leadering™ promotes the use of these talent-based drives.

4. **AN EVENT-DRIVEN TEMPLATE UPGRADE PROCESS**
   Toxicity atrophies
   - Each unpreferred event in reality triggers an automatic belief template upgrade process in the Leadering paradigm which gradually clears problem or interfering beliefs. Over time, your belief template has mare advantageous beliefs to support the application of your key talents.

HOW GROWTH IS BUILT INTO LEADERING™

5. BUILT-IN NATURAL QUANTUM LEAPS CATAPULTING YOUR SYSTEM AHEAD
- The natural quantum leaps inherent in the flow to flow - coincidences, spontaneous knowledge, spontaneous creativity, facilitating events, nature-initiated quantum leaps - ensure that your system is constantly advancing, co-evolving and co-adapting.

6. QUANTUM LEAP EXPERTISE
- Several conditioned reflexes have been installed throughout the Leadering quantum leap process itself so that your expertise will advance with each quantum leap.
- For example, a conditioned reflex has been installed so that the experiential learning of each quantum leap increases the speed, power and span of impact, fluidity, nonlinearity, conditioned reflexes, emotional memory, belief template, belief engineering skill, ability to capitalize on flow to flow, cascading quantum leap thinking, and experiential memory for future quantum leaps.
- Change happens more quickly and safely with Leadering's quantum leap expertise since it provides the ability to advance yourself and other systems nonlinearly from one stable state to the next without having to keep the system stable through linear transitional steps which would slow down progress and might damage the system.
- The Leadering paradigm merges individual and multiple systems with natural processes which are continuously quantum leaping systems to improved congruence and advancement.

15-1C © 2006 Lauren Holmes

Systems Management used by Nature and Natural Leaders

FLOW to GENERATIVE CONGRUENCE DRIVE

FLOW to FLOW DRIVE – THE FLOW ENGINE

Nature pressures all human systems into generative congruence internally and externally. Successful leaders do the same thing.

The 14 paradigm dynamics or leader drives below promote the 15th drive: the flow of systems to generative congruence internally and externally. Congruence is the driving force of the target paradigm of Leadering™.

SYSTEMS MINDSET

A systems-based drive
Everything in the paradigm is a system, including individuals, organizations, and processes.

An expanding consciousness drive to oneness. Consciousness expands due to operating in the flow to congruence and stretching to view interacting systems.

ADVANCEMENT MECHANICS

A quantum leap drive
A templating drive
A self-organizing drive
An emergence drive
Leaders orchestrate abrupt nonlinear system advancements, adaptations, co-evolutions, and re-optimizations using mechanisms available in the flow to congruence. They operate as belief engineers, cultural engineers, reality architects, quantum leap leaders, and emergence leaders: NONLINEAR UPGRADE MECHANISMS

ADVANCEMENT DIRECTIONS

A knowledge-pursuit drive*
Leaders harness a system's innate drives for advancing its talent-based expression in order to achieve multi-system goals and maximization: EVOLUTIONARY PATH DETERMINANT

An adaptation drive*
Externally driven adjustment to advances in the shared contextual system caused by the adaptation / evolution of other subsystems: CHAIN REACTION: THE DANCE

An evolution drive*
'*Growth*' and '*Learning*' help human systems achieve their existing potential. '*Evolution*' advances that potential. Human systems advance by (1) quantum-leap intensifications of their natural core and (2) belief template upgrades: UPGRADED POTENTIAL / FUNCTIONALITY

A co-evolution drive*
Internally driven system upgrade achieved by capitalizing on external upgrading systems: OPPORTUNISTIC SYNERGY + LOCKSTEP ADVANCEMENT

A talent-based flow drive* (internal)
A flow-within-flow drive* (hierarchical)
The flow to internal/external congruence: PEAK-PERFORMING / PEAK-EVOLVING STATE

DRIVES FOR THE UNKNOWN:
the essence of leadership, entrepreneurship, innovation, and career creation

1. **A frontier-pursuit drive***: Penetrate unknown systems.
2. **A creation / creativity-pursuit drive***: Bring unknown into existence.
   NATURE IS ENDLESS MULTI-SYSTEM CREATIVITY - LEADERSHIP IS AN EXTENSION

These dynamics form the toolkit for maximizing any human system in the paradigm whether the system is an individual, organization, market, civilization, or process such as leadership development, career management, or organizational change.

15-2 upgraded © 2006 Lauren Holmes * addicting talent-based

Recording 15: Built-In Growth   78

OUR FLOW ENGINE

OUR CORE FLOW DRIVE COMPLEX:

Your flow engine consists of addictive drives associated with your key talents

Flow is addicting because each of its component drives are addicting: the more you use them the more you want to use them

Our key talent-based drives:
   our flow engine
- flow-pursuit drive
- creativity-pursuit drive
- creative-expression or
  self-expression drive
- frontier-pursuit drive
- knowledge-pursuit drive
- meaning-pursuit drive

Our secondary talent-based drives:
- quantum leap drive
- evolution drive
- co-evolution drive
- self-organization drive

These addictive drives form a unique synergistic thrust within each of us:
   our flow engine

15-3A

Your 5 talent-based operating formulas for top performance in the Leadering paradigm

Lifetime development formula →

Greatest personal performance →

Natural leader formula
(System Maximizer formula) →

Natural leadership development formula →

Greatest leader performance →

© 2006 Lauren Holmes

EVENT PATTERNS TRACKED FOR THEMES
These patterns are indicative of the flow to internal and external congruence or the flow to flow

In the target paradigm, the life-long patterns of the following 'talent-based' or 'work' events are analyzed for themes indicating the flow to generative congruence or flow internally or externally:

- **an unpaid work theme**
- **a knowledge-pursuit theme or learning-pursuit theme**
- **a spontaneous knowledge theme**
- **a frontier-pursuit theme**
- **a creativity-pursuit theme**
- **a talent-based creative expression theme**
- **a meaning-pursuit theme**
- **the theme(s) of talent-based flow states**
- **a flow-to-flow theme, theme(s) of projects**
- **a naturality expansion theme**
- **a resonance theme**
- **a positive emotion theme**

The above themes emerge synchronously when a system is integrated into the flow to congruence - a founding dynamic of the Leading paradigm.

FIVE PERSONAL FORMULAS
for operating in the target Leadering™ paradigm

Based on the themes of the event patterns tracked in the paradigm, the following 5 formulas will emerge to help participants determine how to capitalize on the flow to flow of all human systems.

Your key talents are a system of your strongest capabilities which you are passionate about using and improving which advance reality in some way. This system is what is being acted upon by the flow to flow and your addictive drives.

1. **Talent-based lifetime development formula** or personal evolution formula

2. **Greatest lifetime level of talent-based performance**: the culmination of living one's lifetime development formula.

3. **Talent-based leadership formula**: leadership as an expression of one's lifetime development formula

4. **Talent-based leadership development formula**: merging one's lifetime development formula with one's talent-based leadership formula.

5. **Greatest lifetime level of performance as a leader**: based on the previous 4 formulas.

© 2006 Lauren Holmes

Caution: If you have lived your life directed by external elements (externally referenced) rather than complying with your natural drives internally (internally referenced) you will have less consistent patterns or fewer of them. Become internally referenced and the patterns will emerge.

EXAMPLES OF CONDITIONED REFLEXES
installed for the paradigm shift and operating in the Leading™ paradigm

CONDITIONED REFLEX *TRIGGER*	CONDITIONED REFLEX *RESPONSE*
New goal to advance a system(s)	**SYSTEMS THINKING** Treat every relevant individual, groups of people, processes and bodies of knowledge as systems with a core template and flow engine. Treat every event as part of the patterns indicating the direction of the flow to flow of some system. A system and its reality are a single system with the same template. No events are separate. Upgrade the core of the system first - yours or others - before taking action in compliance with the flow to flow. Expand consciousness to see the patterns and the interconnectedness of all systems in the flow to flow and to determine opportunities for synergy and co-evolution.
Yearning for meaning Need for achievement Every problem or advancement challenge	**KEY TALENTS** Continuously comply with addictive drives pressuring the use of your system of key talents. Shift into talent-based flow state by applying your system of key talents. Translate into terms solvable by one's key talents and the flow to flow associated with your system and the system(s) to be advanced.
A problem situation	**CHALLENGES** Quantum leap to a post-leap state without the problem. Belief engineering to change the template to change the reality. Expand around your core and key talents - expand beyond the problem - to have the capacity and functionality to deal with this challenge. Solve the problem with the emergence, synergy, co-evolution, coincidences, facilitating events, spontaneous knowledge, and spontaneous creativity inherent in the flow to flow.

15-4A　　　　　　　　　　　　　　© 2006 Lauren Holmes

EXAMPLES OF CONDITIONED REFLEXES
installed for the paradigm shift and operating in the Leadering™ paradigm

CONDITONED REFLEX *TRIGGER*	CONDITIONED REFLEX *RESPONSE*
Decision required with no information for making it.	**FLOW TO FLOW** Move into unknown territory in compliance with the flow to flow to collide with the information coincidences which will fuel the emergence process which will result in creative solutions beyond the potential of your system.
the need to penetrate unknown territory quickly and safely: frontiering™	Stop with the blocks and comply with the facilitating events, patterns, themes, natural quantum leaps and signposts of the flow to flow.
the need to bring the unknown into existence: creation/innovation:	Immediately pursue the 3 to 7 information systems which will fuel the emergence process by stopping with the blocks and complying with the facilitating events, patterns, themes, natural quantum leaps and signposts of the flow to flow.
A new project	Select the project in compliance with the flow to flow.
A new project initiated	Immediately pursue the new information, coincidences, facilitating events, spontaneous knowledge and creativity to advance the project in the flow to flow.
A craving for rapid growth in functionality and capabilities	Begin applying your system of key talents in talent-based flow state while complying with the life themes indicative of the flow to flow in your life system.
Unpreferred event or situation in reality	**EVENT-DRIVEN TEMPLATE UPGRADE PROCESS** Make the necessary change to your belief template to change your reality.
A craving for rapid growth in functionality and capabilities	**GROWTH IN CAPACITY** Quantum leap continuously through frontier after frontier of expansion of the application of your system of key talents or those of the system you wish to advance in order to increase your impact and functionality.
Unpreferred event or situation in reality	**REALITY CREATION** Make the necessary change to your belief template to change your reality.
New reality desired	Visualize to the point of feeling the emotions associated with the new reality in order to change the beliefs to change the reality.

15-4B © 2006 Lauren Holmes

EXAMPLES OF CONDITIONED REFLEXES
installed for the paradigm shift and operating in the Leadering™ paradigm

CONDITONED REFLEX *TRIGGER*	CONDITIONED REFLEX *RESPONSE*
	QUANTUM LEAPS
Unknown solution or change required with no idea how it will be achieved	Emotionally blueprint the post-leap state. Quantum leap. Take actions as if the quantum leap was successful.
New goal to advance a system(s)	Quantum leap to advance systems from one stable state to the next, bypassing the need for unstable transitional states.
A problem situation	Quantum leap to a post-leap reality without the problem.
Need for organizational change	Define the post-leap. Source the new template information. Make the template changes. Use the Leadering™ quantum leap process to complete the quantum leap. Operate as if the quantum leap has been successful.
Desire to quantum leap Desire to quantum leap well	Several conditioned reflexes have been installed throughout the Leadering quantum leap process itself. For example: Conditioned reflexes have been installed so that the experiential learning of each quantum leap increases the speed, power and span of impact, fluidity, nonlinearity, conditioned reflexes, emotional memory, belief template, belief engineering skill, ability to capitalize on flow to flow, cascading quantum leap thinking, and experiential memory for future quantum leaps.

15-4C © 2006 Lauren Holmes

LEADERING'S BUILT-IN KEY TALENT DEVELOPMENT

Use these to surmise the potential lifetime impact or legacy of your key talents as an individual, a leader, an entrepreneur, and/or an innovator

Consider the following talent development processes built into the Leadering paradigm and this program when doing the core determination exercises:

If the below assumptions are true,
- How would the art and science behind the use of your system of key talents develop over your lifetime?
- What could be the maximum possible impact of your key talents on reality?
- What would your five operating formulas or strategies be in the Leadering paradigm?

1. Assume you have all of the money and resources and freedom to pursue the use of your key talents to the maximum.

2. Assume your system operates day after day in talent-based flow state within the talent-based flow state of the larger contextual system of which you are a part.

3. Assume your capabilities are extended by nature's capabilities.

4. Assume your drives merge with nature's drives to shift you into overdrive.

5. Assume because you merge with natural forces and these forces are creative, advancing, co-evolving, adapting, you and your talents will be advancing.

6. Assume you will be constantly breaking through new frontiers of the art and science behind applying your key talents.

7. Assume a constant increase in the impact on reality of your key talent system as you constantly expand or intensify around your core. (Figures 14-6A top and 14-6B)

8. Assume years of side ventures which have increased your specialization in various aspects of your art or the creative expression of your key talents

9. Assume the depth of your talent-based flow states increases with each experience thus
    - speeding the increase of your functionality and performance
    - speeding the advancement of your art
    - speeding the increase of your levels of peak performance
    - increasing the speed of your development exponentially.
    - allowing you to advance reality continuously in your peak performance state

15-5A © 2006 Lauren Holmes

LEADERING'S BUILT-IN KEY TALENT DEVELOPMENT

Use these to surmise the potential lifetime impact or legacy of your key talents as an individual, a leader, an entrepreneur, and/or an innovator

10. Assume the addictive drives associated with using your key talents get stronger with each use and pull you to accomplish more without "work" or discipline. Assume the more you use them the more you want to use them.

11. Assume these addictive drives and the growth built into talent-based flow states pull you along the development continuum in Figure 14-6C.

12. Assume a narrowing of your work to using your key talents more precisely and accurately with less baggage and encumbrances around them. You eliminate from your life the things you think you need to do in order to do your art or to be able to do your art but are not your art. (Figure 14-6A bottom)

13. Assume an increase in the level of complexity that you are able to deal with and apply your key talents to (Figures 14-6E and 14-6B):
    - from single system to multiple system impact
    - from transactions to process. from process to quantum leaps
    - from linear to nonlinear
    - more impactful quantum leaps impacting more systems more quickly

14. Assume the adaptivity of your belief template is continuously improved by Leadering's event-driven belief template upgrade process so that your precision for reality creation is improving exponentially and benefiting from the creativity inherent in the flow to flow.

15. Assume that Leadering™ increases the meta-competencies of leaders, entrepreneurs, innovators, and high achievers (figure 14-5D) which will allow you
    - To move more quickly easily and safely into unknown territory and frontiers,
    - To increase your creativity and innovation,
    - To increase your knowledge,
    - To increase your coincidences and facilitating events in order to improve your performance of your art.

16. Assume, as in Figures 14-5C and 14-6E, your consciousness, big picture thinking, and conceptual skills continue to increase and expand so that you can
    - see more patterns, have more information, for decision-making and strategic planning
    - see the flow of systems to congruence or the flow to flow
    - see the interaction of more systems and the opportunities for synergy and co-evolution
    - impact more systems, impact more complex systems, impact larger systems

15-5B © 2006 Lauren Holmes

LEADERING'S BUILT-IN KEY TALENT DEVELOPMENT

Use these to surmise the potential lifetime impact or legacy of your key talents as an individual, a leader, an entrepreneur, and/or an innovator

Note: CONCEPTUAL COMPETENCIES CONSIST OF THE APPROPRIATE PARADIGMS, MINDSETS, AND CONCEPTUAL SKILLS NECESSARY TO:
assess the environment
see the long-range needs and implications of a situation and to build a plan for meeting these needs and
- visualize, address, and capitalize on the complex interrelationships that exist in a workplace in order to set priorities, make decisions, anticipate the future, and formulate strategies and tactics, and
- comprehend the culture of historically developed values, beliefs, and norms in order to visualize its future.

Note: CONCEPTUAL SKILLS INCLUDE:
- concept formation which is the capacity to analyze relationships between objects
- abstraction or the ability to think symbolically
- deductive logic which is the application of general rules or concepts in making a decision for a specific set of stimuli and/or
- inductive logic which is the analysis of feedback or identification of relevant details in formulating a concept to use in decision making,
- problem reframing to enhance creativity
- dealing with multiple perspectives and ambiguity
- frame of reference development including systems understanding, environmental scanning, pattern recognition
- idea and concept development and use to solve complex problems
- envisioning to anticipate the future
- proactive thinking using critical, creative, reflective thinking
- skillful formulation of ends, ways, means
- analysis of complicated events
- trend perception
- change detection
- creative and opportunistic problem-solving
- ability to conceptualize complex ideas
- deployment of models, theories and inferences, and
- pattern recognition.

15-5C   © 2006 Lauren Holmes

THE META-COMPETENCIES
of leaders, entrepreneurs, innovators, and high achievers
unleashed by the Leadering™ Paradigm shift

Systems-Based Approach
systems thinking, systems-based operation, systems-based emotional intelligence, belief system management, quantum leaping, expanded consciousness, conceptual skills, templating

Continuous Development
accelerating growth, co-evolution, re-optimization, agility, fluidity, expanding self-expression, learning/adaptation agility, belief upgrading, expanding consciousness

Cognitive Capabilities
learning agility, knowing, conceptual skills, abstract thinking, expanding consciousness, internally referenced, expanding self-expression and self-awareness, emotional intelligence, deductive reasoning, pattern recognition

Mastering the Unknown
frontiering™, creating, innovating, systems thinking, informationless decision-making, abstract thinking, conceptual skills, expanded consciousness

Performance
talent-based flow and other peak performance states, accelerated implementation, advancement by nonlinear quantum leaps, systems thinking, systems-based operation, expanding self-expression, learning/adaptation agility

15-5D © 2007 Lauren Holmes

INCREASING LEADERSHIP IMPACT
AS YOU EXPAND AROUND YOUR KEY TALENTS

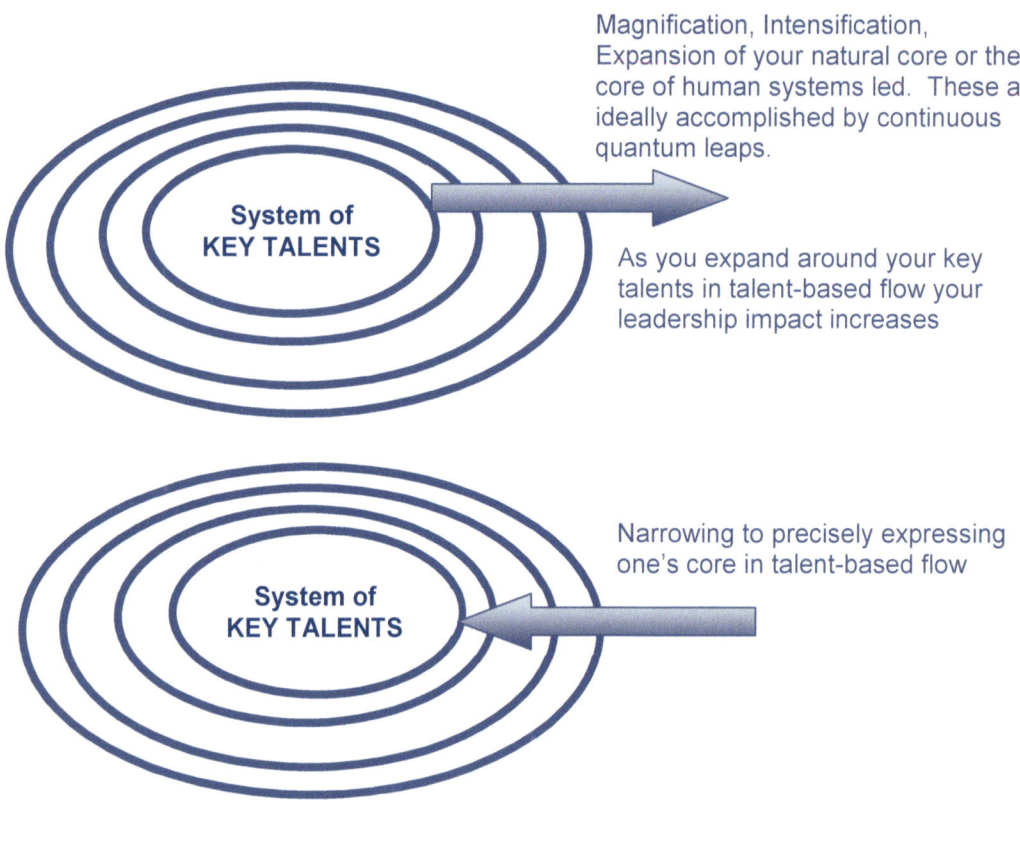

Magnification, Intensification, Expansion of your natural core or the core of human systems led. These are ideally accomplished by continuous quantum leaps.

As you expand around your key talents in talent-based flow your leadership impact increases

Narrowing to precisely expressing one's core in talent-based flow

© 2006 Lauren Holmes

CREATING WORLD LEADERS

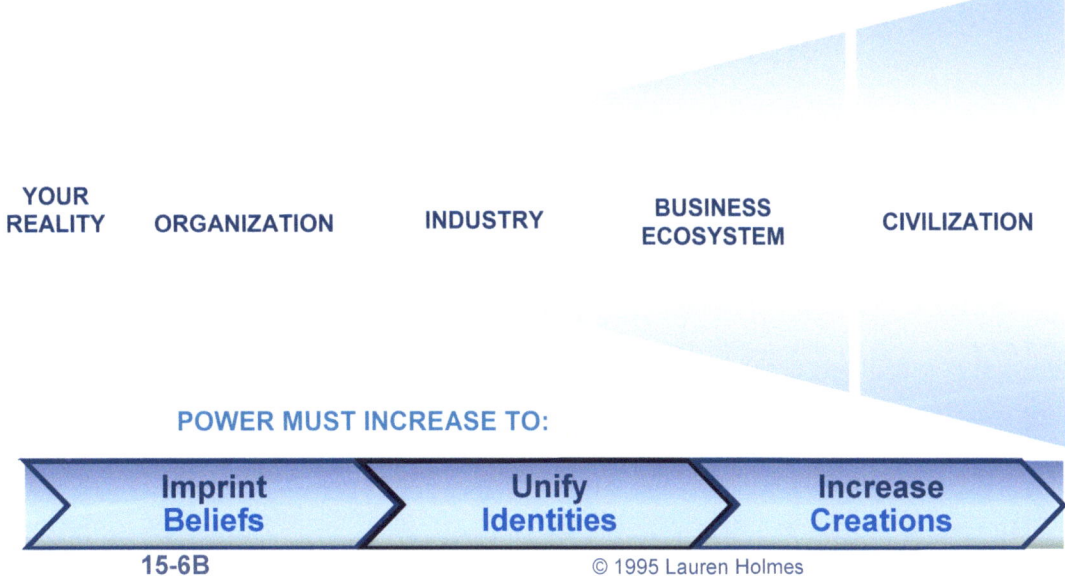

| YOUR REALITY | ORGANIZATION | INDUSTRY | BUSINESS ECOSYSTEM | CIVILIZATION |

POWER MUST INCREASE TO:

> **Imprint Beliefs** › **Unify Identities** › **Increase Creations**

15-6B © 1995 Lauren Holmes

A New Paradigm-based Leadership Development Continuum

LEADERING™ AMPLIFIES LEADER DRIVES

Manager	Transitional Change Leader	Transformational Change Leader	Creational Leader / Frontiering Leader
Run an existing business as is	**Linearly advance an existing business** • Incremental upgrades • Harvest	**Nonlinearly advance an existing business** • Turnarounds • Explosive Growth • Merge 2 existing businesses	**Create the unknown _or_ Penetrate the unknown** • Business startups • Pioneering / Frontiering™ • Re-engineering • New ventures / Innovation

As leader drives strengthen, leader impact increases:
INCREASED DRIVES TO change — frontiering   risk – learning – belief changes – adaptation – growth – congruence ⟶

Leader drive subset

Managers manage what exists ⟹ Leaders bring _the new_ into existence

Many skills taught in leadership development programs emerge naturally as Leadering™ stimulates an increase in the leader drives and dynamics observed in great leaders.

As individuals advance along the leadership development continuum,
their ability to advance reality increases.
If there is no change in beliefs, there is no change in reality.
If there is no change in reality, leadership has not occurred.
The magnitude of change achieved in reality is the measure of leadership strength.

15-6C © 1995 Lauren Holmes

System-Based Key Talent Categories

SYSTEM MAINTENANCE Single / Multi-System	SYSTEM ADVANCEMENT Single / Multi-System	SYSTEM CREATION Single / Multi-System	SYSTEM RELATIONSHIPS Each relationship creates a new system
manager: very little new creation is required. **Creativity and creation increase with each column to the right.** **Since beliefs create reality, this means that the need for belief changes increase as your move to the right.**	strategy development people development organization development multi-organization synergy process development knowledge development technology development **change leadership** • transitional • transformational • facilitative **frontier leadership** **creational leadership** **flow leadership**	**creational leadership** **frontier leadership** **quantum leap leadership** **template leadership** **emergence leadership** system creation strategy system creation implementation entrepreneur company creation intrapreneur project creation new product creation new technology creation new infrastructure creation new process creation new science creation new knowledge creation new skill creation new frontier creation creation research merger-created system acquisition-created system innovation / creativity	System relationships: • to maintain systems • to advance systems • to create systems **co-evolutionary leadership** **co-adaptation leadership** collaboration and synergy business web development CRM: customer relationship management customer development customer chain development supplier chain development network development relationship building team building market development unifying and integrating problem solving conflict resolution peace keeping negotiation mergers and acquisitions relationship strategy/vision relationship-related implementation

- **Increasing belief and information changes**
- **Increasing impact on reality**

- In the Leadering™ paradigm, leadership extends nature's systems management.
- This exercise demonstrates Leadering's single systems maximization toolkit

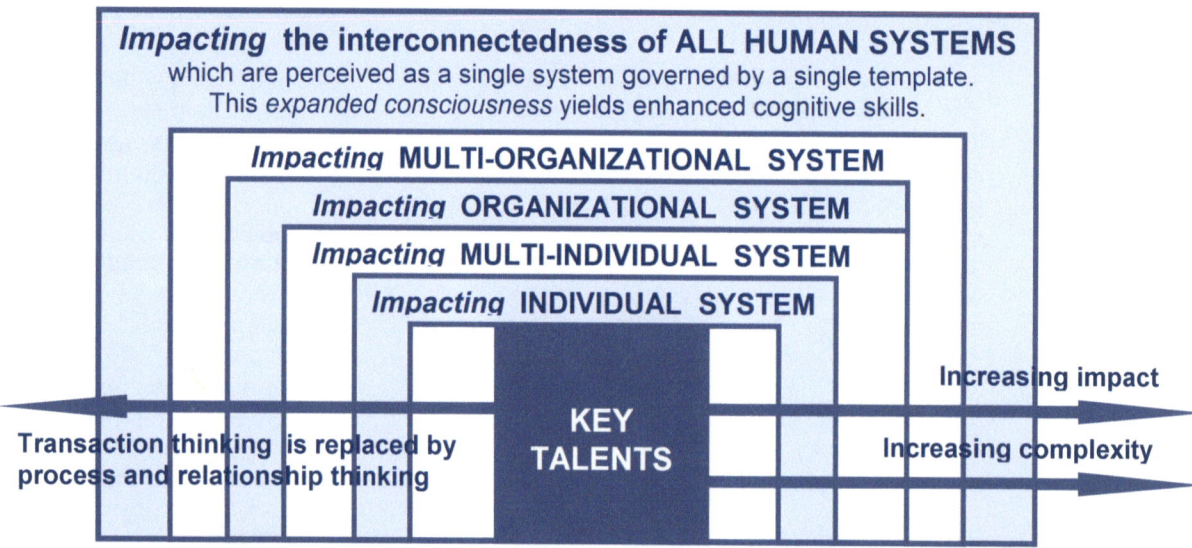

THE LEADERING™ QUANTUM LEAP PROCESS

Design it!   Feel it!   Be it!

PRE-LEAP
1. Choose the right quantum leap or post-leap state
3. Define the post-leap state with clarity
3. Define the post-leap state without previous limitations or toxicity
4. Emotionally template the post-leap state
5. Add the information to fuel emergence
6. Expect the unexpected post-leap

LEAP
1. Release the linear connection to the past
2. Feel yourself 100% fluid
3. Feel the post-leap state
4. Feel who the "post-leap you" will be
5. Commit to the quantum leap
6. Make an abrupt, no-return, reincarnation
7. Trigger spontaneous self-organization by intent

POST-LEAP
1. Operate as if the quantum leap was successful
2. Walk around as the person with the post-leap reality
3. Hold this new identity until reality restructures
4. Ignore evidence of events created by the old template
5. Trigger cascading quantum leaps by intent
6. Establish quantum leaping as a way of life
7. Consolidate your new quantum leap expert beliefs

© 1998 Lauren Holmes

Leadering™ teaches you how to extend your capabilities with those of surrounding systems so you can achieve beyond your potential.

7   PERSONALIZING THE LEADERING™ PARADIGM

I   FLOW MAXIMIZATION EXERCISES   continued

16. Key Talents Exercises   21 minutes   17 figures

Your key talents are a system of your strongest capabilities which you are passionate about using and improving and which advance reality in some way. This system is what is being acted upon by the flow-to-flow and your addictive drives.

Having (a) determined historical patterns from the life themes exercises, (b) projected into the future with the key-talent system-application exercises, and (c) incorporated these to determine key talents, participants will now have the information they need to (d) develop their 5 talent-based operating strategies for moving forward effectively for the rest of their lives in the Leadering™ paradigm.

Once you know your key talents, you can use action learning experimentation to test out the 15 dynamics and especially the flow-to-flow which are acting on your core to accelerate your growth and increase you level of operation and impact reality more substantially. Knowing your key talents is your license for driving the Leadering™ machinery. You can now begin to drive with confidence if you have not already tried the paradigm out.

Recording 16:   Key Talents Exercises   94

THE LEADERING™ CORE CONGRUENCE EXERCISES

These exercises are designed to identify the core of your system which is being acted upon by natural forces inside and outside of you so you can comply with and capitalize on them and avoid operating contrary to them.

FLOW MAXIMIZATION EXERCISES
for maximum performance and advancement

Life Theme exercises
- key talent determination
- flow to flow determination

Key talent Determination exercises
- system-based key talent exercise
- various other exercises

5 Talent-Based Operating Formulas exercises
1: your lifetime development formula
2: your greatest lifetime achievement formula
3: your natural leader formula
4: your leadership development formula
5: your greatest leader performance formula

BELIEF MAXIMIZATION EXERCISES   for Core Congruence

Belief Template Analysis and Upgrade:
- beneficial belief determination:
    ideal talent-based and flow-based beliefs
    identity beliefs, reality creation beliefs
- problem belief determination:
    fear beliefs, toxic beliefs, conflicting beliefs
- event-driven template upgrade process
- quantum leap template exchange process:
    goal-packaging identities, reincarnation

Action Learning Experimentation
- proving beliefs create reality
- improving belief engineering in your own and other systems
- improving template determination / design
- quantum leap experimentation

YOUR FLOW ENGINE:

Natural forces inside and outside of you act on your core

YOUR BELIEF TEMPLATE

Your belief template governs both you and your reality as a single system

Beliefs are information storage units like genes

YOUR CORE CONSISTS OF:

1. **KEY TALENTS**

2. **ADDICTIVE DRIVES**
   pulling you to use your key talents

*Note: Your key talents and associated drives are the immutable beliefs below. They continuously
- create your reality and
- are being acted upon by the flow to flow and Leadering's built-in growth continuums which amplify core impact.

3. **IMMUTABLE BELIEFS**
   (innate gene-based beliefs)
   These define the essence of your system and why it came together in the first place. These beliefs are genetically based and inherent to the built-in creative expression of your system. See *Note above.

4. **CHANGEABLE BELIEFS**
   ideally designed to support the key talents, addictive drives, and immutable beliefs to maximize your performance, development, and survival in biological terms. The goal is core congruence.

16-1A   © 2006 Lauren Holmes

im·mu·ta·ble: unchanging or unchangeable: not changing or not able to be changed

DETERMINE YOUR KEY TALENTS

A Leading™ Core Determination Exercise

PURPOSE OF DETERMINING YOUR KEY TALENTS:
- to identify a major component of the core or nucleus of your system
- to develop 5 talent-based operating formulas or strategies for capitalizing on natural drives or forces acting on the core of your system internally and externally for peak performance, peak advancement, and peak achievement.
- to have working hypotheses for the core and 5 strategies for test-driving your system in the Leadering™ paradigm using action learning experimentation.
- to begin the process of refining these working hypotheses for better future performance.
- to figure out the core that internal and external forces are acting on so you can
    - maximize your performance, and
    - capitalize on those forces for achieving your ongoing goals.
    - reboot your system on your core.

EXERCISE OUTPUT: Listing in a Peer Advisory Database

The ideal output from the Leadering™ Core Determination Exercises is a brief and concise description of your key talents and 5 operating formulas for listing in a Leadering™ Peer Advisory Database. This listing will :
- ensure you have clarity about your core.
- reinforce that core once you have discovered it.
- enable support and creative strategies from Leadering™ peers and advisors for capitalizing on the Leadering™ paradigm for your current and future situations, decisions, and achievements.

With such a listing in front of them, peers and advisors will be in a better position to assess the current challenges and opportunities you are presenting against a bigger-picture understanding of your system and the operation of the flow to flow on it. You want others to quickly understand the core of your system and how natural forces are acting on it so they can assist you with ideas and strategies for capitalizing on nature's machinery.

DETERMINE YOUR KEY TALENTS

A Leadering™ Core Determination Exercise

DEFINITION OF KEY TALENTS

Your key talents are a system of capabilities that you are passionate about using and improving which advance reality in some way. If there is no change in reality, your key talents have not been applied. When you use this system of talents, you perform better than in any other territory of activity. The creative expression of this system of key talents could therefore be called your "art".

Your key talents are interlinked into a system of drives addicting you to using your key talents. These addictive drives form your flow engine. The flow engine is trying to compel you to operate in a special form of peak performance flow state in which you are using your system of key talents. Therefore, we call the forces that the formulas capitalize on the 'flow to flow'. This is the machinery that Leadering™ provides the toolkit and expertise to drive. The goal is to enable you to operate 100% of the time in your talent-based flow state.

One needs to know one's key talents being acted on by this flow engine in order to determine one's 5 Leadering™ operating formulas or strategies for capitalizing on this flow to flow.

DETERMINING YOUR KEY TALENTS

Assume you have the freedom, resources, and opportunities to use your greatest talents to the maximum. Your key talents are identifiable by territories where:
- there is work you love to do
- you love to change reality (creation and creativity)
- you love to learn more or develop new skills or knowledge (frontiering™)
- you would love to be paid to learn and create: your ideal territory of paid peak evolution
- you would like to make your greatest contribution to the world
- you could leave your greatest legacy because your perform so well
- the activities to be done would be work to others but are compelling play to you
- given total freedom and resources, you would feel compelled to create and learn

DETERMINE YOUR KEY TALENTS

A Leadering™ Core Determination Exercise

DEFINING YOUR SYSTEM OF KEY TALENTS
A generic descriptor describing how you like to change reality
Your descriptor(s) should not be a job
The descriptor(s) you use for you key talents should be generic and refers to the way in which using your system of key talents changes reality. They should not refer to a job. A 'teacher' is both a job and a generic descriptor. However, the dimension of 'teaching' most relevant to you would be a more effective choice. For example, your system of key talents for 'teaching' could perhaps be more effectively described to relate more to

- 'people development' or
- 'the communication of knowledge', or
- 'a passion for assimilating new information, repackaging it to be more effective, and conveying it to others in such a way that they can apply the new information'
- or 'to *quantum leap* people to new levels of being'.

Notice that none of these descriptors is an actual job. Rather they prescribe generic creativity based on the individual's key talents. Try to avoid labels which are defined careers or jobs that can be done by people with a multitude of different systems of key talents. It is the generic application of your key talents that we are trying to identify, not traditional career strategy. Natural forces act on the former but not the latter.

Your generic descriptor(s) will evolve over time as you do.
Refer to Leadering's built-in growth recording for more details on what to lifetime growth continuums are launched by the Leadering™ paradigm and paradigm shift. For example, you will be continuously expanding the impact of your key talents over time requiring the definition to adjust to larger systems or more complex systems, or a greater number of systems, or a different category of systems, etc. At the same time, your key talents will become more specialized with use, requiring your descriptor(s) to hone in with more precision.

Try to avoid labels that might only be relevant to where your life is now
Don't be distracted by the specialization side ventures. (figure 16-2)
The flow to flow will often lead you to alternate between developing your system of key talents as a whole and developing the expertise in a component of the system and then integrating that learning back into the larger system. You will want to avoid thinking that one of those component areas is your key talent. Find out what the common threads are that link up the specialization side ventures. What are the key talents that link them up? What is the core around which the specialization side ventures revolve?

Many life contexts can be adapted to using your key talents.
It just takes a little creativity. Try not to make any drastic changes until you are sure of your themes and that you have mastered the flow to flow and driving nature's machinery sufficiently. There are likely an infinite number of applications of your generic key talents.

DETERMINE YOUR KEY TALENTS

4

A Leadering™ Core Determination Exercise

INPUT FROM THE CORE DETERMINATION EXERCISES:
Review your findings from the **Life Themes exercise** (figure 16-3) and the **Systems-Based Key Talent Exercise** (figures 16-4A and 16-4B) as input to your first hypothesis as to your key talents. I have also added some **additional Key Talent Determination Exercises** should you need them. Figure 16-5A provides an overview and figures 16-5B through 16-5E provides more detailed instruction.

YOUR KEY TALENT HYPOTHESIS MUST AGREE WITH
YOUR LIFE THEMES EVIDENCE:
The first check on the accuracy of the selection of your system of key talents is that it must agree with all of your findings in the Life Themes exercise. Those themes are derived from the patterns of events which indicate the flow to flow and your internal drives and nature's external drives trying to get you to operate with your key talents. Logically then, these themes have to be flagging both your key talents and the flow to flow operating in your life. Therefore, the agreement between your key talent descriptor(s) and your life themes and the historical pattern of events behind them is the first validation of the accuracy of your selected descriptor(s).

The second is for you to conduct action learning experimentation with driving the Leadering™ paradigm machinery having re-centered your system or core (and your life) on your key talents and the rest of the core of your system. You will expect to experience signposts of being in the flow to flow such as the natural quantum leaps in figure 16-6.

YOUR 5 FORMULAS MUST AGREE WITH
EVIDENCE FROM LIFE THEMES EXERCISE
Because the 5 operating formulas are also founded on your key talents and their development, they too must agree with your findings from the historical events of the Life Themes exercise.

16-1E

© 2006 Lauren Holmes

DETERMINE YOUR KEY TALENTS

A Leadering™ Core Determination Exercise

TEST DRIVE YOUR KEY TALENTS
Use Leadering's action-learning experimentation process to drive the Leadering™ paradigm machinery having re-centered yourself and your life on your key talents and the rest of the core of your system. Do the themes and patterns of events highlighted in the life themes exercise continue to validate your hypothesis? Figure 16-6 demonstrates the telltale signs of the facilitating events we expect to experience in flow to flow. Are the signposts there when you start to operate in the Leadering paradigm?

There are certain ways you expect reality to react when you have your formula right. When it does not, it is time to refine and reassess. If the signposts disappear in the future, refine your working hypotheses again and use reality like a gigantic computer to find the accurate hypothesis again. Look for telltale signs that natural forces agree with your choice: that you have correctly identified the core of your system that your drives and nature's drives are acting on. Allow your working hypotheses to evolve over time as you do so you continue they continue to be accurate predictors of where the flow to flow and your flow engine are going so you can capitalize on them.

USE YOUR KEY TALENTS TO DEVELOP YOUR
5 TALENT-BASED OPERATING FORMULAS
Each of your 5 personalized formulas is a different strategy for the application of your key talents. All 5 must agree be cohesive and congruent with your flow engine – the addictive drives trying to get you to peak performance and peak evolution flow state using your key talents.

QUANTUM LEAP I   (figure 16-8)
- to lock in the change into your template
- to reinforce your core and your key talents
- to re-centre your system
- to lay the foundation for operating to your maximum for the rest of your life.
- to consolidate your knowledge for how to apply the same core management approach to any human system in the service of mutually beneficial goals.

QUANTUM LEAP II   (figure 15-16A)
There is a pressure of internal and external drives to expand your system around its core with its system of key talents. Why not simply quantum leap to the next wider expansion of your system or series of expansions. It is a quantum leap that should be supported by natural forces. It makes sense to incorporate these expansion quantum leaps into your modus operandi for the rest of your life.

ANOTHER EVOLUTIONARY DIRECTION

Side ventures to develop the component skills of your 'art'

Since the flow engine often causes component skill development to progress sequentially, it can appear as if any one of these component skill development phases is actually your evolutionary formula - especially since, at the time you investigate them, you are very passionate about learning them and using them. However, keep focused on what binds them all together to determine your evolutionary formula.

EVENT PATTERNS TRACKED FOR THEMES

These patterns are indicative of the flow-to-flow

In the target paradigm, the life-long patterns of the following 'talent-based' or 'work' events are analyzed for themes indicating the flow to generative congruence or flow internally or externally:

- **an unpaid work theme** based on patterns of events in which you freely give away "work" that others would charge for or that you are so passionate about that you would pay for the opportunity to do.
- **a talent-based knowledge-pursuit or learning-pursuit theme** based on patterns of events of seeking knowledge passionately and willingly for the application of key talents (learning-pursuit theme)
- **a talent-based spontaneous knowledge theme** based on patterns of events in which spontaneous knowledge emerged to support the application of key talents
- **a talent-based frontier-pursuit theme** based on patterns of events of new territories of growth, learning and achievement the system was drawn to pursue for the application of key talents
- **a talent-based creativity-pursuit theme** based on patterns of events of preferred creative expression or creative expression which you or system was drawn to pursue for the application of key talents along with events in which creativity or creative invention or innovation spontaneously emerged for the application of key talents
- **a talent-based creative expression theme** based on patterns of events of creative expression in which your passion and enthusiasm were inflamed
- **a talent-based meaning-pursuit theme** based on patterns of events of work or achievements or contributions considered a meaningful application of key talents
- **the theme(s) of talent-based flow states** indicated by patterns of events whereby you went into flow state during the application of key talents
- **a talent-based flow-to-flow theme, theme(s) of projects** requiring the application of key talents which were supported by lots of coincidences, flows, spontaneous knowledge / creativity (figure 16-6)
- **talent-based naturality expansion theme** (figure 15-6A) indicated by patterns of expansions or intensifications of your system around its core to greater impact on reality - the key direction of growth and advancement of any system in the Leadering™ paradigm.
- **a talent-based resonance theme** based on patterns of subjects or activities for the application of key talents with which you resonated
- **a talent-based positive emotion theme** based on patterns of events in which passion, excitement, and enthusiasm emerged during the application of key talents

All of the above themes indicate when a system is integrated into the flow to congruence.

System-Based Key Talent Categories

SYSTEM MAINTENANCE Single / Multi-System	SYSTEM ADVANCEMENT Single / Multi-System	SYSTEM CREATION Single / Multi-System	SYSTEM RELATIONSHIPS Each relationship creates a new system
manager: very little new creation is required. **Creativity and creation increase with each column to the right.** **Since beliefs create reality, this means that the need for belief changes increase as your move to the right.**	strategy development people development organization development multi-organization synergy process development knowledge development technology development **change leadership** • transitional • transformational • facilitative **frontier leadership creational leadership flow leadership**	**creational leadership frontier leadership quantum leap leadership template leadership emergence leadership** system creation strategy system creation implementation entrepreneur company creation intrapreneur project creation new product creation new technology creation new infrastructure creation new process creation new science creation new knowledge creation new skill creation new frontier creation creation research merger-created system acquisition-created system innovation / creativity	System relationships: • to maintain systems • to advance systems • to create systems **co-evolutionary leadership co-adaptation leadership** collaboration and synergy business web development CRM: customer relationship management customer development customer chain development supplier chain development network development relationship building team building market development unifying and integrating problem solving conflict resolution peace keeping negotiation mergers and acquisitions relationship strategy/vision relationship-related implementation

- **Increasing belief and information changes**
- **Increasing impact on reality**

- In the Leadering™ paradigm, leadership extends nature's systems management.
- This exercise demonstrates Leadering's single systems maximization toolkit

EXAMPLES OF AREAS OF ONE'S ADDICTIVE KEY TALENTS	INDIV'L SYSTEM	MULTI-INDIV'L SYSTEM	ORG'L SYSTEM	MULTI-ORG'L SYSTEM	KNOW-LEDGE SYSTEM	PROCESS SYSTEM
Description and/or Examples	*You *a person *a follower *your child	Individuals en masse: a consumer market, a university	A group of people: an organization or company	A business web or community	A science, field, discipline	*Leadership development * Business process reengineering

16-4B © 2006 Lauren Holmes

SUMMARY OF ADDITIONAL ANALYSES AND EXERCISES FOR DETERMINING YOUR KEY TALENTS

Talents you are addicted to using and improving

These exercises in addition to the **Life themes exercise** and the **Systems-based key talents exercise** could help you to determine your key talents:

Total gratification exercise: What work would you do to creatively express your natural talents and passion for learning within a specific territory associated with those talents if you had 100% security of having revenues of millions of dollars every year for the rest of your life.

The amnesia exercise: If you had no memory of your past, what work would choose to do to creatively express your natural talents and passion for learning within a specific territory associated with those talents if you already had a lot of money and it wasn't a factor.

Childhood talents exercise: When you felt totally free as a child, what were the childhood talents you chose to improve, pursue, cultivate, or express as a child. How did you like to change reality?

Preferred creations exercise: Determine the common theme to your preferred activities or preferred creative expression. It is important to think generically and look for the common thread. This will be a recurring theme that exists in all of the things that you love to do. What is the common pattern among all of the things that you love to do?

Dream or fantasy exercise: Is there a common theme that emerges spontaneously in any dreams or daydreams that you have with respect to work that you are doing which changes reality.

The enthusiasm and resonance exercise: Of the list of possible learning/creative expression themes that could be the foundation of you your natural evolutionary path, which ones cause your resonance (frequency sensing) or enthusiasm to go up when you think of spending a lifetime pursuing them.

Meaningful work exercise: What is meaningful to you? What work using your natural talents, knowledge-pursuit themes, creativity-pursuit, and frontiering-pursuit themes would give your life the greatest meaning and give you the most pride in your achievements if you spent a lifetime pursuing them.

Clusters of natural quantum leaps (coincidences, spontaneous knowledge, spontaneous creativity, talent-based flow states, facilitating events). Natural quantum leaps occur more frequently when you are using your key talents in talent-based flow state. Examining the occurrence of clusters of natural quantum leaps should indicate your key talents. Quantum leaps to the next amplification or expansions of your talent-based expression are included in these clusters.

Natural states inventory: What is the common theme running through times in which you felt most naturally yourself while you were changing reality in some way. Inventory what skills you were applying. Is there a label for the creativity you were using or your preferred creations which also defines your system of key talents?

Action learning experiments: These will allow you to both determine and to verify your key talents and 5 talent-based operating formulas for the Leadering™ paradigm The natural quantum leaps which will emerge and the built-in growth processes will both facilitate your immediate and long-term performance and achievement.

16-5A overview © 2006 Lauren Holmes

EXERCISES FOR DETERMINING YOUR KEY TALENTS

Talents you are addicted to using and improving

> "The truth is that all of us attain the greatest success and happiness possible in this life whenever we use our native capacities to their greatest extent."
> — Smiley Blanton, psychiatrist

Total gratification exercise: What work would you do to creatively express your natural talents and passion for learning within a specific territory associated with those talents if you had 100% security of having revenues of millions of dollars every year for the rest of your life.

Most people have some goals they have been pursuing for some time . . . money, a job title, contribution, or success in some form. Imagine you've already achieved your goals and achieved them a hundredfold beyond what you were striving for.

If your goal was money, for example, assume you have a guaranteed income of a million dollars a year for the rest of your life. As a result, picture yourself doing all of the things you would do immediately upon learning this. Perhaps you would take some time off and take your family around the world. Perhaps you would spend time buying everything you've always wanted to own . . . . a certain kind of house, recreational property, cars and other vehicles, electronic gadgetry . . . . If your goal was contribution, picture you have already done monumental things to change the world which would satisfy most people with respect to their lifetime achievement.

Now picture yourself relaxing on a beach for a couple of months with nothing to do, having gratified whatever goals you have had in the past. In that state of satiation, abundance, and relaxation, what do you then choose to do? When you get the answer to that question, what you are likely looking at is the application of your key talents. This is your art: creation using your key talents.

The amnesia exercise: If you had no memory of your past, what work would choose to do to creatively express your natural talents and passion for learning within a specific territory associated with those talents if you already had a lot of money and it wasn't a factor.

Assume you have lost your memory and are dropped into a foreign country. What is it that you want to do? Assume you have more money than you know what to do with, so it is not an issue. What would you choose to do? Consider a number of possible catch-phrases for you to "wear" to describe your art. "Wear" them for a week or two to see which ones fit. Try them out on your friends and family. By trial and error, you will eventually arrive at a right fit.

16-5B detail   © 2006 Lauren Holmes   Adapted from Peak Evolution (Lauren Holmes, 2001)

EXERCISES FOR DETERMINING YOUR KEY TALENTS

Talents you are addicted to using and improving

Childhood talents exercise: When you felt totally free as a child, what were the childhood talents you chose to improve, pursue, cultivate, or express. How did you choose to change realty?

Look back to your childhood before your identity and art had been interfered with. You were probably more authentic and natural as a child. Think about the categories of things you liked to do as a child. Think about the kinds of activities that you excelled at. Extrapolate those categories or themes into your adult world to determine the ideal creative expressions of your key talents.

Preferred creations exercise: Determine the common theme to your preferred activities which change reality: your preferred creations. Think generically and look for the common thread. This will be a recurring theme that exists in all of the 'work' that you love to do which changes reality in some way.

Your "*art*" is the natural creative expression of your key talents. It is that thing or category of things you love to do and are naturally good at. Other people might think of your *art* as work if they had to do it, but for you, doing your *art* is its own reward. You would put in long hours of work for no pay in order to do it. It is something you would describe as "*the effortless effort.*" You continually seek opportunities to do it. You have undoubtedly enjoyed doing your *art* since you were a small child.
If you can't determine what it is, think back to your childhood and look for the common themes among the things you enjoyed doing.

Even though I call it your "*art*," it is not necessarily artistic. For some people, their *art* might be their gift for parenting or building relationships or teaching. These are not occupations but rather natural talents and desires which can then be applied to creating what is meaningful to your system. Your creations are a form of self-expression. You know who you are by your creations. Your creations also reinforce who you are. Your creations serve to facilitate self-expression, self-knowledge, and self-creation. What you choose to create also tells you what is meaningful to you.

Dream or fantasy exercise: Is there a common theme that emerges spontaneously in any dreams or daydreams that you have with respect to work that you enjoy doing which changes reality.

Take your fantasies and day dreams seriously. They likely hold clues to the "true you". They are telling you your passions - a sure sign of your key talents. Look for consistent themes in your passions. Wherever you experience or think about doing things that generate positive emotional states, you are likely being shown your key talents and their associated addictive drives.

16-5C detail   © 2006 Lauren Holmes   Adapted from Peak Evolution (Lauren Holmes, 2001)

EXERCISES FOR DETERMINING YOUR KEY TALENTS

Talents you are addicted to using and improving

"To do good things in the world, first you must know who you are and what gives meaning in your life."   Paula P. Brownlee

The enthusiasm and resonance exercise: Of your list of possible learning/creative expression themes that could be the foundation of your natural evolutionary path, which ones cause your resonance (frequency sensing) or enthusiasm to go up when you think of spending a lifetime pursuing them.

Clusters of natural quantum leaps (coincidences, spontaneous knowledge, spontaneous creativity, talent-based flow states, facilitating events). Natural quantum leaps occur more frequently when you are using your key talents in talent-based flow state. Examining the occurrence of clusters of natural quantum leaps should indicate your key talents. Quantum leaps to the next amplification or expansions of your talent-based expression are included in these clusters.

You'll be surprised by the tremendous orderliness of nature continuously trying to optimize your system. The swirl of natural quantum leaps which occur in the flow to flow is unmistakable over one's lifetime when you know what to look for. Are there common themes that suggest the direction that the flow to flow is attempting to take you to increase the expression of your key talents? Review the high points in your life right back to childhood. Look at the pattern of natural quantum leaps over your lifetime. You'll find strong flow events around activities using and improving your key talents. You can know your key talents by these patterns of events. You can therefore have some reasoned foundation from which to select categories of activities for the future. As you do those activities, they will be supported.

Meaningful work exercise: What is meaningful to you? What work using your natural talents, knowledge-pursuit themes, creativity-pursuit, and frontiering-pursuit themes would give your life the greatest meaning and give you the most pride in your achievements if you spent a lifetime pursuing them.

If you have some overriding purpose you have been pursuing in your life, you might be able to deduce your key talents from that. Alternatively, you may see patterns and themes in the meaningful events and activities of your life. What you choose to create can tell you what is meaningful to you. What you are excited about creating is linked to your key talents. If you simply begin to operate with your resonance moment by moment, in no time at all you'll find yourself only doing things that are meaningful and natural to you. Creation using your key talents is at the foundation of what is meaningful to you.

EXERCISES FOR DETERMINING YOUR KEY TALENTS

Talents you are addicted to using and improving

Natural states inventory: What is the common theme running through times in which you felt most naturally yourself while you were changing reality in some way. Inventory what skills you were applying. Is there a label for the creativity you were using or your preferred creations which also defines your system of key talents?

Each time we do activities consistent with our naturality, we strengthen it. The more we use our naturality, the stronger it gets. Naturality is an addictive drive. Accordingly, it is a good idea to check in with your resonance periodically through the day to determine if you are doing activities in sync with the natural you. Are you doing things you are enthusiastic about or that you have an inner knowing are the right things for you right now?

Naturality results from being, every moment, the person you truly are. It results from your system being centred on its natural core. This is the only foundation on which to achieve your full potential. This is the only way to turn yourself up to your full possible volume - your full strength of character. In order to become core-centred, you simply need to begin. This moment. Then the next moment and the next. All of a sudden, you'll find you're not only living naturally but have become addicted to it. Before long, you will not be able to do "unnatural" things even if they are things you have tolerated for years. Ask yourself periodically, "Does this activity feel natural or not?"

By far the most powerful tool for amplifying our naturality is to operate strictly in the present with our resonance - our frequency-sensing capability. To develop this new habit, start by checking in with your resonance at each decision point of your day to choose your next activity. Pretend you are a tuning fork and when you find the right next activity that is natural to you and adaptive, it will feel as if the second tuning fork is starting to resonate. If you find you are operating in sync with your resonance each moment, you are core-centred. Over time, your life will align with your natural core and all of the benefits of living in the Leadering™ paradigm will accrue. Another approach to amplifying your natural core is to cease and desist doing unnatural acts.

Action learning experiments: These will allow you to both determine and to verify your key talents and 5 talent-based operating formulas for the Leadering™ paradigm. The natural quantum leaps which will emerge and the built-in growth processes will both facilitate your immediate and long-term performance and achievement.

Action learning exercises allow you to gain proficiency in complying with the external and internal pressures to talent-based flow and flow to flow. Complying with all of the patterns for both combined will amplify power and creative expression through increased time in talent-based flow state and reinforcement from internal and external drives of your system and its contextual system.
Quantum leaps to the next amplification of your talent-based expression will occur spontaneously.

16-5E detail © 2006 Lauren Holmes

The advantage of operating in talent-based flow within the talent-based flow of the contextual system

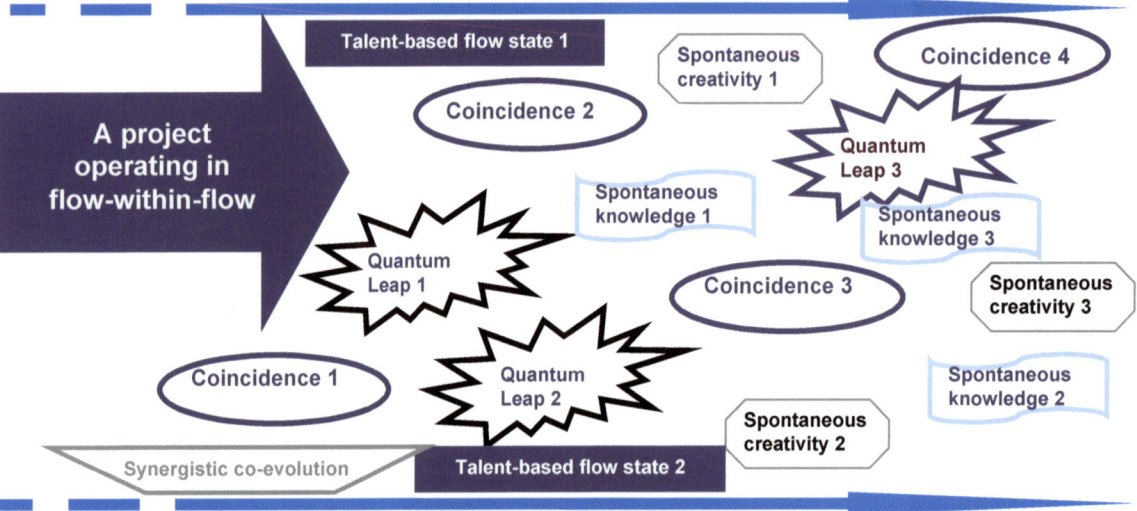

Increasing functionality with each flow experience:
- expanding consciousness and conceptual capacity
- peak performance
- peak evolution
- increasing creative capability
- expansion / intensification / enlargement of the system's natural creative expression

Proof of the Leadering™ paradigm – Proof of the accuracy of your 5 formulas
If you are operating in talent-based flow and the clustering of natural quantum leaps above emerge in your reality, then you have proof that the Leadering paradigm™ and nature's machinery inside and outside of you do indeed operate in the way Leadering™ describes.

YOUR FIVE PERSONALIZED OPERATING FORMULAS
for maximizing in the Leadering™ paradigm

Key talents being acted on by the flow to flow

Your key talents are a system of your strongest capabilities which you are addicted to using and improving. When used, they advance reality in some way. All 5 formulas are operating strategies for capitalizing on your key talents. Therefore they are interlinked. Your key talents are also interlinked into a system of addictive drives which form your flow engine. The flow engine promotes operating in a peak performance flow state in which you are using your key talents. The key talents being acted on by the flow engine need to be known in order to determine one's 5 operating formulas for the Leadering™ paradigm.

1. Your talent-based lifetime development formula: advancing your system

If natural forces continuously pressure you to expand or intensify your ability to use your key talents for creation - to advance reality - what will be the development path or theme of that intensification process underpinning your life?

2. Your greatest talent-based performance as an individual:

If you were to pursue the continuous expansion of your key talents over a lifetime and at top speeds, what is the highest level of creative impact or reality creation that you would likely achieve. What is the highest possible culmination of living your lifetime development formula? What is your maximum attainment based on a lifetime of accelerating development of your key talents?

3. Your talent-based leadership formula: advancing other systems

If you complied with the addictive drives pulling you to the continuous expansion of your key talents, what would be the territory and form of your leadership? How would formulas 1 and 2 define you as a leader by logical extension? What would your leadership formula look like if it was 100% based on your greatest performance with your key talents and their continuous expansion?

4. Your talent-based leadership development formula:

Your leadership development formula just allows you a more specialized lens with which to examine and strategize your personal development. The continuous expansion of the intensity and impact of your key talents define both your development as an individual and a leader. Therefore, leadership development and lifetime development form the same single continuum. The advancement of your key talents increases your strength, impact, and creativity as a leader. How would the previous 3 formulas define a leadership development formula? For those on the Leadering™ program who assume they will never be a leader, it is built in. (figure 16-6E)

5. Your greatest talent-based performance as a leader:

Based on your 4 previous formulas, determine your greatest lifetime level of performance as a leader. Given your advancement as an individual and a leader based on the continuous intensification of your key talents, and given the formula for your greatest performance as an individual, what would be the dimensions of your ultimate performance level as a leader: generically, what will be your greatest levels of capability for causing reality advances?

© 2006 Lauren Holmes

THE LEADERING™ QUANTUM LEAP PROCESS

Design it!   Feel it!   Be it!

PRE-LEAP
1. Choose the right quantum leap or post-leap state
4. Define the post-leap state with clarity
3. Define the post-leap state without previous limitations or toxicity
4. Emotionally template the post-leap state
5. Add the information to fuel emergence
6. Expect the unexpected post-leap

LEAP
1. Release the linear connection to the past
2. Feel yourself 100% fluid
3. Feel the post-leap state
4. Feel who the "post-leap you" will be
5. Commit to the quantum leap
6. Make an abrupt, no-return, reincarnation
7. Trigger spontaneous self-organization by intent

POST-LEAP
1. Operate as if the quantum leap was successful
2. Walk around as the person with the post-leap reality
3. Hold this new identity until reality restructures
4. Ignore evidence of events created by the old template
5. Trigger cascading quantum leaps by intent
6. Establish quantum leaping as a way of life
7. Consolidate your new quantum leap expert beliefs

RECORDING 17

Leadering™ is about operating and advancing naturally. If somehow, over the course of your life, you have moved away from the natural modus operandi for your system, Leadering™ puts you right back into the centre of your being so you can operate continuously to the maximum capacity of your system, expressing the meaningful creativity your system has evolved to express, and achieving the level of greatness latent within your system.

7 PERSONALIZING THE LEADERING™ PARADIGM

I FLOW MAXIMIZATION EXERCISES continued

17. **5 Formulas Exercise Preparation**   51 minutes   19 figures
    More information is provided about the 5 formulas in light of what you have discovered to this point. This prepares you for beginning the 5 formula exercises with the next recording.

THE LEADERING™ CORE DETERMINATION EXERCISES

These exercises are designed to identify the core of your system which is being acted upon by natural forces inside and outside of you so you can comply with and capitalize on them and avoid operating contrary to them.

FLOW EXPLOITATION EXERCISES
for maximum performance and advancement

Life Theme exercises
- key talent determination
- flow to flow determination

Key talent Determination exercises
- system-based key talent exercise
- various other exercises

5 Talent-Based Operating Formulas exercises
1: your lifetime development formula
2: your greatest lifetime achievement formula
3: your natural leader formula
4: your leadership development formula
5: your greatest leader performance formula

BELIEF MAXIMIZATION EXERCISES for Core Congruence

Belief Template Analysis and Upgrade:
- beneficial belief determination:
  ideal talent-based and flow-based beliefs
  identity beliefs, reality creation beliefs
- problem belief determination:
  fear beliefs, toxic beliefs, conflicting beliefs
- event-driven template upgrade process
- quantum leap template exchange process:
  goal-packaging identities, reincarnation

Action Learning Experimentation
- proving beliefs create reality
- improving belief engineering in your own and other systems
- improving template determination / design
- quantum leap experimentation

YOUR FLOW ENGINE:

Natural forces inside and outside of you act on your core

YOUR BELIEF TEMPLATE

Your belief template governs both you and your reality as a single system

Beliefs are information storage units like genes

YOUR CORE CONSISTS OF:

1. **KEY TALENTS**

2. **ADDICTIVE DRIVES**
   pulling you to use your key talents

   *Note: Your key talents and associated drives are the immutable beliefs below. They continuously
   - create your reality and
   - are being acted upon by the flow to flow and Leadering's built-in growth continuums which amplify core impact.

3. **IMMUTABLE BELIEFS**
   (**innate gene-based beliefs**)
   These define the essence of your system and why it came together in the first place. These beliefs are genetically based and inherent to the built-in creative expression of your system. See *Note above.

4. **CHANGEABLE BELIEFS**
   ideally designed to support the key talents, addictive drives, and immutable beliefs to maximize your performance, development, and survival in biological terms. The goal is core congruence.

© 2006 Lauren Holmes

Evolution

FORMULAS 1 and 2: Advancing your personal system

Formula 2 is the culmination of the Formula 1 development continuum.

Formula 1 lifetime key talent development continuum

Move up and down the continuum to let the big picture inform your current implementation tactics and, vice versa, use your current findings to inform the big picture.

Formula 2 defines the ultimate level of talent-based performance at which you can operate as a result of implementing the Formula 1 lifetime key talent development strategy for capitalizing on innate drives and natural forces internally and externally.

© 2006 Lauren Holmes

Co-Evolution

FORMULAS 3, 4, and 5: Advancing your personal system by creating, advancing, and maximizing other systems:

Leadering™ Leadership and Leadership Development

Continuum Start Point:
Formula 3:
talent-based leadership

Continuum End Point:
Formula 5: greatest level
of talent-based leadership

Formulas 1 and 4 share a development continuum:
Formula 4 talent-based leader development continuum is a subset development stream of the Formula 1 lifetime key talent development continuum.

Lifetime development and leadership development define the same continuum in the Leadering™ paradigm:
the expansion of the innate core of your system while creating and expanding the foundational core of other systems.

© 2006 Lauren Holmes

Evolution + Co-Evolution

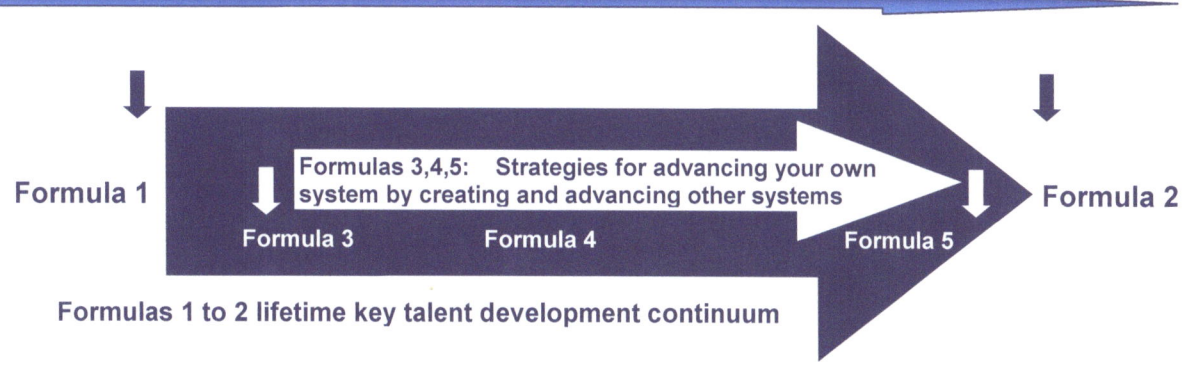

All 5 FORMULAS: Advancing your personal system by creating, advancing, and maximizing other systems:

Flow to Flow - Flow to Congruence - Flow to Unity

Formula 1

Formulas 3,4,5: Strategies for advancing your own system by creating and advancing other systems

Formula 3   Formula 4   Formula 5

Formula 2

Formulas 1 to 2 lifetime key talent development continuum

Projected direction of your historical talent-based life themes

All 5 formulas are interlinked. The 5 formulas define both a continuum and a continuum within that continuum: a subset. Formulas 1 and 2 define the continuum and formulas 3, 4, and 5 define a continuum subset.

All are about advancing your system core in the direction of the growth continuums built into the Leadering™ paradigm.

The human evolutionary continuum, the lifetime key talent development continuum and the leadership development continuum are the same continuum. The flow to flow defines a single continuum into which all human systems are pressured. Therefore, to capitalize on those forces, all 5 of the formulas have to relate to that continuum.

Since your themes identified by the Life Themes exercise demonstrate the flow to flow acting on your core and its system of key talents, your 5 formulas must agree with the evidence you discovered in the patterns throughout your life.

All 5 formulas relate specifically to the application of your key talents to advance reality.

Leadership is core-based in the Leadering™ paradigm because internal and external drives are acting on your system core and the cores of all human systems.

Maximum strength as an individual, leader, entrepreneur, innovator and top performer come from complying with and capitalizing on the forces defining this continuum.

FORMULA 2

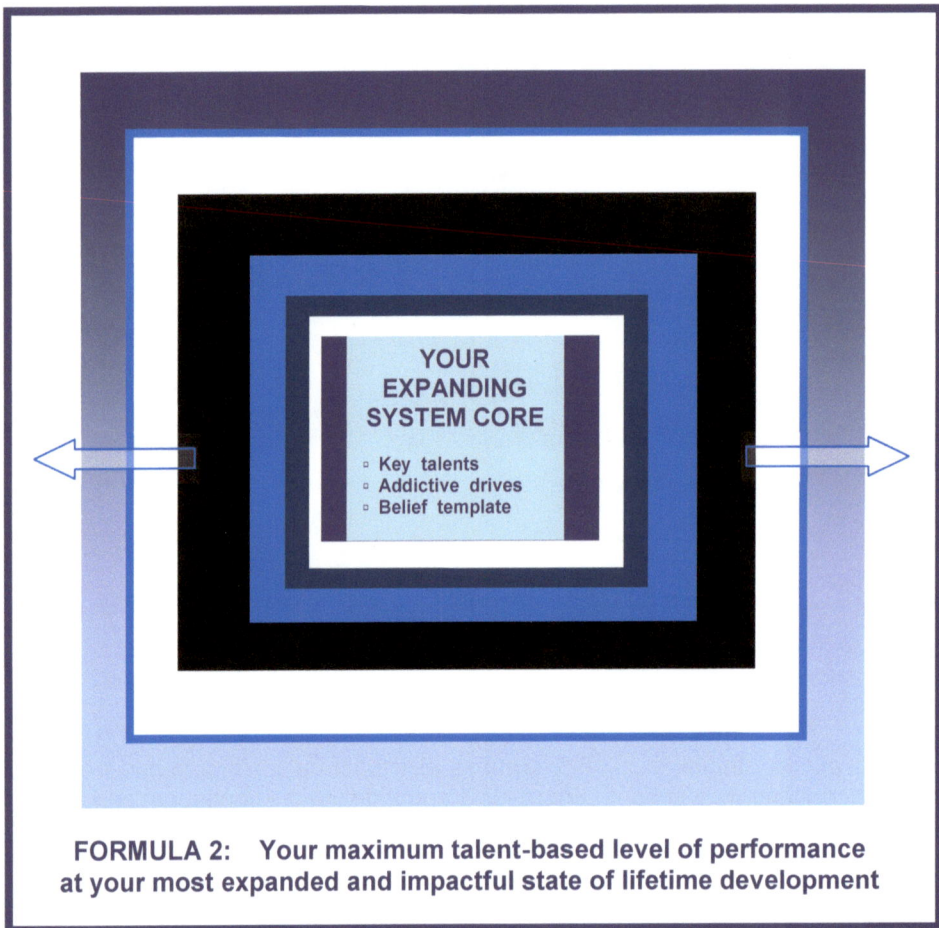

FORMULA 2: Your maximum talent-based level of performance at your most expanded and impactful state of lifetime development

1. At this level of expansion of your core and your key talents in particular, what kind of work are you doing?
2. How are you changing reality?
3. What new functionality are you applying?
4. How are you capitalizing on natural forces to change reality with your key talents?
5. What is your ideal identity at this greatest level of performance?

Evolution

FORMULAS 1 and 2: Advancing your personal system

Formula 1 lifetime key talent development continuum

Move up and down the continuum to let the big picture inform your current implementation tactics and, vice versa, use your current findings to inform the big picture.

Formula 2 is the culmination of the Formula 1 development continuum.

Formula 2 defines the ultimate level of talent-based performance at which you can operate as a result of implementing the Formula 1 lifetime key talent development strategy for capitalizing on innate drives and natural forces internally and externally.

17-6A (17-2)   © 2006 Lauren Holmes

Nonlinear continuum direction

Amplification of the strength and impact of your system of **KEY TALENTS**

Amplification, Intensification, Expansion of your system's innate core. Core expansions in the Leadering™ paradigm are achieved by quantum leap - a method for core replacement.

As your key talents expand as a result of operating in talent-based flow state and the flow to flow, your impact on reality increases. The magnitude of change you cause in reality increases. Your creative impact increases.

17-6B   © 2006 Lauren Holmes

Nonlinear reality advancement

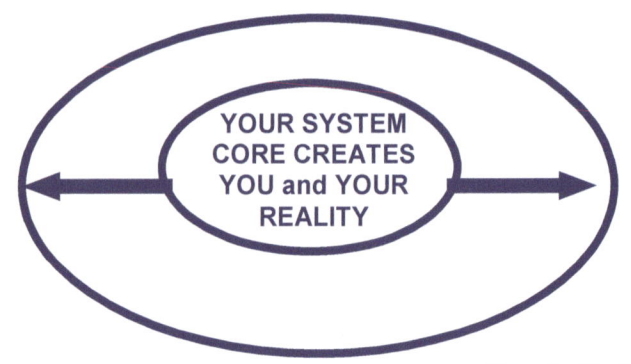

You and your reality are a single system in the Leading™ paradigm. Realities are self-created by your system core.

Change your core to change your reality: the situations and events you will experience.

Formulas 1 and 2 not only advance your core but your reality or experience by reflection.

YOUR EXPANDING SYSTEM CORE
The foundation of all human system development in the Leading™ paradigm

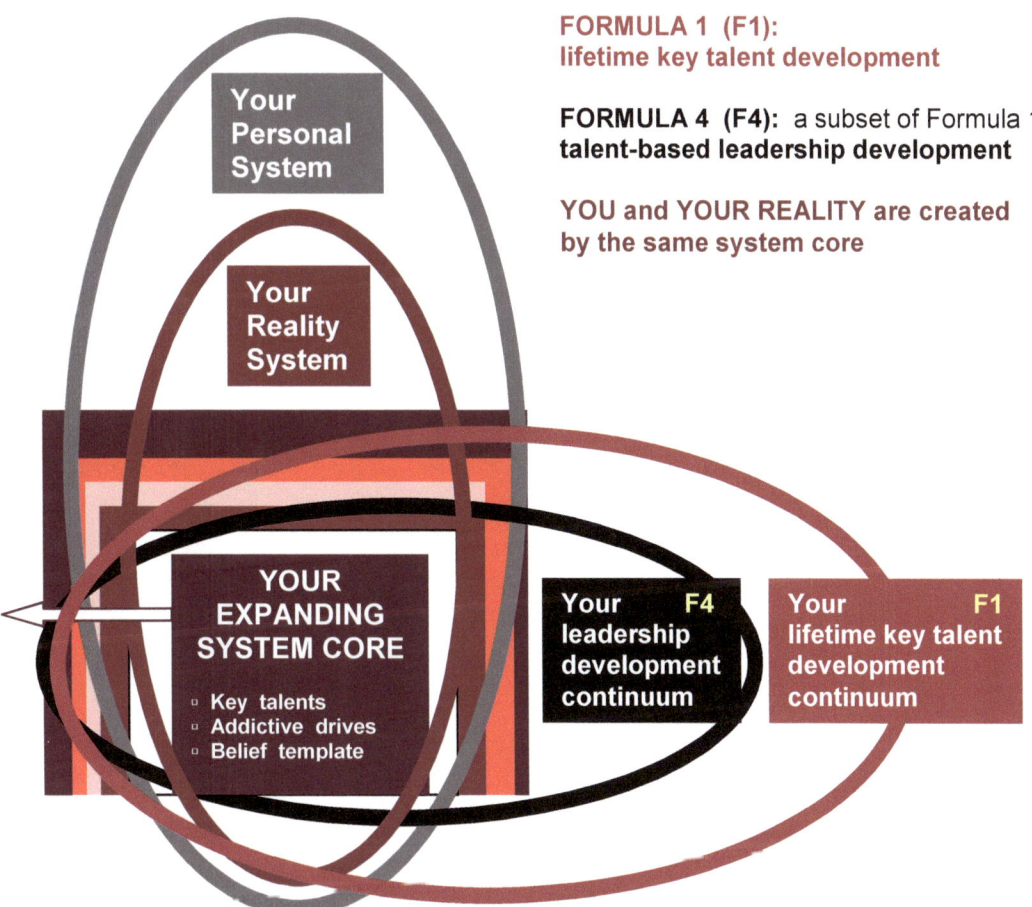

FORMULA 1 (F1):
lifetime key talent development

FORMULA 4 (F4): a subset of Formula 1
talent-based leadership development

YOU and YOUR REALITY are created by the same system core

NONLINEAR DEVELOPMENT IN THE LEADERING PARDIGM

The progression of the continuum defined by formulas 1 and 2 is not linear but the amplification of the core of each human system by quantum leaps.

FORMULAS 3, 4, and 5:
Amplification of your Impact on Human Systems
Go up and down this continuum to develop and express your key talents

Impacting the interconnectedness of ALL HUMAN SYSTEMS
which are perceived as a single system governed by a single template:
This *expanded consciousness* yields enhanced cognitive skills.

Impacting MULTI-ORGANIZATIONAL SYSTEM

Impacting ORGANIZATIONAL SYSTEM

Impacting MULTI-INDIVIDUAL SYSTEM

Impacting INDIVIDUAL SYSTEM

KEY TALENTS applied to systems

Increasing impact

Increasing complexity

Transaction thinking is replaced by process and relationship thinking

Use side ventures to experiment on simple systems then take what you have learned to more complex systems

© 2006 Lauren Holmes

FORMULAS 3, 4, and 5: Advancing your personal system by creating, advancing, and maximizing other systems:

Leadering™ Leadership and Leadership Development

Continuum Start Point:
Formula 3:
talent-based leadership

Continuum End Point:
Formula 5: greatest level of talent-based leadership

Formulas 1 and 4 share a development continuum:
Formula 4 talent-based leader development continuum is a subset development stream of the Formula 1 lifetime key talent development continuum.

Lifetime development and leadership development define the same continuum in the Leadering™ paradigm:
the expansion of the innate core of your system while creating and expanding the foundational core of other systems.

Nonlinear continuum directions

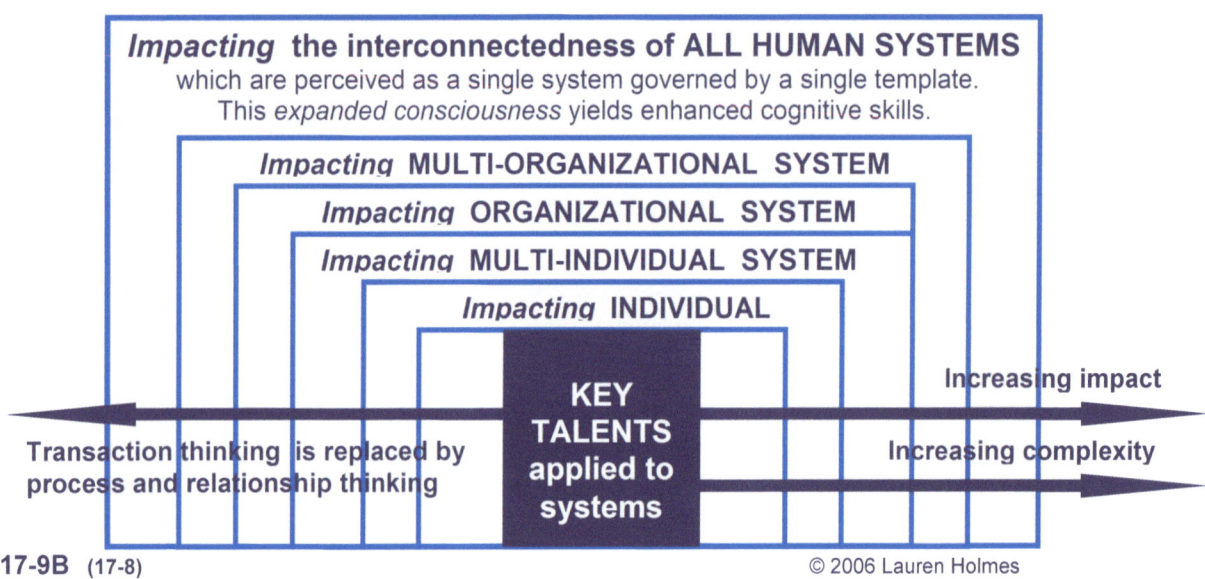

17-9B (17-8) © 2006 Lauren Holmes

Evolution

FORMULAS 1 and 2: Advancing your personal system

Identified by Core Determination Exercises:
- Life themes exercises
- Key talent determination exercises

Co-Evolution - Co-Adaptation - Co-Creation - Synergy

FORMULAS 3, 4, and 5: Advancing your personal system by creating, advancing, and maximizing other system:

- Determined by the lifetime development continuum defined by formulas 1 and 2
- Core Determination Exercises: systems-based key-talent application exercise

17-10 © 2006 Lauren Holmes

Recording17: 5 Formula Exercise Prep 124

Co-Evolution

FORMULAS 3, 4, and 5: Advancing your system by creating, maximizing, and capitalizing on other human systems

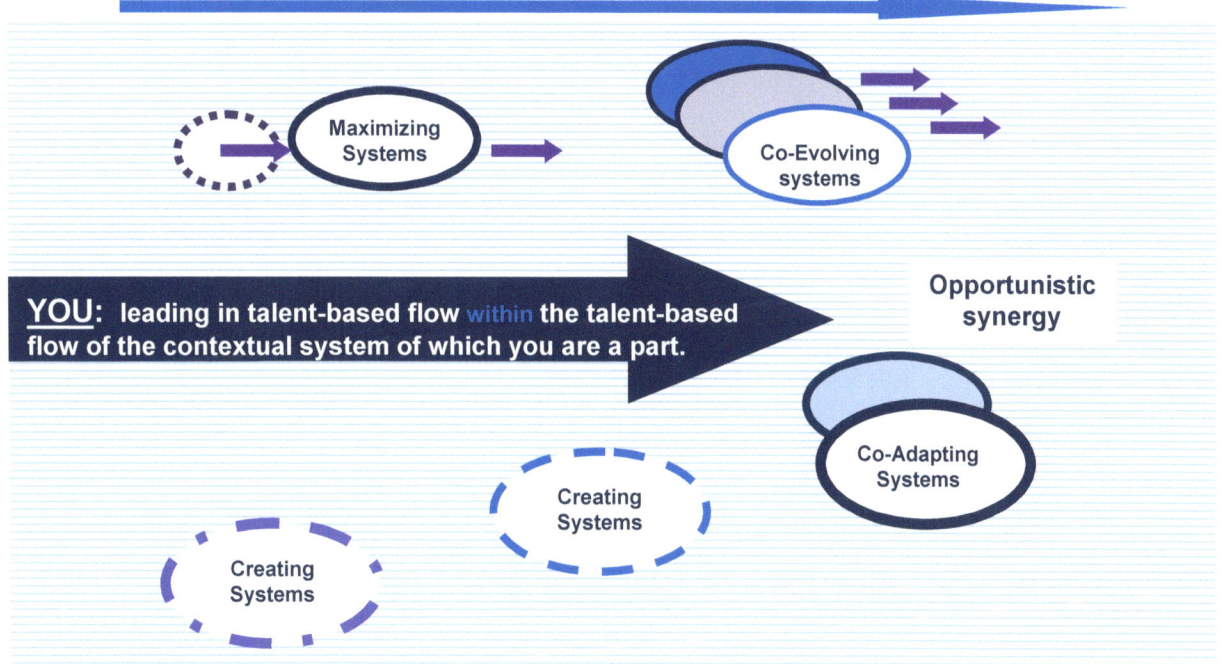

Talent-based system leadership in the flow to flow

Maximizing Systems → Co-Evolving systems

YOU: leading in talent-based flow *within* the talent-based flow of the contextual system of which you are a part.

Opportunistic synergy

Co-Adapting Systems

Creating Systems

Creating Systems

Advancing your system by applying your key talents to other systems	Individual Systems	Multi-Individual Systems	Organization Systems	Multi-Organization Systems	Knowledge Systems	Process Systems

Leadering™ provides a single systems maximization toolkit for advancing your personal system or those that you choose to lead for *peak legacy*.

17-11 © 2006 Lauren Holmes

Where are you on the leadership development continuum
with respect to maximizing systems for your legacy goals?

LEADERING™ AMPLIFIES LEADER DRIVES

Manager	Transitional Change Leader	Transformational Change Leader	Creational Leader / Frontiering Leader
Run an existing business as is	**Advance an existing business linearly** • Incremental upgrades • Harvest	**Change an existing business nonlinearly** • Turnarounds • Explosive Growth • Merge 2 existing businesses	**Create the unknown or Penetrate the unknown** • Business startups • Pioneering / Frontiering™ • Re-engineering • New ventures / • Innovation

As leader drives strengthen, leader impact increases:
INCREASED DRIVES to change – creativity/creation – frontiering™
INCREASED BELIEF CHANGES MADE

| Systems maintenance | Increasing systems advancement → | | Systems Creation: new and new from grouping existing systems |

Managers run existing systems ➡ Leaders advance and create systems

As managers progress along the leadership development continuum,
their ability to advance reality increases.
Their ability to make belief changes increases.
If there is no change in beliefs, there is no change in reality.
If there is no change in reality, leadership has not occurred.
The magnitude of change achieved in reality is the measure of leadership strength.

© 1995 Lauren Holmes

SAMPLE CATEGORIES OF LEADERING'S BUILT-IN GROWTH

CONTINUOUS DEVELOPMEMT
Addiction to continuous development:
- the continuous increase in drives which addict you to using and improving your system of core talents
- these addictive drives cause the continuous improvement of your system of core talents becomes the founding dynamic of your life to which the other segments of your life are integrated.
- an accelerating increase in speed of development of your system of core talents
- the continuous increase in the development of drives associated with meta-competencies such as frontiering, creativity, learning to learn, and learning agility which promote continuous development
- addiction to peak performance and peak advancement flow states

CONTINUOUSLY IMPROVING PERFORMANCE
1. Continuous increase in time spent operating in peak performance and peak advancement flow states
2. Depth of your talent-based flow states increases with each experience thus increasing performance further
3. Event-driven belief upgrade process continually improves performance through more supportive beliefs

CONTINUOUSLY INCREASING IMPACT
1. Continuous increase in impact of creations
2. Reality creation precision
3. Continuous increase in creativity and innovation
4. Continuous increase in your impact on reality
5. An increase in the level of complexity handled from single system to multiple systems impact; from transactions to process; from process to quantum leaps; from linear to nonlinear; more impactful quantum leaps impacting more systems more quickly

CONTINUOUSLY INCREASING FUNCTIONALITY
1. Continuous increase in the specialization of your system of core talents
2. Accelerating improvement of abilities to use your core talents
3. Increasing ability to penetrate the unknown or bring the unknown into existence and a craving for both: frontiering and creativity.
4. Continuous improvement in your facility for nonlinear quantum leaps to speed advancement of your system and other systems
5. Systems-based modus operandi: single toolkit for advancing systems, continuous increase in your ability to advance systems and to create new systems
6. Continuous acquisition and improvement of meta-competencies associated with successful leaders, entrepreneurs, innovators and high achievers. (Meta-competencies improve the ability to assimilate and use competencies): continuous development, improved cognitive capabilities, improved performance. These allow you to move more quickly easily and safely into unknown territory and frontiers, increase your creativity and innovation, increase your knowledge-acquisition capabilities, and increase your ability to court coincidences and facilitating events which will improve your performance of your art.
7. Continuous improvement to cognitive skills:
    - concept formation, conceptualization of complex ideas, abstract thinking, deductive and inductive logic, problem reframing, dealing with multiple perspectives and ambiguity, skillful formulation of ends, ways, means
    - frame of reference development: systems understanding, environmental scanning, pattern recognition
    - proactive thinking using critical, creative, and reflective thinking
    - analysis of complicated events, trend perception, change detection, creative and opportunistic problem-solving
    - deployment of models, theories and inferences
    - visualization, addressing, and capitalization of complex interrelationships: see the interaction of more systems and the opportunities for synergy and co-evolution; impact more systems, impact more complex systems, impact larger systems
    - big-picture thinking and see more patterns to have more information for decision-making and strategic and tactical planning

EVENT PATTERNS TRACKED FOR THEMES
These patterns are indicative of the flow to internal and external congruence or the flow to flow

In the target paradigm, the life-long patterns of the following 'talent-based' or 'work' events are analyzed for themes indicating the flow to generative congruence or flow internally or externally:

- **an unpaid work theme**
- **a knowledge-pursuit theme or learning-pursuit theme**
- **a spontaneous knowledge theme**
- **a frontier-pursuit theme**
- **a creativity-pursuit theme**
- **a talent-based creative expression theme**
- **a meaning-pursuit theme**
- **the theme(s) of talent-based flow states**
- **a flow-to-flow theme, theme(s) of projects**
- **a naturality expansion theme**
- **a resonance theme**
- **a positive emotion theme**

Choose one or more of the above themes to identify when your system is integrated into the flow to congruence.

5 PERSONAL FORMULAS
for operating in the target Leading™ paradigm

Based on the themes of the event patterns tracked in the paradigm, the following 5 formulas will emerge to help participants determine how to capitalize on the flow to flow of all human systems.

Your key talents are a system of your strongest capabilities which you are passionate about using and improving which advance reality in some way. This system is what is being acted upon by the flow to flow and your addictive drives.

1. **Talent-based lifetime development formula** or personal evolution formula

2. **Greatest lifetime level of talent-based performance**: the culmination of living one's lifetime development formula.

3. **Talent-based leadership formula**: leadership as an expression of one's lifetime development formula

4. **Talent-based leadership development formula**: merging one's lifetime development formula with one's talent-based leadership formula.

5. **Greatest lifetime level of performance as a leader**: based on the previous 4 formulas.

© 2006 Lauren Holmes

Caution: If you have lived your life directed by external elements (externally referenced) rather than complying with your natural talent-based drives internally (internally referenced) you will have less consistent patterns or fewer of them. Operate internally referenced for awhile and the patterns will become evident.

EVENT PATTERNS TRACKED FOR THEMES
These patterns are indicative of the flow to flow

In the target paradigm, the life-long patterns of the following 'talent-based' or 'work' events are analyzed for themes indicating the flow to generative congruence or flow internally or externally:

- **an unpaid work theme** based on patterns of events in which you freely give away "work" that others would charge for or that you are so passionate about that you would pay for the opportunity to do.

- **a talent-based knowledge-pursuit or learning-pursuit theme** based on patterns of events of seeking knowledge passionately and willingly for the application of key talents (learning-pursuit theme)

- **a talent-based spontaneous knowledge theme** based on patterns of events in which spontaneous knowledge emerged to support the application of key talents

- **a talent-based frontier-pursuit theme** based on patterns of events of new territories of growth, learning and achievement the system was drawn to pursue for the application of key talents

- **a talent-based creativity-pursuit theme** based on patterns of events of preferred creative expression or creative expression which you or system was drawn to pursue for the application of key talents along with events in which creativity or creative invention or innovation spontaneously emerged for the application of key talents

- **a talent-based creative expression theme** based on patterns of events of creative expression in which your passion and enthusiasm were inflamed

- **a talent-based meaning-pursuit theme** based on patterns of events of work or achievements or contributions considered a meaningful application of key talents

- **the theme(s) of talent-based flow states** indicated by patterns of events whereby you went into flow state during the application of key talents

- **a talent-based flow-to-flow theme, theme(s) of projects** requiring the application of key talents which were supported by lots of coincidences, flows, spontaneous knowledge / creativity (figure 16-6)

- **talent-based naturality expansion theme** (figures 15-6A, 17-5, 17-6C, 17-7, and 17-8) indicated by patterns of expansions or intensifications of your system around its core to greater impact on reality - the key direction of growth and advancement of any system in the Leadering™ paradigm.

- **a talent-based resonance theme** based on patterns of subjects or activities for the application of key talents with which you resonated

- **a talent-based positive emotion theme** based on patterns of events in which passion, excitement, and enthusiasm emerged during the application of key talents

All of the above themes indicate when a system
is integrated into the flow to congruence.

YOUR FIVE PERSONALIZED OPERATING FORMULAS
for maximizing in the Leading™ paradigm

Key talents being acted on by the flow-to-flow
Your key talents are a system of your strongest capabilities which you are innately addicted to using and improving. When used, your key talents advance reality in some way. All 5 formulas are operating strategies for capitalizing on your key talents. Therefore they are interlinked. Your key talents are also interlinked into a system of addictive drives which form your flow engine. The flow engine promotes operating in a peak performance flow state in which you are using your key talents. The key talents being acted on by the flow engine need to be known in order to determine one's 5 operating formulas for the Leading™ paradigm.

1. Your lifetime key talent development formula: **advancing your system**
If natural forces continuously pressure you to expand or intensify your ability to use your key talents for creation - to advance reality - what will be the development path or theme of that intensification process underpinning your life?

2. Your greatest talent-based performance as an individual:
If you were to pursue the continuous expansion of your key talents over a lifetime and at top speeds, what is the highest level of creative impact or reality creation that you would likely achieve. What is the highest possible culmination of living your lifetime development formula? What is your maximum attainment based on a lifetime of accelerating development of your key talents?

3. Your talent-based leadership formula: **advancing other systems**
If you complied with the addictive drives pulling you to the continuous expansion of your key talents, what would be the territory and form of your leadership? How would formulas 1 and 2 define you as a leader by logical extension? What would your leadership formula look like if it was 100% based on your greatest performance with your key talents and their continuous expansion?

4. Your talent-based leadership development formula:
Your leadership development formula just allows you a more specialized lens with which to examine and strategize your personal development. The continuous expansion of the intensity and impact of your key talents define both your development as an individual and a leader. Therefore, leadership development and lifetime development form the same single continuum. The advancement of your key talents increases your strength, impact, and creativity as a leader. How would the previous 3 formulas define your personalized talent-based leadership development formula? For those on the Leading™ program who assume they will never be a leader, it is built in. (figure 17-3)

5. Your greatest talent-based performance as a leader:
Based on your 4 previous formulas, determine your greatest lifetime level of performance as a leader. Given your advancement as an individual and a leader based on the continuous intensification of your key talents, and given the formula for your greatest performance as an individual (Formula 2), what would be the dimensions of your ultimate performance level as a leader: generically, what will be your greatest levels of capability for causing reality advances?

THE LEADERING™ QUANTUM LEAP PROCESS

Design it!   Feel it!   Be it!

PRE-LEAP
1. Choose the right quantum leap or post-leap state
5. Define the post-leap state with clarity
3. Define the post-leap state without previous limitations or toxicity
4. Emotionally template the post-leap state
5. Add the information to fuel emergence
6. Expect the unexpected post-leap

LEAP
1. Release the linear connection to the past
2. Feel yourself 100% fluid
3. Feel the post-leap state
4. Feel who the "post-leap you" will be
5. Commit to the quantum leap
6. Make an abrupt, no-return, reincarnation
7. Trigger spontaneous self-organization by intent

POST-LEAP
1. Operate as if the quantum leap was successful
2. Walk around as the person with the post-leap reality
3. Hold this new identity until reality restructures
4. Ignore evidence of events created by the old template
5. Trigger cascading quantum leaps by intent
6. Establish quantum leaping as a way of life
7. Consolidate your new quantum leap expert beliefs

© 1998 Lauren Holmes

Categories of Quantum Leaps to apply to each Formula

CORE UPGRADE QUANTUM LEAPS
- quantum leaps to new functionality such as increased cognitive skills, leader meta-competencies, and an increasingly supportive belief template.

CORE EXPANSION QUANTUM LEAPS
Internal and external drives pressure your system to expand around its core system of key talents and drives. The best way to comply with these pressures to expand is to routinely quantum leap as a modus operandi for the rest of your life. These quantum leaps are facilitated by natural forces. These expansions include:
- quantum leaps to the next wider iteration of power and impact of your system.
- a series of quantum leaps which break through frontier after frontier with respect to improving your prowess and skill for applying your key talents to advance reality. Expansion quantum leaps advance the art and science behind your F1-F2 development of your key talents.
- 10-year maximum quantum leaps: a quantum leap to a category of expansion or capability as if you have been operating at that level of intensification and impact of your system for the last 10 years. This speeds the advancement of your capabilities.

REALIGNMENT QUANTUM LEAPS
- quantum leaps to re-boot your system onto its natural core in compliance with natural forces continuously pressuring this re-centering.
- quantum leaps to merge your system into the-flow-to-flow or to the flow of other dynamics and built-in growth continuums within the Leadering™ paradigm.

NOTES FOR ALL 5 LEADERING™ OPERATING FORMULAS

1. **Leaders:** For those taking Leadering™ with the intention of becoming visible leaders in positions of authority and commanding others, you should attempt to include in formulas 3, 4, and 5, a specific theme for your leadership which is based on the expansion of your key talents over your lifetime as prescribed by formula 1.

2. **Non-Leaders:** For those who do not plan to become visible leaders with followers reporting, please use this exercise to identify a strategy for developing your systems advancement capabilities as you develop around your key talents in the Leadering paradigm.

3. **For those pursuing Entrepreneuring, Innovation, Recareering™ and Peak Performance:** For those taking Leadering™ for recareering™, for peak performance, and for maximum lifetime achievement, you should translate all 5 formulas in terms of your career and being paid for continuously scaling new frontiers of application of your talents. The pursuit of p*aid peak evolution* should be the determinant for your career choices. You want to be paid for pursuing your lifetime maximum.

4. **The 5 formulas are logically interlinked:**
   All 5 formulas should be logically integrated into a single cohesive whole based on the advancement of your core.
   Each formula is based on the intensification of your key talents.
   Each formula is about how those key talents will advance reality.
   Each formula must agree with the evidence you uncovered in the patterns of historical events in the talent-based life themes exercise. The themes indicate where the flow-to-flow internally and externally has been pressuring the expansion of your key talents. Formula 1 has already been operating throughout your life. Your 5 formulas enable you to proactively support its strategy.
   Formulas 3 to 5 should agree with your findings in the systems-based key talents exercise.

5. **Quantum leaps** should be used to lock new information uncovered by the process into your system as permanent template changes rather than simply new information being applied to old machinery.

6. Assume you have all of **the resources and freedom** required to maximize your system over your lifetime.

The Leadering paradigm is composed of an integrated system of meta-competencies, drives, instincts, reflexes, beliefs, dynamics, and cognitive capabilities shared by adept leaders, entrepreneurs, innovators, and achievers.

7 PERSONALIZING THE LEADERING™ PARADIGM

I   FLOW MAXIMIZATION EXERCISES   continued

18. **Determining your 5 Maximizing Formulas:**   34 minutes   18 figures

Exercises for determining each of your 5 formulas for maximizing within the Leadering™ paradigm. Information about each of the 5 formulas is presented for individual formulas and in combination. The structure and content of the figures for each 5-formula exercise is introduced as well as some general advice before proceeding with the exercises designed to assist you in developing your personalized formulas for operating the Leadering™ the machinery.

It is not necessary to do all of the exercises, only what is required for you to develop your first working hypotheses for operating in the Leadering™ paradigm. Action learning experimentation will tell you whether your working hypotheses are correct. The notes are in-depth and more than most require in order to provide you with something to come back to for the first pass at your hypotheses or for new iterations and refinements as may be required for the rest of your life.

Exercises, notes, and questions are provided to assist you in determining each of your 5 formulas for maximizing yourself, other human systems, and the Leadering™ paradigm for goal achievement. The repetition of some figures is to enable you to have everything in one place for determining each formula. It is only necessary to derive your best hypothesis to test out for confirmation of each personal formula. Use as much or as little of this support material as is necessary for you to achieve this goal. Everyone's needs are different.

| Formula 1: 14 figures | Formula 3: 17 figures | Formula 5: 13 figures |
| Formula 2: 8 figures | Formula 4: 18 figures | |

THE LEADERING™ CORE DETERMINATION EXERCISES

These exercises are designed to identify the core of your system which is being acted upon by natural forces inside and outside of you so you can comply with and capitalize on them and avoid operating contrary to them.

FLOW EXPLOITATION EXERCISES
for maximum performance and advancement

Life Theme exercises
- key talent determination
- flow to flow determination

Key talent Determination exercises
- system-based key talent exercise
- various other exercises

5 Talent-Based Operating Formulas exercises
1: your lifetime development formula
2: your greatest lifetime achievement formula
3: your natural leader formula
4: your leadership development formula
5: your greatest leader performance formula

BELIEF MAXIMIZATION EXERCISES
for Core Congruence

Belief Template Analysis and Upgrade:
- beneficial belief determination:
  ideal talent-based and flow-based beliefs
  identity beliefs, reality creation beliefs
- problem belief determination:
  fear beliefs, toxic beliefs, conflicting beliefs
- event-driven template upgrade process
- quantum leap template exchange process:
  goal-packaging identities, reincarnation

Action Learning Experimentation
- proving beliefs create reality
- improving belief engineering in your own and other systems
- improving template determination / design
- quantum leap experimentation

YOUR FLOW ENGINE:

Natural forces inside and outside of you act on your core

YOUR BELIEF TEMPLATE

Your belief template governs both you and your reality as a single system

Beliefs are information storage units like genes

YOUR CORE CONSISTS OF:

1. **KEY TALENTS**

2. **ADDICTIVE DRIVES**
   pulling you to use your key talents

   *Note: Your key talents and associated drives are the immutable beliefs below. They continuously
   - create your reality and
   - are being acted upon by the flow to flow and Leadering's built-in growth continuums which amplify core impact.

3. **IMMUTABLE BELIEFS** (**innate gene-based beliefs**) These define the essence of your system and why it came together in the first place. These beliefs are genetically based and inherent to the built-in creative expression of your system. See *Note above.

4. **CHANGEABLE BELIEFS** ideally designed to support the key talents, addictive drives, and immutable beliefs to maximize your performance, development, and survival in biological terms. The goal is core congruence.

© 2006 Lauren Holmes

Evolution

FORMULAS 1 and 2:   Advancing your personal system

Formula 1 lifetime key talent development continuum

Move up and down the continuum to let the big picture inform your current implementation tactics and, vice versa, use your current findings to inform the big picture.

Formula 2 is the culmination of the Formula 1 development continuum.

Formula 2 defines the ultimate level of talent-based performance at which you can operate as a result of implementing the Formula 1 lifetime key talent development strategy for capitalizing on innate drives and natural forces internally and externally.

Co-Evolution

FORMULAS 3, 4, and 5:   Advancing your personal system by creating, advancing, and maximizing other systems:

Leadering™ Leadership and Leadership Development

Continuum Start Point:
Formula 3:
talent-based leadership

Continuum End Point:
Formula 5: greatest level of talent-based leadership

Formulas 1 and 4 share a development continuum:
Formula 4 talent-based leader development continuum is a subset development stream of the Formula 1 lifetime key talent development continuum.

Lifetime development and leadership development define the same continuum in the Leadering™ paradigm:
the expansion of the innate core of your system while creating and expanding the foundational core of other systems.

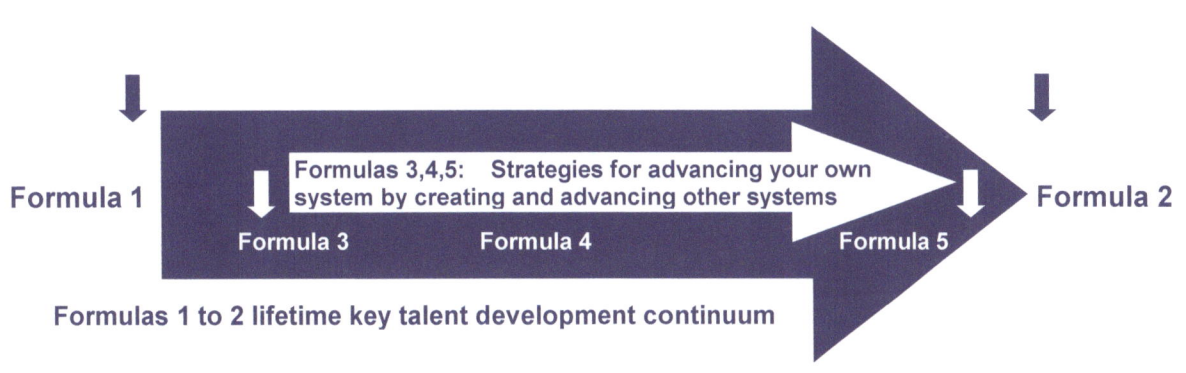

All 5 formulas are interlinked. The 5 formulas define both a continuum and a continuum within that continuum: a subset. Formulas 1 and 2 define the continuum and formulas 3, 4, and 5 define a continuum subset.

All are about advancing your system core in the direction of the growth continuums built into the Leadering™ paradigm.

The human evolutionary continuum, the lifetime key talent development continuum and the leadership development continuum are the same continuum. The flow to flow defines a single continuum into which all human systems are pressured. Therefore, to capitalize on those forces, all 5 of the formulas have to relate to that continuum.

Since your themes identified by the Life Themes exercise demonstrate the flow to flow acting on your core and its system of key talents, your 5 formulas must agree with the evidence you discovered in the patterns throughout your life.

All 5 formulas relate specifically to the application of your key talents to advance reality.

Leadership is core-based in the Leadering™ paradigm because internal and external drives are acting on your system core and the cores of all human systems.

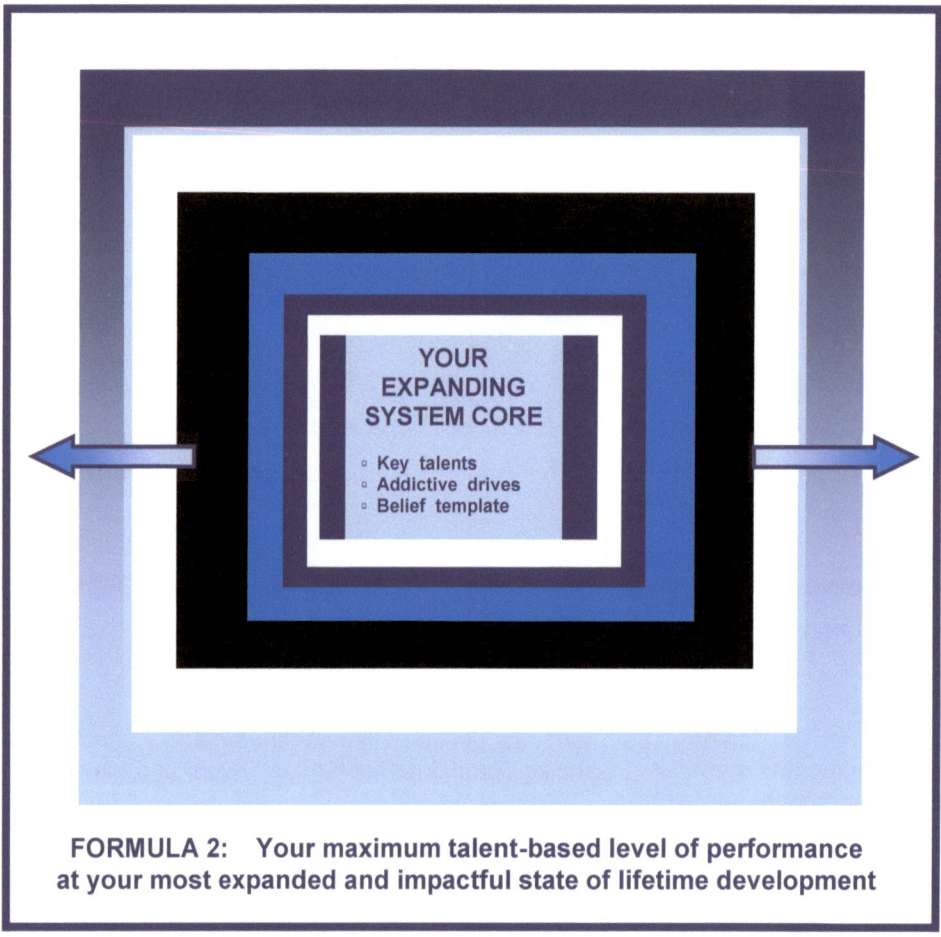

FORMULA 2: Your maximum talent-based level of performance at your most expanded and impactful state of lifetime development

1. At this level of expansion of your core and your key talents in particular, what kind of work are you doing?
2. How are you changing reality?
3. What new functionality are you applying?
4. How are you capitalizing on natural forces to change reality with your key talents?
5. What is your ideal identity at this greatest level of performance?

FORMULAS 1 and 2: Advancing your personal system

Formula 1 lifetime key talent development continuum

Move up and down the continuum to let the big picture inform your current implementation tactics and, vice versa, use your current findings to inform the big picture.

Formula 2 is the culmination of the Formula 1 development continuum.

Formula 2 defines the ultimate level of talent-based performance at which you can operate as a result of implementing the Formula 1 lifetime key talent development strategy for capitalizing on innate drives and natural forces internally and externally.

18-6A (18-2)   © 2006 Lauren Holmes

Nonlinear continuum direction

Amplification, Intensification, Expansion of your system's innate core. Core expansions in the Leadering™ paradigm are achieved by quantum leap - a method for core replacement.

As your key talents expand as a result of operating in talent-based flow state and the flow to flow, your impact on reality increases. The magnitude of change you cause in reality increases. Your creative impact increases.

18-6B   © 2006 Lauren Holmes

Nonlinear reality advancement

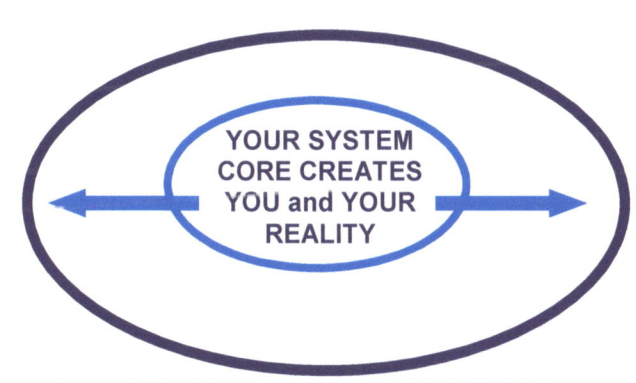

You and your reality are a single system in the Leadering™ paradigm. Realities are self-created by your system core.

Change your core to change your reality: the situations and events you will experience.

Formulas 1 and 2 not only advance your core but your reality or experience by reflection.

18-6C   © 2006 Lauren Holmes

YOUR EXPANDING SYSTEM CORE
The foundation of all human system development in the Leading™ paradigm

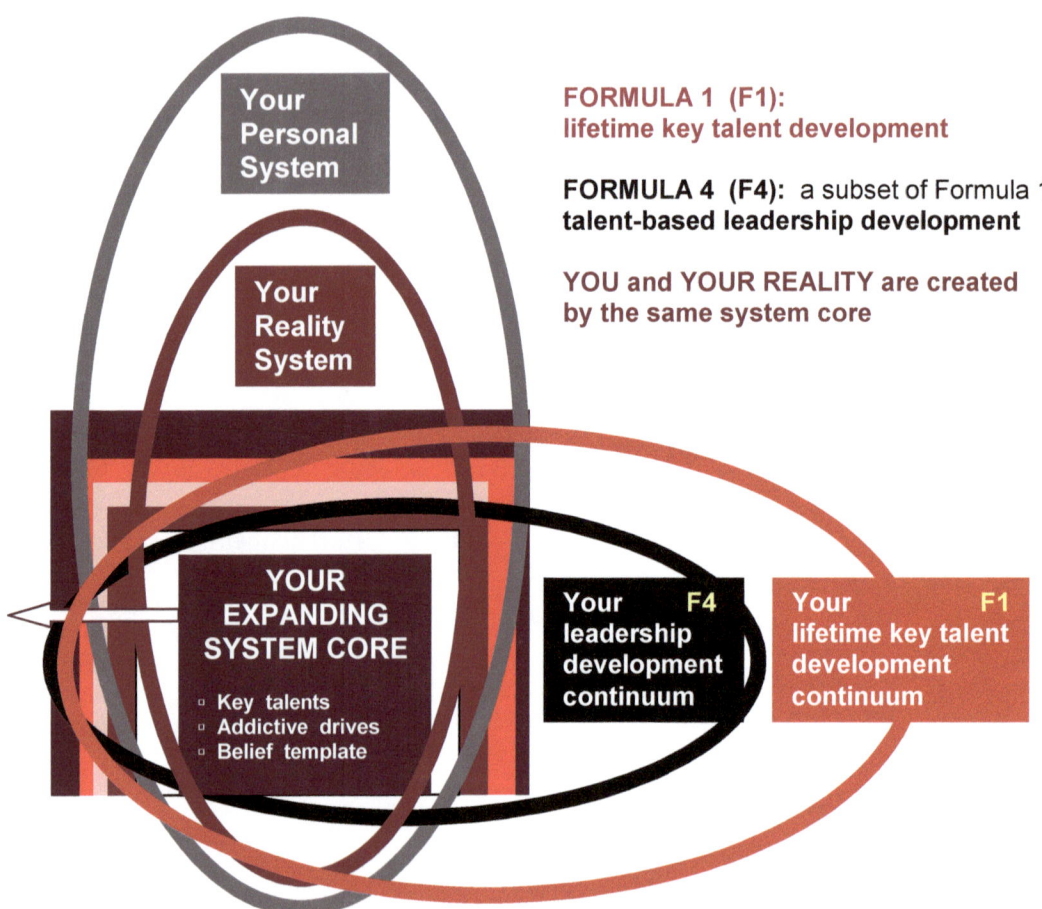

FORMULA 1 (F1):
lifetime key talent development

FORMULA 4 (F4): a subset of Formula 1
talent-based leadership development

YOU and YOUR REALITY are created by the same system core

NONLINEAR DEVELOPMENT IN THE LEADERING PARDIGM

The progression of the continuum defined by formulas 1 and 2 is not linear but the amplification of the core of each human system by quantum leaps.

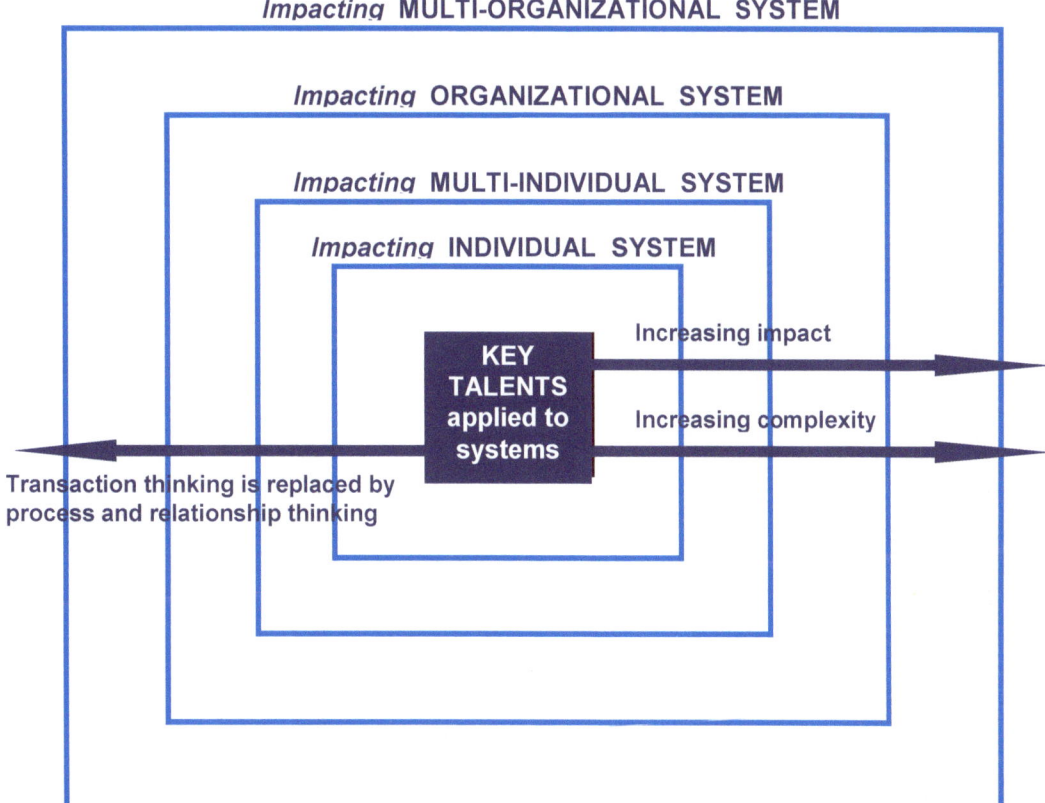

Co-Evolution

FORMULAS 3, 4, and 5: Advancing your personal system by creating, advancing, and maximizing other systems:

Leadering™ Leadership and Leadership Development

Continuum Start Point:
Formula 3:
talent-based leadership

Continuum End Point:
Formula 5: greatest level of talent-based leadership

Formulas 1 and 4 share a development continuum:
Formula 4 talent-based leader development continuum is a subset development stream of the Formula 1 lifetime key talent development continuum.

Lifetime development and leadership development define the same continuum in the Leadering™ paradigm:
the expansion of the innate core of your system while creating and expanding the foundational core of other systems.

18-9A (18-3) © 2006 Lauren Holmes

Nonlinear continuum directions

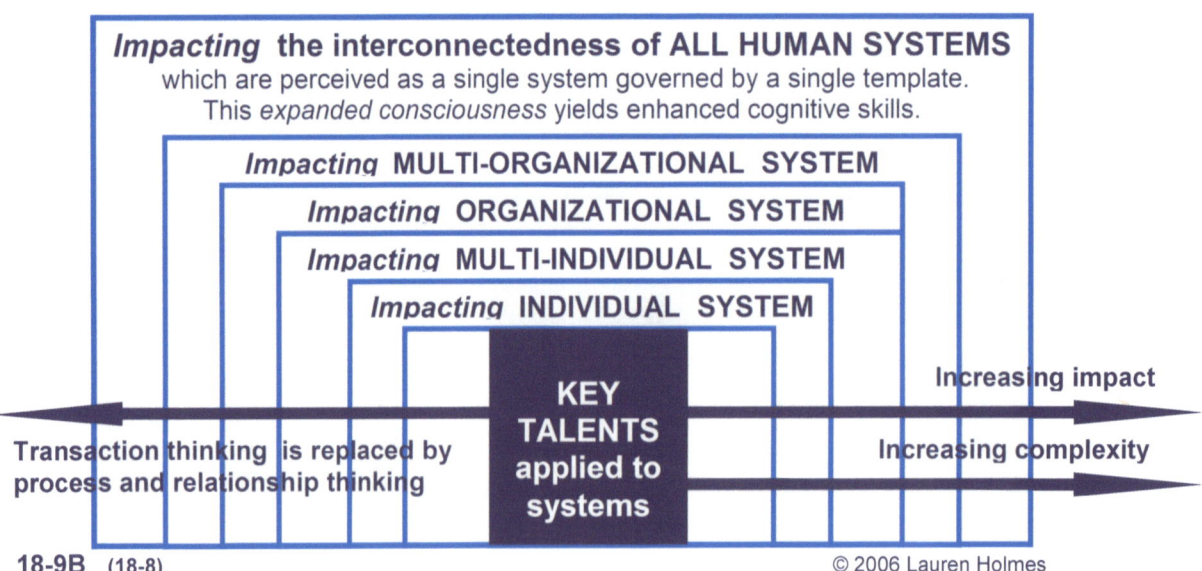

18-9B (18-8) © 2006 Lauren Holmes

FORMULAS 1 and 2:   Advancing your personal system

Identified by Core Determination Exercises:
- Life themes exercises
- Key talent determination exercises

FORMULAS 3, 4, and 5:   Advancing your personal system by creating, advancing, and maximizing other system:

- Determined by the lifetime development continuum defined by formulas 1 and 2
- Core Determination Exercises: systems-based key-talent application exercise

Co-Evolution

FORMULAS 3, 4, and 5: Advancing your personal system by creating, advancing, and maximizing other systems:

Talent-based system leadership in the flow-to-flow

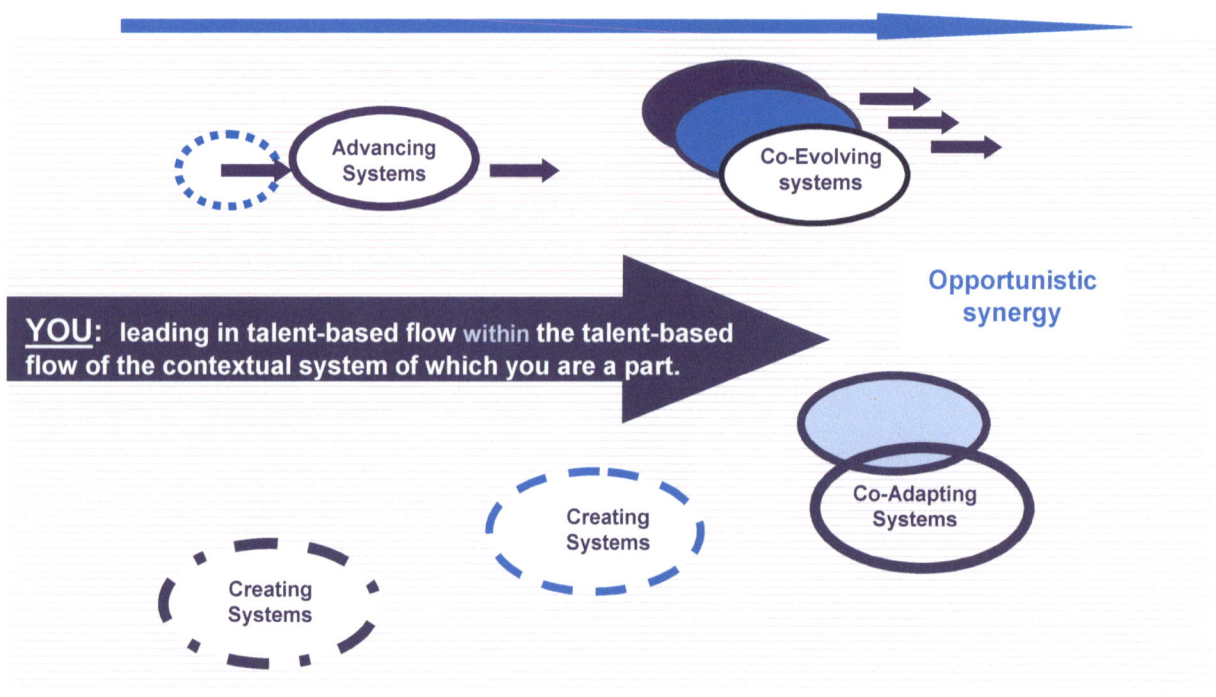

YOU: leading in talent-based flow *within* the talent-based flow of the contextual system of which you are a part.

Opportunistic synergy

Advancing your system by applying your key talents to other systems	Individual Systems	Multi-Individual Systems	Organization Systems	Multi-Organization Systems	Knowledge Systems	Process Systems

Leadering™ provides a single systems maximization toolkit for advancing

18-11 © 2006 Lauren Holmes

Where are you on the leadership development continuum with respect to advancing systems?

LEADERING™ AMPLIFIES LEADER DRIVES

Manager	Transitional Change Leader	Transformational Change Leader	Creational Leader / Frontiering Leader
Run an existing business as is	**Advance an existing business linearly** • Incremental upgrades • Harvest	**Change an existing business nonlinearly** • Turnarounds • Explosive Growth • Merge 2 existing businesses	**Create the unknown or Penetrate the unknown** • Business startups • Pioneering / Frontiering • Re-engineering • New ventures / Innovation

As leader drives strengthen, leader impact increases:
INCREASED DRIVES to change – creativity/creation – frontiering™
INCREASED BELIEF CHANGES MADE

| Systems maintenance | Increasing systems advancement | | Systems Creation: new and new from grouping existing systems |

Managers run existing systems ➡ Leaders create and advance systems

As managers progress along the leadership development continuum, their ability to advance reality increases. Their ability to make belief changes increases. If there is no change in beliefs, there is no change in reality. If there is no change in reality, leadership has not occurred. The magnitude of change achieved in reality is the measure of leadership strength.

© 1995 Lauren Holmes

SAMPLE CATEGORIES OF LEADERING'S BUILT-IN GROWTH

CONTINUOUS DEVELOPMENT
Addiction to continuous development:
- the continuous increase in drives which addict you to using and improving your system of core talents
- these addictive drives cause the continuous improvement of your system of core talents becomes the founding dynamic of your life to which the other segments of your life are integrated.
- an accelerating increase in speed of development of your system of core talents
- the continuous increase in the development of drives associated with meta-competencies such as frontiering, creativity, learning to learn, and learning agility which promote continuous development
- addiction to peak performance and peak advancement flow states

CONTINUOUSLY IMPROVING PERFORMANCE
1. Continuous increase in time spent operating in peak performance and peak advancement flow states
2. Depth of your talent-based flow states increases with each experience thus increasing performance further
3. Event-driven belief upgrade process continually improves performance through more supportive beliefs

CONTINUOUSLY INCREASING IMPACT
1. Continuous increase in impact of creations
2. Reality creation precision
3. Continuous increase in creativity and innovation
4. Continuous increase in your impact on reality
5. An increase in the level of complexity handled from single system to multiple systems impact; from transactions to process; from process to quantum leaps; from linear to nonlinear; more impactful quantum leaps impacting more systems more quickly

CONTINUOUSLY INCREASING FUNCTIONALITY
1. Continuous increase in the specialization of your system of core talents
2. Accelerating improvement of abilities to use your core talents
3. Increasing ability to penetrate the unknown or bring the unknown into existence and a craving for both: frontiering and creativity.
4. Continuous improvement in your facility for nonlinear quantum leaps to speed advancement of your system and other systems
5. Systems-based modus operandi: single toolkit for advancing systems, continuous increase in your ability to advance systems and to create new systems
6. Continuous acquisition and improvement of meta-competencies associated with successful leaders, entrepreneurs, innovators and high achievers. (Meta-competencies improve the ability to assimilate and use competencies): continuous development, improved cognitive capabilities, improved performance. These allow you to move more quickly easily and safely into unknown territory and frontiers, increase your creativity and innovation, increase your knowledge-acquisition capabilities, and increase your ability to court coincidences and facilitating events which will improve your performance of your art.
7. Continuous improvement to cognitive skills:
   - concept formation, conceptualization of complex ideas, abstract thinking, deductive and inductive logic, problem reframing, dealing with multiple perspectives and ambiguity, skillful formulation of ends, ways, means
   - frame of reference development: systems understanding, environmental scanning, pattern recognition
   - proactive thinking using critical, creative, and reflective thinking
   - analysis of complicated events, trend perception, change detection, creative and opportunistic problem-solving
   - deployment of models, theories and inferences
   - visualization, addressing, and capitalization of complex interrelationships: see the interaction of more systems and the opportunities for synergy and co-evolution; impact more systems, impact more complex systems, impact larger systems
   - big-picture thinking and see more patterns to have more information for decision-making and strategic and tactical planning

Recording 18: Determining your 5 Maximizing Formulas

EVENT PATTERNS TRACKED FOR THEMES These patterns are indicative of the flow to internal and external congruence or the flow to flow	FIVE PERSONAL FORMULAS for operating in the target Leading™ paradigm
In the target paradigm, the life-long patterns of the following 'talent-based' or 'work' events are analyzed for themes indicating the flow to generative congruence or flow internally or externally: - an unpaid work theme - a knowledge-pursuit theme or learning-pursuit theme - a spontaneous knowledge theme - a frontier-pursuit theme - a creativity-pursuit theme - a talent-based creative expression theme - a meaning-pursuit theme - the theme(s) of talent-based flow states - a flow-to-flow theme, theme(s) of projects - a naturality expansion theme - a resonance theme - a positive emotion theme **All of the above themes indicate when a system is integrated into the flow to congruence.**	Based on the themes of the event patterns tracked in the paradigm, the following 5 formulas will emerge to help participants determine how to capitalize on the flow to flow of all human systems. Your key talents are a system of your strongest capabilities which you are passionate about using and improving which advance reality in some way. This system is what is being acted upon by the flow to flow and your addictive drives. 1. **Talent-based lifetime development formula** or personal evolution formula 2. **Greatest lifetime level of talent-based performance**: the culmination of living one's lifetime development formula. 3. **Talent-based leadership formula**: leadership as an expression of one's lifetime development formula 4. **Talent-based leadership development formula**: merging one's lifetime development formula with one's talent-based leadership formula. 5. **Greatest lifetime level of performance as a leader** based on the previous 4 formulas.

18-4A   © 2006 Lauren Holmes

Caution: If you have lived your life directed by external elements (externally referenced) rather than complying with your natural talent-based drives internally (internally referenced) you will have less consistent patterns or fewer of them. Operate internally referenced for awhile and the patterns will become evident.

EVENT PATTERNS TRACKED FOR THEMES
These patterns are indicative of the flow-to-flow

In the target paradigm, the life-long patterns of the following 'talent-based' or 'work' events are analyzed for themes indicating the flow to generative congruence or flow internally or externally:

- **an unpaid work theme** based on patterns of events in which you freely give away "work" that others would charge for or that you are so passionate about that you would pay for the opportunity to do.
- **a talent-based knowledge-pursuit or learning-pursuit theme** based on patterns of events of seeking knowledge passionately and willingly for the application of key talents (learning-pursuit theme)
- **a talent-based spontaneous knowledge theme** based on patterns of events in which spontaneous knowledge emerged to support the application of key talents
- **a talent-based frontier-pursuit theme** based on patterns of events of new territories of growth, learning and achievement the system was drawn to pursue for the application of key talents
- **a talent-based creativity-pursuit theme** based on patterns of events of preferred creative expression or creative expression which you or system was drawn to pursue for the application of key talents along with events in which creativity or creative invention or innovation spontaneously emerged for the application of key talents
- **a talent-based creative expression theme** based on patterns of events of creative expression in which your passion and enthusiasm were inflamed
- **a talent-based meaning-pursuit theme** based on patterns of events of work or achievements or contributions considered a meaningful application of key talents
- **the theme(s) of talent-based flow states** indicated by patterns of events whereby you went into flow state during the application of key talents
- **a talent-based flow-to-flow theme, theme(s) of projects** requiring the application of key talents which were supported by lots of coincidences, flows, spontaneous knowledge / creativity (figure 16-6)
- **talent-based naturality expansion theme** (figures 17-5, 17-6B, 17-6C, 17-7, and 17-8) indicated by patterns of expansions or intensifications of your system around its core to greater impact on reality - the key direction of growth and advancement of any system in the Leadering™ paradigm.
- **a talent-based resonance theme** based on patterns of subjects or activities for the application of key talents with which you resonated
- **a talent-based positive emotion theme** based on patterns of events in which passion, excitement, and enthusiasm emerged during the application of key talents

All of the above themes indicate when a system is integrated into the flow to congruence.

YOUR FIVE PERSONALIZED OPERATING FORMULAS
for maximizing in the Leadering™ paradigm

Key talents being acted on by the flow-to-flow
Your key talents are a system of your strongest capabilities which you are innately addicted to using and improving. When used, your key talents advance reality in some way. All 5 formulas are operating strategies for capitalizing on your key talents. Therefore they are interlinked. Your key talents are also interlinked into a system of addictive drives which form your flow engine. The flow engine promotes operating in a peak performance flow state in which you are using your key talents. The key talents being acted on by the flow engine need to be known in order to determine one's 5 operating formulas for the Leadering™ paradigm.

1. Your lifetime key talent development formula: <mark>advancing your system</mark>
If natural forces continuously pressure you to expand or intensify your ability to use your key talents for creation - to advance reality - what will be the development path or theme of that intensification process underpinning your life?

2. Your greatest talent-based performance as an individual:
If you were to pursue the continuous expansion of your key talents over a lifetime and at top speeds, what is the highest level of creative impact or reality creation that you would likely achieve. What is the highest possible culmination of living your lifetime development formula? What is your maximum attainment based on a lifetime of accelerating development of your key talents?

3. Your talent-based leadership formula: <mark>advancing other systems</mark>
If you complied with the addictive drives pulling you to the continuous expansion of your key talents, what would be the territory and form of your leadership? How would formulas 1 and 2 define you as a leader by logical extension? What would your leadership formula look like if it was 100% based on your greatest performance with your key talents and their continuous expansion?

4. Your talent-based leadership development formula:
Your leadership development formula just allows you a more specialized lens with which to examine and strategize your personal development. The continuous expansion of the intensity and impact of your key talents define both your development as an individual and a leader. Therefore, leadership development and lifetime development form the same single continuum. The advancement of your key talents increases your strength, impact, and creativity as a leader. How would the previous 3 formulas define your personalized talent-based leadership development formula? For those on the Leadering™ program who assume they will never be a leader, it is built in. (figure 18-3)

5. Your greatest talent-based performance as a leader:
Based on your 4 previous formulas, determine your greatest lifetime level of performance as a leader. Given your advancement as an individual and a leader based on the continuous intensification of your key talents, and given the formula for your greatest performance as an individual (Formula 2), what would be the dimensions of your ultimate performance level as a leader: generically, what will be your greatest levels of capability for causing reality advances?

THE LEADERING™ QUANTUM LEAP PROCESS

Design it!   Feel it!   Be it!

PRE-LEAP
1. Choose the right quantum leap or post-leap state
2. Define the post-leap state with clarity
3. Define the post-leap state without previous limitations or toxicity
4. Emotionally template the post-leap state
5. Add the information to fuel emergence
6. Expect the unexpected post-leap

LEAP
1. Release the linear connection to the past
2. Feel yourself 100% fluid
3. Feel the post-leap state
4. Feel who the "post-leap you" will be
5. Commit to the quantum leap
6. Make an abrupt, no-return, reincarnation
7. Trigger spontaneous self-organization by intent

POST-LEAP
1. Operate as if the quantum leap was successful
2. Walk around as the person with the post-leap reality
3. Hold this new identity until reality restructures
4. Ignore evidence of events created by the old template
5. Trigger cascading quantum leaps by intent
6. Establish quantum leaping as a way of life
7. Consolidate your new quantum leap expert beliefs

© 1998 Lauren Holmes

Categories of Quantum Leaps to apply to each Formula

CORE UPGRADE QUANTUM LEAPS
- quantum leaps to new functionality such as increased cognitive skills, leader meta-competencies, and an increasingly supportive belief template.

CORE EXPANSION QUANTUM LEAPS
Internal and external drives pressure your system to expand around its core system of key talents and drives. The best way to comply with these pressures to expand is to routinely quantum leap as a modus operandi for the rest of your life. These quantum leaps are facilitated by natural forces. These expansions include:
- quantum leaps to the next wider iteration of power and impact of your system.
- a series of quantum leaps which break through frontier after frontier with respect to improving your prowess and skill for applying your key talents to advance reality. Expansion quantum leaps advance the art and science behind your F1-F2 development of your key talents.
- 10-year maximum quantum leaps: a quantum leap to a category of expansion or capability as if you have been operating at that level of intensification and impact of your system for the last 10 years. This speeds the advancement of your capabilities.

REALIGNMENT QUANTUM LEAPS
- quantum leaps to re-boot your system onto its natural core in compliance with natural forces continuously pressuring this re-centering.
- quantum leaps to merge your system into the-flow-to-flow or to the flow of other dynamics and built-in growth continuums within the Leadering™ paradigm.

NOTES FOR ALL 5 LEADERING™ OPERATING FORMULAS

1. **Leaders:** For those taking Leadering™ with the intention of becoming visible leaders in positions of authority and commanding others, you should attempt to include in formulas 3, 4, and 5, a specific theme for your leadership which is based on the expansion of your key talents over your lifetime as prescribed by formula 1.

2. **Non-Leaders:** For those who do not plan to become visible leaders with followers reporting, please use this exercise to identify a strategy for developing your systems advancement capabilities as you develop around your key talents in the Leadering paradigm.

3. **For those pursuing Entrepreneuring, Innovation, Recareering™ and Peak Performance:** For those taking Leadering™ for recareering™, for peak performance, and for maximum lifetime achievement, you should translate all 5 formulas in terms of your career and being paid for continuously scaling new frontiers of application of your talents. The pursuit of p*aid peak evolution* should be the determinant for your career choices. You want to be paid for pursuing your lifetime maximum.

4. **The 5 formulas are logically interlinked:**
   All 5 formulas should be logically integrated into a single cohesive whole based on the advancement of your core.
   Each formula is based on the intensification of your key talents.
   Each formula is about how those key talents will advance reality.
   Each formula must agree with the evidence you uncovered in the patterns of historical events in the talent-based life themes exercise. The themes indicate where the flow-to-flow internally and externally has been pressuring the expansion of your key talents. Formula 1 has already been operating throughout your life. Your 5 formulas enable you to proactively support its strategy.
   Formulas 3 to 5 should agree with your findings in the systems-based key talents exercise.

5. **Quantum leaps** should be used to lock new information uncovered by the process into your system as permanent template changes rather than simply new information being applied to old machinery.

6. Assume you have all of **the resources and freedom** required to maximize your system over your lifetime.

FORMULA 1

A great deal of the power of the Leadering™ paradigm shift to transform you and how you will operate derives from excess capacity built into the Leadering™ experience. Leadering™ works by throwing you into overwhelm. You must be stretched beyond your previous capabilities for new functionality and performance to emerge, especially cognitive skills such as conceptual, abstract, relational, and systems thinking.

7 PERSONALIZING THE LEADERING™ PARADIGM

I FLOW MAXIMIZATION EXERCISES continued

Determining your 5 Formulas:

Exercises, notes, and questions are provided to assist you in determining each of your 5 formulas for maximizing yourself, other human systems, and the Leadering™ paradigm for goal achievement. The repetition of some figures is to enable you to have everything in one place for determining each formula. It is only necessary to derive your best hypothesis to test out for confirmation of each personal formula. Use as much or as little of this support material as is necessary for you to achieve this goal. Everyone's needs are different.

Formula 1: 14 figures   Formula 3: 17 figures   Formula 5: 13 figures
Formula 2:   8 figures   Formula 4: 18 figures

Leadering™ talent-based operating formulas exercises
as a means to capitalize on the flow-to-flow to maximize yourself and your life

Formula 1: Your lifetime key talent development formula
DESCRIPTION

Development

ADVANCING YOUR PERSONAL SYSTEM

Formula 1 is a strategy for complying with natural forces pressuring your system to maximum performance. Specifically, it is a strategy for maximizing the creative expression of your core system of key talents and the drives which draw you to use and improve those key talents to advance reality in some way.

Formula 1 and Formula 2 define a lifetime development continuum for maximizing your key talents using all of the growth continuums built into the Leadering™ paradigm. The Formula1-Formula 2 continuum (F1-F2) thus becomes the foundational or underlying dynamic organizing your system and your life to which everything else attaches. Formula 1 therefore determines the other 4 formulas.

Formulas 3, 4, and 5 are subsets of Formula 1. Together they define a continuum which is a subset of the Formula1-Formula2 continuum. Formulas 1 and 2 address the advancement of your system to greater impact on advancing reality. Formulas 3, 4, and 5 are strategies for using the advancement of other systems to advance your own system and its impact on reality.

The progression of the continuum defined by Formulas 1 and 2 is not linear but the amplification of the core of each human system by quantum leaps.

All 5 formulas are about advancing your system core in the direction of the growth continuums built into the Leadering™ paradigm.

The human evolutionary continuum, the lifetime key talent development continuum and the leadership development continuum are the same continuum. The flow to flow defines a single continuum into which all human systems are pressured. Therefore, to capitalize on those forces, all 5 of the formulas have to relate to that continuum.

Since your themes identified by the Life Themes exercise demonstrate the flow to flow acting on your core and its system of key talents, your 5 formulas must agree with the evidence you discovered in the patterns throughout your life.

All 5 formulas relate specifically to the application of your key talents to advance reality.

Leadership is core-based in the Leadering™ paradigm because internal and external drives are acting on your system core and the cores of all human systems.

Maximum strength as an individual, leader, entrepreneur, innovator and top performer come from complying with and capitalizing on the forces defining this continuum.

Evolution

FORMULAS 1 and 2: Advancing your personal system

Formula 1 lifetime key talent development continuum

Move up and down the continuum to let the big picture inform your current implementation tactics and, vice versa, use your current findings to inform the big picture.

Formula 2 is the culmination of the Formula 1 development continuum.

Formula 2 defines the ultimate level of talent-based performance at which you can operate as a result of implementing the Formula 1 lifetime key talent development strategy for capitalizing on innate drives and natural forces internally and externally.

18-1B   Formula 1   © 2006 Lauren Holmes

Evolution + Co-Evolution

All 5 FORMULAS: Advancing your personal system by creating, advancing, and maximizing other human systems

Flow to Flow - Flow to Congruence - Flow to fusion

Formula 1

Formulas 3,4,5: Strategies for advancing your own system by creating and advancing other systems

Formula 3   Formula 4   Formula 5

Formula 2

Formulas 1 to 2 lifetime key talent development continuum

Projected direction of your historical talent-based life themes

18-1C   Formula 1   © 2006 Lauren Holmes

Formula 1: Your lifetime key talent development formula
INSTRUCTIONS
Development.

Formula 1 is determined by projecting into the future two previously identified bodies of information about the advancement of your key talents:
1. the talent-based themes discovered from the historical patterns of events in the life themes exercise, and
2. the talent-based growth directions built into the Leading™ paradigm identified in recording 15 dedicated to that subject matter (figure 18-13).

IDEAL OUTCOME
The outcome of the formula 1 exercise is a working hypothesis that can be tested by trying to live it and looking for the tell-tale signs that you have moved into the flow-to-flow as a result.

The outcome is a working hypothesis for how your system will achieve its lifetime maximum based on the single underpinning dynamic of your system of key talents going through iteration after iteration of expansion of functionality and impact on reality.

The cumulative outcome of the 5 formulas is a fully integrated customized foundation for greatness as an individual, a leader, an entrepreneur, and an innovator upon which classic leader and performance competencies can be embedded.

The 5 formulas can be written individually or as a single cohesive strategy for the peer advisory database. Leading™ peers and co-workers should be able to quickly grasp the core of your system now and where it will ultimately advance over your lifetime. They can then interpret how the flow-to-flow is acting on your core at any time to advise you how to synergistically capitalize on the situations at hand.

Peer Advisory Database
A personal talent-based formulas list is begun which will contain the most up-to-date version of each participant's lifetime development formula, talent-based leadership formula, talent-based leadership development formula, and creativity-pursuit, frontier-pursuit, knowledge-pursuit and meaning-pursuit themes is provided to all participants
- to enable the best input and advice and
- to reinforce these personal formulas and themes within each participant so there is no backsliding.

FORMULAS 1 and 2: Advancing your personal system

Identified by Core Determination Exercises:
- Life themes exercises
- Key talent determination exercises

FORMULAS 3, 4, and 5: Advancing your personal system by creating, advancing, and maximizing other system:

- Determined by the lifetime development continuum defined by formulas 1 and 2
- Core Determination Exercises: systems-based key-talent application exercise

Leadering™ talent-based operating formulas exercises
as a means to capitalize on the flow-to-flow to maximize yourself and your life

Formula 1: Your lifetime key talent development formula
QUESTIONS
Development

QUESTIONS to help you determine your ideal lifetime key talent development formula based on the advancement of your key talents as prescribed in the Leadering™ paradigm:

1. **Reality impact theme:**
   - What are the characteristics of the 'work' you truly love to do, work which brings something new into the world or leaves reality changed in some way?
   - What is the 'work' that is play to you, that you would do for free but others would demand to be paid for?

2. **Expansion continuum of reality impact:**
   - How will your impact on reality advance as you expand and develop?
   - If the underlying dynamics of your life will be a continuous expansion of the ability to apply your key talents for creation, or what is, in effect, to change reality, what will that intensification process look like?
   - If natural forces continuously pressure you to expand or intensify your ability to use your key talents for creation - to advance reality - what will be the development path or theme of that intensification process underpinning your life?
   - If your lifetime development is based on the continuous expansion of your impact on reality through the application of your key talents, what will that intensification continuum look like?

   Try to release your linear thinking to contemplate this formula 1 expansion around the core of your system.

3. **Projection of historical life themes:**
   If you projected out the themes you discovered in the talent-based life themes exercise to the end of your life, what would be your path to maximum lifetime advancement based on the development of those key talents? Formula 1 must agree with the historical patterns of events in your past you uncovered in the talent-based life themes.

4. **Nature's neutral perspective:**
   - If you were nature, how would you objectively maximize your personal system over your lifetime?
   - What would you do with this core and this set of capabilities inherent in your system to ensure survival and maximization?

   Try to overlook the limitations and toxicity you might have accumulated over the years which might limit or sway your thinking. Assume nature only looks at your system as it stands and the opportunities to capitalize on existing internal and external drives, dynamics, and capabilities to advance your system.

18-1F   Formula 1   © 2006 Lauren Holmes

Formula 1: Your lifetime key talent development formula
QUANTUM LEAP SUGGESTIONS

Development

CORE UPGRADE QUANTUM LEAPS
1. Quantum leaps to new functionality such as increased cognitive skills, leader meta-competencies, and an increasingly supportive belief template.

2. Paid peak evolution quantum leap:
   Quantum leap to a life founded on your knowledge-pursuit, creativity-pursuit, meaning-pursuit, and frontiering-pursuit themes so that you are
   - earning revenues doing only the work you are most passionately drawn to do,
   - using your key talents to their maximum, then continuously increasing that maximum
   - being paid to learn the information and skills you would pursue anyway to improve your key talent capabilities if you had total freedom and all the resources you needed.

CORE EXPANSION QUANTUM LEAPS
1. Quantum leap to new expansions of the power and impact of your key talents on advancing reality one after the next after the next.
   - Internalize your next 5 expansions. Quantum leap to a post leap in which you have been operating 5 expansions out for the last 10 years.
   - Repeat this exercise and quantum leap often for the rest of your life.
   - Continuously quantum leap to the next amplification of the power and impact of your key talents as a way of life so that you are constantly scaling new frontiers of the art and science behind using your key talents.

REALIGNMENT QUANTUM LEAPS
1. Quantum leap to re-boot your system onto its natural core in compliance with natural forces continuously pressuring this re-centering.

2. Quantum leap to realign your life to the flow to internal and external congruence or, in other words, the flow-to-flow or the flow-within-flow.

3. Quantum leap to operating for the rest of your life in 100% talent-based flow state for peak performance and peak advancement.

4. Quantum leap to living in alignment with all of the historical themes you discovered in the talent-based life themes exercises.

HOW GROWTH IS BUILT INTO LEADERING™

The Key Leadering™ Paradigm Growth Players

System Core:
System Flow engine:
- flow pursuit of the system`
- key talents
- core addictive drives

System Template:
- immutable beliefs
- changeable beliefs: event-driven template upgrade process

System Meta-Competencies

Conditioned Reflexes

Leadering™ System Maximization Toolkit: the 15 dynamics or leader drives

Systems Mindset
- systems-based dynamic
- expanding consciousness

Advancement Mechanics
- quantum leap dynamic
- templating dynamic
- self-organizing dynamic
- emergence dynamic

Advancement Directions
- knowledge-pursuit drive
- adaptation drive
- evolution drive
- co-evolution drive
- talent-based flow drive
- flow-within-flow drive

Drives for the Unknown:
- frontier-pursuit drive
- creation / creativity-pursuit drive

Five Talent-based Operating Formulas
lifetime development, greatest lifetime performance, leadership, leadership development, greatest leader lifetime performance

Self- or System-Initiated Quantum Leaps

Nature-Initiated Quantum Leaps imbedded in the flow-to-flow
- coincidences (multi-system synergy, co-evolution, co-adaptation)
- spontaneous knowledge
- spontaneous creativity
- facilitating events
- flow states

for opportunistic synergy, co-evolution, co-adaptation, creative problem-solving, and flow-within-flow

Talent-Based Themes of your 'Life System'
- an unpaid work theme
- a knowledge-pursuit theme
- a spontaneous knowledge theme
- a frontier-pursuit theme
- a creativity-pursuit theme
- a talent-based creative expression theme
- a meaning-pursuit theme
- the theme(s) of talent-based flow states
- a flow-to-flow theme,
- theme(s) of talent-based projects
- a naturality expansion theme
- a resonance theme
- a positive emotion theme

18-1H   Formula 1

© 2006 Lauren Holmes

SAMPLE CATEGORIES OF LEADERING'S BUILT-IN GROWTH

CONTINUOUSLY IMPROVING PERFORMANCE
1. Increasing time operating in peak performance and peak advancement flow states
2. Depth of your talent-based flow states increases with each experience thus increasing performance further
3. Event-driven belief upgrade process continually improves performance through more supportive beliefs

CONTINUOUSLY INCREASING IMPACT
1. Increasing impact of creations, magnitude of advancement of reality, and reality creation precision
2. Reality creation precision
3. Increasing creativity and innovation
4. An increase in the level of complexity handled: from single system to multiple systems impact; from transactions to process; from process to quantum leaps; from linear to nonlinear; more impactful quantum leaps impacting more systems more quickly

CONTINUOUS DEVELOPMENT
Addiction to continuous development:
- the continuous increase in drives which addict you to using and improving your system of core talents
- these addictive drives cause the continuous improvement of your system of core talents becomes the founding dynamic of your life to which the other segments of your life are integrated.
- an accelerating increase in speed of development of your system of core talents
- the continuous increase in the development of drives associated with meta-competencies such as frontiering, creativity, learning to learn, and learning agility which promote continuous development
- addiction to flow states which continuously improve your key talents, functionality, and performance

CONTINUOUSLY INCREASING FUNCTIONALITY
1. Continuous increase in the specialization of your system of core talents
2. Accelerating improvement of abilities to use your core talents
3. Increasing ability to penetrate the unknown or bring the unknown into existence and a craving for both: frontiering and creativity.
4. Continuous improvement in your facility for nonlinear quantum leaps to speed advancement of your system and other systems
5. Systems-based modus operandi: single toolkit for advancing systems, continuous increase in your ability to advance systems and to create new systems
6. Continuous acquisition and improvement of meta-competencies associated with successful leaders, entrepreneurs, innovators and high achievers. (Meta-competencies improve the ability to assimilate and use competencies): continuous development, improved cognitive capabilities, improved performance. These allow you to move more quickly easily and safely into unknown territory and frontiers, increase your creativity and innovation, increase your knowledge-acquisition capabilities, and increase your ability to court coincidences and facilitating events which will improve your performance of your art.
7. Continuous improvement to cognitive skills:
    - concept formation, conceptualization of complex ideas, abstract thinking, deductive and inductive logic, problem reframing, dealing with multiple perspectives and ambiguity, skillful formulation of ends, ways, means
    - frame of reference development: systems understanding, environmental scanning, pattern recognition
    - proactive thinking using critical, creative, and reflective thinking
    - analysis of complicated events, trend perception, change detection, creative and opportunistic problem-solving
    - deployment of models, theories and inferences
    - visualization, addressing, and capitalization of complex interrelationships: see the interaction of more systems and the opportunities for synergy and co-evolution; impact more systems, impact more complex systems, impact larger systems
    - big-picture thinking and seeing more patterns to have more information for decision-making and strategic and tactical planning

Determining your Formula 1   162

THE LEADERING™ CORE DETERMINATION EXERCISES

These exercises are designed to identify the core of your system which is being acted upon by natural forces inside and outside of you so you can comply with and capitalize on them and avoid operating contrary to them.

FLOW EXPLOITATION EXERCISES
for maximum performance and advancement

Life Theme exercises
- key talent determination
- flow to flow determination

Key talent Determination exercises
- system-based key talent exercise
- various other exercises

5 Talent-Based Operating Formulas exercises
1: your lifetime development formula
2: your greatest lifetime achievement formula
3: your natural leader formula
4: your leadership development formula
5: your greatest leader performance formula

BELIEF MAXIMIZATION EXERCISES
for Core Congruence

Belief Template Analysis and Upgrade:
- beneficial belief determination:
    ideal talent-based and flow-based beliefs
    identity beliefs, reality creation beliefs
- problem belief determination:
    fear beliefs, toxic beliefs, conflicting beliefs
- event-driven template upgrade process
- quantum leap template exchange process:
    goal-packaging identities, reincarnation

Action Learning Experimentation
- proving beliefs create reality
- improving belief engineering in your own and other systems
- improving template determination / design
- quantum leap experimentation

YOUR FLOW ENGINE:

Natural forces inside and outside of you act on your core

YOUR BELIEF TEMPLATE

Your belief template governs both you and your reality as a single system

Beliefs are information storage units like genes

YOUR CORE CONSISTS OF:

1. **KEY TALENTS**

2. **ADDICTIVE DRIVES**
   pulling you to use your key talents

   *Note: Your key talents and associated drives are the immutable beliefs below. They continuously
   - create your reality and
   - are being acted upon by the flow to flow and Leadering's built-in growth continuums which amplify core impact.

3. **IMMUTABLE BELIEFS**
   (**innate gene-based beliefs**)
   These define the essence of your system and why it came together in the first place. These beliefs are genetically based and inherent to the built-in creative expression of your system. See *Note above.

4. **CHANGEABLE BELIEFS**
   ideally designed to support the key talents, addictive drives, and immutable beliefs to maximize your performance, development, and survival in biological terms. The goal is core congruence.

18-1K   Formula 1   © 2006 Lauren Holmes

LIFE-LONG FORMULA REFINEMENT

Refinements to these 5 formulas are a life-long process based on action-learning experimentation.

Refinements are required as one continuously intensifies and expands around one's dynamic core:

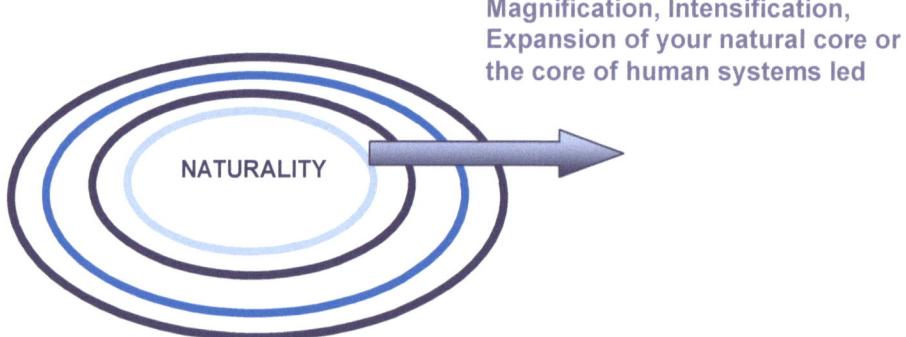

Magnification, Intensification, Expansion of your natural core or the core of human systems led

Refinements are required as one's use of one's key talents narrows to specialization.

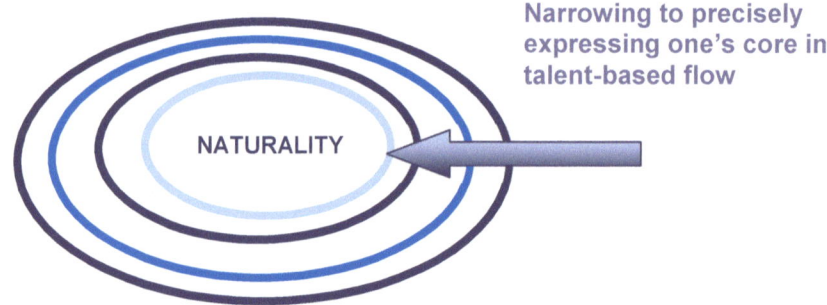

Narrowing to precisely expressing one's core in talent-based flow

Refinements will also be necessary as the flow-to-flow changes direction and/or brings different co-evolving systems into your context.

18-1L   Formula 1   © 2006 Lauren Holmes

Determining your Formula 1   164

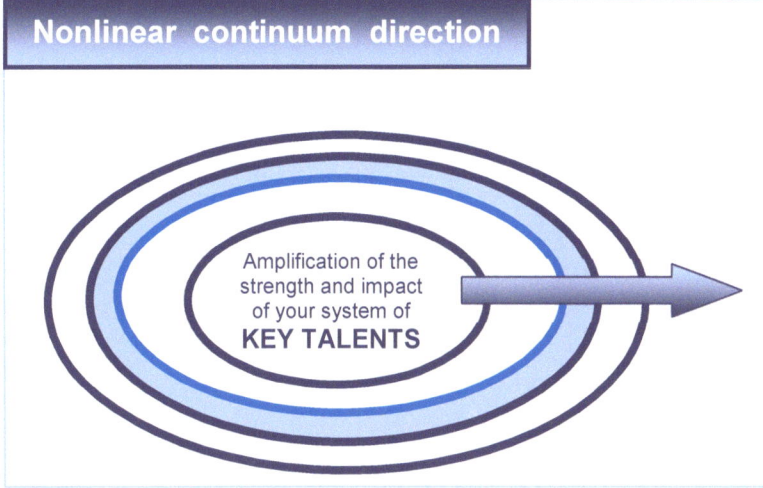

Nonlinear continuum direction

Amplification, Intensification, Expansion of your system's innate core. Core expansions in the Leadering™ paradigm are achieved by quantum leap - a method for core replacement.

As your key talents expand as a result of operating in talent-based flow state and the flow-to-flow, your impact on reality increases. The magnitude of change you cause in reality increases. Your creative impact increases.

18-1M   © 2006 Lauren Holmes

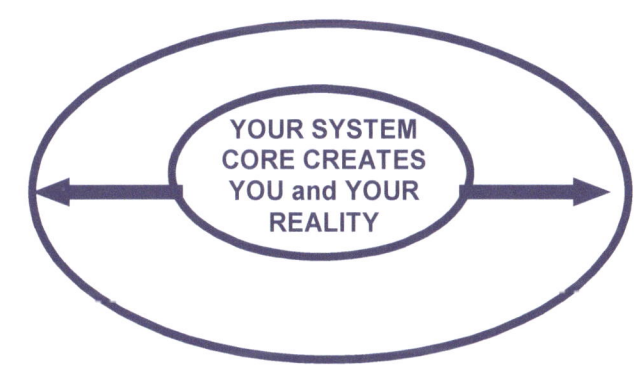

Nonlinear reality advancement

You and your reality are a single system in the Leadering™ paradigm. Realities are self-created by your system core.

Change your core to change your reality: the situations and events you will experience.

Formulas 1 and 2 not only advance your core but your reality or your experience by reflection.

18-1N   © 2006 Lauren Holmes

THE LEADERING™ QUANTUM LEAP PROCESS

Design it!   Feel it!   Be it!

PRE-LEAP
1. Choose the right quantum leap or post-leap state
6. Define the post-leap state with clarity
3. Define the post-leap state without previous limitations or toxicity
4. Emotionally template the post-leap state
5. Add the information to fuel emergence
6. Expect the unexpected post-leap

LEAP
1. Release the linear connection to the past
2. Feel yourself 100% fluid
3. Feel the post-leap state
4. Feel who the "post-leap you" will be
5. Commit to the quantum leap
6. Make an abrupt, no-return, reincarnation
7. Trigger spontaneous self-organization by intent

POST-LEAP
1. Operate as if the quantum leap was successful
2. Walk around as the person with the post-leap reality
3. Hold this new identity until reality restructures
4. Ignore evidence of events created by the old template
5. Trigger cascading quantum leaps by intent
6. Establish quantum leaping as a way of life
7. Consolidate your new quantum leap expert beliefs

18-1P   Formula 1   © 1998 Lauren Holmes

Categories of Quantum Leaps to apply to each Formula

CORE UPGRADE QUANTUM LEAPS
- quantum leaps to new functionality such as increased cognitive skills, leader meta-competencies, and an increasingly supportive belief template.

CORE EXPANSION QUANTUM LEAPS
Internal and external drives pressure your system to expand around its core system of key talents and drives. The best way to comply with these pressures to expand is to routinely quantum leap as a modus operandi for the rest of your life. These quantum leaps are facilitated by natural forces. These expansions include:
- quantum leaps to the next wider iteration of power and impact of your system.
- a series of quantum leaps which break through frontier after frontier with respect to improving your prowess and skill for applying your key talents to advance reality. Expansion quantum leaps advance the art and science behind your F1-F2 development of your key talents.
- 10-year maximum quantum leaps: a quantum leap to a category of expansion or capability as if you have been operating at that level of intensification and impact of your system for the last 10 years. This speeds the advancement of your capabilities.

REALIGNMENT QUANTUM LEAPS
- quantum leaps to re-boot your system onto its natural core in compliance with natural forces continuously pressuring this re-centering.
- quantum leaps to merge your system into the-flow-to-flow or to the flow of other dynamics and built-in growth continuums within the Leading™ paradigm.

18-1Q   Formula 1

NOTES FOR ALL 5 LEADERING™ OPERATING FORMULAS

1. **Leaders:** For those taking Leadering™ with the intention of becoming visible leaders in positions of authority and commanding others, you should attempt to include in formulas 3, 4, and 5, a specific theme for your leadership which is based on the expansion of your key talents over your lifetime as prescribed by formula 1.

2. **Non-Leaders:** For those who do not plan to become visible leaders with followers reporting, please use this exercise to identify a strategy for developing your systems advancement capabilities as you develop around your key talents in the Leadering paradigm.

3. **For those pursuing Entrepreneuring, Innovation, Recareering™ and Peak Performance:** For those taking Leadering™ for recareering™, for peak performance, and for maximum lifetime achievement, you should translate all 5 formulas in terms of your career and being paid for continuously scaling new frontiers of application of your talents. The pursuit of p*aid peak evolution* should be the determinant for your career choices. You want to be paid for pursuing your lifetime maximum.

4. **The 5 formulas are logically interlinked:**
All 5 formulas should be logically integrated into a single cohesive whole based on the advancement of your core.
Each formula is based on the intensification of your key talents.
Each formula is about how those key talents will advance reality.
Each formula must agree with the evidence you uncovered in the patterns of historical events in the talent-based life themes exercise. The themes indicate where the flow-to-flow internally and externally has been pressuring the expansion of your key talents.
Formula 1 has already been operating throughout your life. Your 5 formulas enable you to proactively support its strategy.
Formulas 3 to 5 should agree with your findings in the systems-based key talents exercise.

5. **Quantum leaps** should be used to lock new information uncovered by the process into your system as permanent template changes rather than simply new information being applied to old machinery.

6. Assume you have all of **the resources and freedom** required to maximize your system over your lifetime.

FORMULA 2

To maximize, one must operate the way one's system is meant to. Leadering™ capitalizes on one's natural drives and mechanisms to pull one into the Leadering paradigm and maximization. Leadering™ intensifies and extends the natural

7 PERSONALIZING THE LEADERING™ PARADIGM

I FLOW MAXIMIZATION EXERCISES continued

Determining your 5 Formulas:

Exercises, notes, and questions are provided to assist you in determining each of your 5 formulas for maximizing yourself, other human systems, and the Leadering™ paradigm for goal achievement. The repetition of some figures is to enable you to have everything in one place for determining each formula. It is only necessary to derive your best hypothesis to test out for confirmation of each personal formula. Use as much or as little of this support material as is necessary for you to achieve this goal. Everyone's needs are different.

Formula 1: 14 figures   Formula 3: 17 figures   Formula 5: 13 figures
Formula 2:   8 figures   Formula 4: 18 figures

Leadering™ talent-based operating formulas exercises
as a means to capitalize on the flow-to-flow to maximize yourself and your life

Formula 2: Your greatest level of talent-based operation
Maximized individual formula

DESCRIPTION

Destination

Formula 2 defines your highest level of creative impact or reality creation that you can achieve.

Formula 2 is your greatest lifetime level of talent-based operation attainable for advancing reality based on
- the culmination of living your formula 1 lifetime development formula
- Leadering's key talent determination exercises
- Leadering's life themes exercises suggesting the direction of your future growth
- the built-in growth continuums of the Leadering™ paradigm
- the amplification of your key talents over time.
- operating in talent based flow state for peak performance and peak advancement: the most likely foundation for your greatest lifetime performance.
- what your maximum way of operating would be if your life was dedicated to an accelerating expansion of your key talents with your income paying you to dedicate yourself to that advancement.

Formula 1 and 2 define your lifetime development continuum.

Formulas 3, 4, and 5 define a subset continuum of this F1-F2 continuum.

Formula 2 is logically linked with formula 5:
- formula 2 is your greatest operating destination as an individual.
- formula 5 is your greatest operating destination or state of being as a leader or as an expert who in advances other human systems as the means advance your own to achieve your formula 2 maximum.

The progression of the continuum defined by formulas 1 and 2 is not linear but the amplification of the core of each human system by quantum leaps.

18-2A   Formula 2   © 2006 Lauren Holmes

Evolution

FORMULAS 1 and 2: Advancing your personal system

Formula 1 lifetime key talent development continuum

Move up and down the continuum to let the big picture inform your current implementation tactics and, vice versa, use your current findings to inform the big picture.

Formula 2 is the culmination of the Formula 1 development continuum.

Formula 2 defines the ultimate level of talent-based performance at which you can operate as a result of implementing the Formula 1 lifetime key talent development strategy for capitalizing on innate drives and natural forces internally and externally.

18-2B   Formula 2   © 2006 Lauren Holmes

Evolution + Co-Evolution

All 5 FORMULAS: Advancing your personal system by creating, advancing, and maximizing other human systems

Flow to Flow - Flow to Congruence - Flow to fusion

Formula 1

Formulas 3,4,5: Strategies for advancing your own system by creating and advancing other systems

Formula 3   Formula 4   Formula 5

Formula 2

Formulas 1 to 2 lifetime key talent development continuum

Projected direction of your historical talent-based life themes

18-2C   Formula 2   © 2006 Lauren Holmes

Formula 2: Your greatest level of talent-based operation
Maximized individual formula

INSTRUCTIONS

Destination

Assume your functionality and potential will increase

You have likely not yet achieved the level of functionality that is your full potential. We therefore do not want to limit your greatest creations and performance to what you are capable of right now. Rather, project out years of perpetual advancement in talent-based flow state and years of creations in which you have been operating at your maximum in a particular field or discipline which maximizes your system of key talents or your art. This is the ultimate goal state that you want to envision to define formula 2.

Analyze the following data and situations to determine your Formula 2

- the culmination of living your formula 1 lifetime development formula
- Leadering's key talent determination exercises
- Leadering's life themes exercises suggesting the direction of your future growth
- the built-in growth continuums of the Leadering™ paradigm
- the amplification of your key talents over time.
- operating in talent based flow state for peak performance and peak advancement: the most likely foundation for your greatest lifetime performance.
- what your maximum way of operating would be if your life was dedicated to an accelerating expansion of your key talents with your income paying you to dedicate yourself to that advancement.
- nature's perspective on the maximum potential of your ability to impact reality with your key talents as a state of being

IDEAL OUTCOME:

A working hypothesis concisely written for the peer advisory database that can be tested by trying to live it and looking for the tell-tale signs that you have moved into the flow-to-flow as a result.

18-2D   Formula 2   © 2006 Lauren Holmes

FORMULAS 1 and 2: Advancing your personal system

Identified by Core Determination Exercises:
- Life themes exercises
- Key talent determination exercises

FORMULAS 3, 4, and 5: Advancing your personal system by creating, advancing, and maximizing other system:

- Determined by the lifetime development continuum defined by formulas 1 and 2
- Core Determination Exercises: systems-based key-talent application exercise

Formula 2: Your greatest level of talent-based operation
Maximized individual formula

QUESTIONS

Destination

QUESTIONS to help you determine the maximum level of talent-based performance at which you could be operating within your lifetime based on the advancement of your key talents as prescribed in the Leading™ paradigm:

1. What is your greatest possible talent-based operation as an individual

2. If you pursue the continuous expansion of your key talents over a lifetime and at top speeds, what is the highest level of creative impact or reality creation that you would likely attain?

3. What is the highest possible culmination of living your formula 1 lifetime key-talent development strategy? What is your maximum lifetime attainment based on a on an accelerating intensification of your key talents over your life? What would be your greatest possible legacy or creation in reality or change to reality?

4. If you lived the strategy that you determined for formula 1 and had pursued the continuous and rapid expansion of your key talents over your lifetime, what is the highest level of creative impact or reality creation that you would achieve? Generically,
   - what would you be creating or
   - how would you be advancing reality or
   - what would be the goal state of capability or functionality you would achieve rather than what is a particular goal you might wish to achieve?
   - What level of performance of using your system of key talents would you like to be operating at before you die?

5. What does the science behind the use of your key talents look like after operating for 10 years at your formula 2 maximum?

6. What state of operation would you achieve if you turned yourself over to the ever-increasing addictive drives drawing you to use and improve your key talents.

18-2F   Formula 2   © 2006 Lauren Holmes

Formula 2: Your greatest level of talent-based operation
Maximized individual formula
QUANTUM LEAP SUGGESTIONS

Destination

CORE UPGRADE QUANTUM LEAPS
1. Quantum leap to a state of paid peak evolution in which your job pays you to continuously advance your key talents to attain your formula 2 lifetime maximum.

CORE EXPANSION QUANTUM LEAPS
2. Quantum leap to your greatest lifetime level of talent-based operation:

   - quantum leap to a state of peak advancement to achieve the lifetime maximum of the impact, capabilities, and functionality of your key talents.

   - quantum leap to being a person who has successfully operated for over 10 years at the level of your maximum ability to advance reality based on the application of your key talents, and your knowledge-pursuit, creativity-pursuit, meaning-pursuit, and frontiering-pursuit themes.

   - quantum leap to being a person who has operated 10 years at the highest levels of your talent-based creative expression or the highest creative expression of your talents or your maximum level of impacting and creating reality

REALIGNMENT QUANTUM LEAPS
3. Quantum leap to alignment with your F1-F2 continuum as a way of life to achieve your greatest level of talent-based operation and greatest impact on reality.

4. Quantum leap to a life aligned with your talent-based knowledge-pursuit theme so that you're the expansion path of your key talents is the foundational dynamic for your daily and lifetime operation.

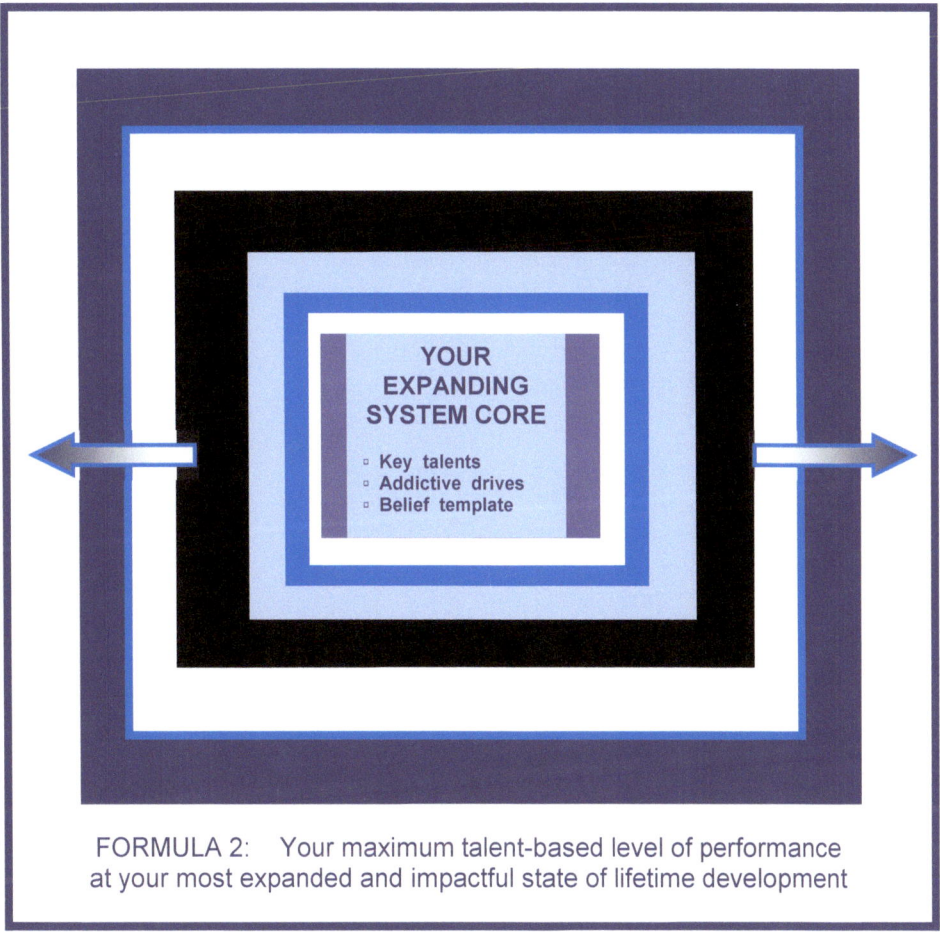

FORMULA 2: Your maximum talent-based level of performance at your most expanded and impactful state of lifetime development

1. At this level of expansion of your core and your key talents in particular, what kind of work are you doing?
2. How are you changing reality?
3. What new functionality are you applying?
4. How are you capitalizing on natural forces to change reality with your key talents?
5. What is your ideal identity at this greatest level of performance?

18-2H   Formula 2   © 2006 Lauren Holmes

THE LEADERING™ QUANTUM LEAP PROCESS

Design it!   Feel it!   Be it!

PRE-LEAP
1. Choose the right quantum leap or post-leap state
2. Define the post-leap state with clarity
3. Define the post-leap state without previous limitations or toxicity
4. Emotionally template the post-leap state
5. Add the information to fuel emergence
6. Expect the unexpected post-leap

LEAP
1. Release the linear connection to the past
2. Feel yourself 100% fluid
3. Feel the post-leap state
4. Feel who the "post-leap you" will be
5. Commit to the quantum leap
6. Make an abrupt, no-return, reincarnation
7. Trigger spontaneous self-organization by intent

POST-LEAP
1. Operate as if the quantum leap was successful
2. Walk around as the person with the post-leap reality
3. Hold this new identity until reality restructures
4. Ignore evidence of events created by the old template
5. Trigger cascading quantum leaps by intent
6. Establish quantum leaping as a way of life
7. Consolidate your new quantum leap expert beliefs

Formula 2   © 1998 Lauren Holmes

FORMULA 3

Leadering™ is not a course. It is an experiential process designed to incite a paradigm shift into a paradigm that is continuously advancing. As a result, individuals will not only continually advance but stay in sync with progress. Leadering™ can therefore accomplish so much more than a course.

7 PERSONALIZING THE LEADERING™ PARADIGM

I FLOW MAXIMIZATION EXERCISES continued

Determining your 5 Formulas:

Exercises, notes, and questions are provided to assist you in determining each of your 5 formulas for maximizing yourself, other human systems, and the Leadering™ paradigm for goal achievement. The repetition of some figures is to enable you to have everything in one place for determining each formula. It is only necessary to derive your best hypothesis to test out for confirmation of each personal formula. Use as much or as little of this support material as is necessary for you to achieve this goal. Everyone's needs are different.

Formula 1: 14 figures   **Formula 3: 17 figures**   Formula 5: 13 figures
Formula 2: 8 figures   Formula 4: 18 figures

Formula 3: Your talent-based leadership formula
DESCRIPTION - 1
Development.

Formula 3 is a system co-evolution strategy

Formula 3 is a co-evolution strategy which includes both co-evolving other systems with each other and other systems with your own system to achieve goals.

Formula 3 is a strategy for co-evolutionary leadership or system advancement base on using and improving your system of key talents and strengths.

Formula 3 is a strategy for maximizing your own system through advancing other human systems both singly and in synergy to achieve your goals.

Maximizing your system requires maximizing the performance and impact of your system of key talents and associated drives on reality. In other words, Formula 3 is about using your best skills for your greatest level of meaningful reality creation by harnessing and capitalizing on other human systems.

A goal of the Leadering™ program is to ensure that once you learn how to advance your own system using Leadering's systems maximization toolkit, you will then be able to apply that toolkit to advance any human system to achieve more profound goals more quickly and effectively.

Formula 3 capitalizes on Leadering's built-in growth continuums

Formula 3 is about accelerating yourself through the endless expansions of the lifetime development continuum defined by Formulas 1 and 2, by amplifying the impact of your key talents on reality through applying them to human systems of increasing size and complexity. Formula 3 is a subset of Formula 1's strategy for maximizing the best strengths of your system over your lifetime.

Formulas 1 and 2 are about advancing your system. Formulas 3, 4, and 5 are about advancing other systems as a strategy for maximizing your system.

All 5 formulas capitalize on the growth forces built into the Leadering™ paradigm which have been identified in a recording detailing that built-in growth. You will want to have a strategy for not only complying with these forces but capitalizing on them for increasing the impact of your key talents on reality. This is your Formula 3 talent-based leadership strategy.

Formula 3: Your talent-based leadership formula
DESCRIPTION - 2

Development

Formula 3 is a strategy for operating the Leadering™ machinery

Formula 3 is your strategy for operating the Leadering™ machinery using its systems maximization toolkit in a way that has been personalized to your key talents.

The Leadering™ machinery is the integrated flow-to-flow of human systems in the paradigm. It is advanced by your use of the Leadering™ systems maximization toolkit which has been customized to the key talents at the core of your system.

Formulas 3, 4, and 5 are strategies for this personalization of the Leadering™ toolkit and machinery.

You must be centered on your core system of key talents to drive the machinery of the Leadering™ paradigm: that is the engine that drives the machinery. All of nature's systems maximization forces are focused on driving that engine.

Formula 3 is a way to personalize your Leadering™ systems maximization toolkit and the Leadering™ paradigm

Formula 3 is about copying, complying with, and capitalizing on nature's systems maximization process which we have used as a metaphor for the Leadering™ paradigm.

Leaders do what nature does in orchestrating the synergistic advancement of systems using the 15 dynamics. This is the ideal natural systems maximization process that is at the foundation of leadership in the Leadering™ paradigm. Leadering's leadership development then adds skills on how to do that on top of this layer of meta-competencies.

Everything in the Leadering™ paradigm is a system. Therefore, to operate in the paradigm you need to create and advance systems using Leadering's 15 dynamics or drives inherent in human systems. But to do that, the Leadering™ systems maximization toolkit must be customized or personalized to your art or system of key talents: your system core. Therefore you need to determine your personal Leadering™ operating formulas to customize the paradigm and the systems maximization toolkit to your system.

In the Leadering™ paradigm than, not just leaders will use the single systems maximization toolkit for creating and advancing systems, but everyone will use it - the same toolkit, customized to the system of key talents at the core of each person's own system.

Formula 3 personalizes the Leadering™ paradigm and the Leadering™ systems maximization toolkit to your natural growth path defined in formulas 1 and 2.

How each person operates in the paradigm is determined by their natural core and is based on their key talents. This is because all of the dynamics in the paradigm are acting on that core. To harness them, one must be operating consistent with those dynamics.

Formula 3: Your talent-based leadership formula
DESCRIPTION - 3
Development.

Formula 3 is a subset of Formula 1

Formula 3 is a subset of the formula1-to-formula2 lifetime key talent development continuum based on the amplification of your core. This especially includes advancement of the impact and performance of your key talents.

All 5 formulas are refinements of a single lifetime maximization of your system and all of the systems you choose to lead. The additional formulas break out the first one to allow you to see the dimensions of the overarching strategy and to put it into more practical terms whereby progress is achievable and measurable.

Formula 3 is your personal strategy for developing your key talents by applying them to the creation and advancement of other human systems. It represents one category or one subset or one dimension of development within the lifetime development strategy you have already defined with formulas 1 and 2.

Systems Advancement Work defined by Formula 3

Examples of systems advancement work that your Formula 3 strategy will help you to accomplish will include:
- using the 15 dynamics and drives in the Leadering™ systems maximization toolkit.
- evolving individual systems or co-evolving them in groups, or
- adapting systems to each other,
- quantum leaping them alone or in groups and capitalizing on natural quantum leaps and the synergy between/among systems in the flow.
- putting them into their peak performing and peak advancing flow state and
- then integrating them together into the flow state of the contextual system of which they are a part.
- merging systems into the flow-to-flow
- advancing them through creativity, creation, and frontiering into new territory and new levels of performance
- orchestrating them to the new information that they need to advance their own art or level of application of their core talents.
- re-booting systems to be centred on their innate core for maximum performance and achievement
- leading more systems, creating new systems, both single systems and new systems from grouping existing systems
- impacting more complex systems with more far-reaching results: more reality changing or world changing outcomes
- causing greater impact on reality to change reality more

18-3C   Formula 3   © 2006 Lauren Holmes

Formula 3: Your talent-based leadership formula
DESCRIPTION - 4
Development

NOTE: Customize your terminology for Formulas 3, 4, and 5

The leader meta-competencies cultivated by the Leadering™ paradigm will enhance performance on many fronts beyond leadership such as entrepreneurship, innovation and career achievement.   The Leadering™ meta-competencies are not restricted to leadership. Choose terminology that works for you with respect to maximizing and advancing systems:

ALTERNATE NAMES FOR YOUR FORMULA 3

leadership formula	systems facilitator formula
facilitative leadership formula	systems leadership formula
systems maximization formula	systems advancement formula
systems orchestration formula	systems co-evolution formula
system synergy formula	systems advancer formula
talent-based system advancement formula	your Leadering™ formula

18-3D   Formula 3

© 2006 Lauren Holmes

Formula 3: Your talent-based leadership formula
INSTRUCTIONS - 1

Development

IDEAL OUTCOME of the Formula 3 exercise:

The ideal outcome is a working hypothesis that can be tested by trying to live it and looking for the tell-tale signs that you have moved into the flow-to-flow as a result.

Formula 3 defines your formula for advancing your key talents while using them to advance other human systems based on their own core talents.

The cumulative outcome of the 5 formulas is a fully integrated customized foundation for greatness as a leader / individual upon which classic leader competencies can be embedded.

The 5 formulas can be written individually or as a single cohesive strategy for the peer advisory database. Leadering™ peers and co-workers should be able to quickly grasp the core of your system now and where it will advance over your lifetime so as to be able interpret how the flow-to-flow is acting on your core at any time for you or them to capitalize on the situations at hand.

18-3E   Formula 3   © 2006 Lauren Holmes

FORMULAS 1 and 2:   Advancing your personal system

Identified by Core Determination Exercises:
- Life themes exercises
- Key talent determination exercises

FORMULAS 3, 4, and 5:   Advancing your personal system by creating, advancing, and maximizing other system:

- Determined by the lifetime development continuum defined by formulas 1 and 2
- Core Determination Exercises: systems-based key-talent application exercise

Formula 3: Your talent-based leadership formula
INSTRUCTIONS - 2

Development

RULES FOR FORMULA 3

Your talent-based leadership formula must:

- provide a strategy for developing your key talents by applying them to the creation and advancement of other human systems.

- incorporate how you will be changing reality using your key talents. Creating or changing reality in increasingly more impactful ways is the means to both consolidate and prove your new learning and advancement.

- provide a talent-based leadership strategy personalized to your system core

- provide a systems-based leadership strategy personalized to your system core

- extrapolate your leadership and leadership development formula from your formula 1 lifetime key-talent development formula. What is the best interpretation of leadership for you based on your lifetime key-talent development formula or continuum?

- provide a strategy for accelerating yourself along the lifetime key-talent development continuum defined by formula 1 and 2, by amplifying the impact of your key talents on reality through their application to advancing systems of increasing size and complexity.

- agree with the evidence you uncovered from the historical event patterns in your past that you examined in the life themes exercise.

- agree with your determinations in the system-based key talent exercise

- agree with your key talent determination exercises

- assume you are nature. How would nature neutrally solve the challenges of integrating and maximizing the human systems at hand as the means to develop your own system's key talents? Be as objective as nature is in neutrally maximizing your system vis-à-vis the current flow-to-flow. Forget your past toxicity, failures, or limitations which are now irrelevant.

Formula 3: Your talent-based leadership formula
INSTRUCTIONS - 3

Development

Use previously identified information

Formula 3 is determined by projecting into the future the below bodies of information previously identified in the Leadering™ process about the advancement of your key talents:

Input from the core determination exercises:

1. **Life themes exercise**: All 5 formulas must be consistent with the evidence you uncovered in your life themes exercise: the talent-based themes discovered from the historical patterns of events in the life themes exercise which have been used to determine formulas 1 and 2. The key themes relevant to your talent-based leadership formula are your knowledge-pursuit, creativity-pursuit, frontiering-pursuit, and meaning-pursuit themes.

2. **Systems-based key talent application exercise**:
   The key talents system application exercise gives you a glimpse into the ideal systems to which your key talents can be ideally applied. This then identifies your ideal context for maximizing your leadership.
   - What kind of systems are your key talents ideally suited to advance now and as they develop? (recording 14, figures 17-11, 16-4A and 16-4B)
   - What are the most complex systems you will be impacting at the height of your leadership strength?

3. **Key talent determination exercises:**
   - Given what you know about the key talents at your system core from the core determination exercises, what would be your natural leadership theme, strategy, or formula based on the natural bias to use and improve those key talents?
   - What do you now know about your ideal formula for leadership or the advancement of human systems?

4. **Leadering™ paradigm built-in growth continuums:** the talent-based growth pressures built into the Leadering™ paradigm identified in the audio dedicated to that subject matter.

5. **Leadering™ paradigm systems maximization toolkit:** the 15 dynamics copied from the metaphor of nature's systems maximization process.

18-3G   Formula 3   © 2006 Lauren Holmes

Formula 3: Your talent-based leadership formula
QUESTIONS - 1

Development

Your Formula1-to-Formula2 lifetime key-talent development continuum

1. What is your best leadership strategy that is:
   - consistent with your formulas 1 and 2 continuum.
   - a logical extension of and a subset of your lifetime key-talent development continuum.
   - consistent with the projected advancement and amplification of your key talents.
   - consistent with the built-in growth directions of the Leadering™ paradigm.
   - consistent with the addictive talent-based drives pulling you to your greatest performance based on your key talents.

2. Given what you know about the Leadering™ process advancing your own system, how would you advance other human systems through using and improving your key talents? How do you merge your advancement with your orchestration of the advancement of other human systems?

3. Where are you on the leadership development continuum? (figure 18-12)

4. If you were a creational leader, a frontiering leader, and a talent-based leader, what would be your ideal leadership strategy? (figure 18-12) Your key talents are the only foundation for your greatest performance as an individual or a leader.
   How will your key talents define your leadership?
   How will you interpret your leadership to capitalize on your key talents?
   If you complied with the addictive drives pulling you to the continuous expansion of your key talents, what would be the territory and form of your leadership?
   How will you capitalize on human systems to achieve your growth and creation goals

5. What kind of leadership and/or system maximizer roles will progress you along your lifetime key-talent development continuum (F1-F2)?

Talent-based leadership:
Advancing your key talents as the foundation for your leadership strength.

6. What is your personalized formula or strategy for your talent-based leadership?

7. What would your leadership formula be if it was 100% based on the continuous advancement and amplification of your key talents to your greatest performance as an individual and a leader? In other words, what would be your leadership formula if you were true to the innate nature and growth path of your system?

8. What will your leadership formula be if your underlying dynamic of your system and your life is the continuous advancement and amplification of your key talents?

Formula 3: Your talent-based leadership formula
QUESTIONS - 2

Development

QUESTIONS continued

Orchestrating the Co-Evolution of your system and other human systems

9. Given the Leadering™ systems maximization process and toolkit, how will you orchestrate your co-evolution and the co-evolution of the human systems you wish to advance or capitalize on to achieve your goals?

10. How will you progress from being able to advance only your personal system to orchestrating many human systems to cause dramatic change in reality?

11. What do you know about the human systems you will be creating, advancing, linking into new systems, co-evolving, co-adapting, and combining in opportunistic synergy?

12. How would you capitalize other human systems as fodder for advancing the creative expression of your system and the reality you create?

Systems-based leadership:
Using the Leadering™ systems maximization toolkit and operating the Leadering™ machinery to advance systems

13. What is your personalized formula or strategy for your systems-based leadership in the Leadering™ paradigm?

14. In the Leadering™ paradigm not just leaders but everyone will use Leadering's single systems maximization toolkit for creating, advancing, and capitalizing on human systems. The toolkit will be the same but its very nature will require it to be customized to the system of key talents at the core of each person's own system.
How will you marry your key talents and the 15 dynamics to operate the Leadering™ machinery to achieve your goals or those of other human systems you wish to advance?

15. What does your Leadership formula look like if you can easily command Leadering's systems maximization toolkit?
Think in terms of :
    - using the 15 dynamics and drives in the Leadering™ systems maximization toolkit
    - evolving systems
    - adapting systems to each other
    - co-evolving systems
    - quantum leaping systems alone or in groups
    - putting systems into their peak performing and peak advancing flow state and
    - integrating systems together into the flow state of the contextual system of which they are a part
    - advancing human systems through creativity, creation, and frontiering into new territory and new levels of performance
    - orchestrating human systems to the new information that they need to advance their own art or the level of impact of their core talents.

18-3J   Formula 3   © 2006 Lauren Holmes

Formula 3: Your talent-based leadership formula
QUANTUM LEAP SUGGESTIONS

Development

CORE UPGRADE QUANTUM LEAPS

1. Quantum leap to the identity of leader and/or human system maximizer.

2. Quantum leap to a leader who has been operating successfully with your natural leadership formula for the last 10 years using the systems maximization toolkit and all of the advanced functionality and modus operandi of the Leadering™ paradigm.

3. Quantum leap from externally referenced and created by one's reality to internally referenced and creating one's reality.

CORE EXPANSION QUANTUM LEAPS

4. Quantum leap to a leader with expanding consciousness and expanding capabilities to catalyze the co-evolution of human systems in the flow-to-flow in greater numbers, and with increasing complexity, meaning and impact.

REALIGNMENT QUANTUM LEAPS

5. Quantum leap to align with the projection into the future of the historical life themes you have identified from your past. These are associated with the use and improvement of your key talents within the flow-to-flow. This quantum leap then is a practical means to merge you with the flow-to-flow and to sustain that integration to keep yourself firmly in the driver's seat of the Leadering™ machinery.

   - Quantum leap to integration within the flow of all human systems so that you capitalize on opportunities for co-evolution, adaptation, and synergy. Assume you can operate as successfully as nature with respect to capitalizing on the dance of creativity among all human systems as they pursue maximization.

   - Quantum leap to a smart partner with all human systems relevant to your goals in your path in the flow-to-flow.

6. Quantum leap to align with your F1-F2 development continuum which is on the flow-to-flow so as to routinely capitalize on all of the human systems relevant to your goals that you would expect to find there.

7. Quantum leap to a system maximizer who routinely re-centers all relevant human systems to their natural core including your own. Not only do you re-centre your system other human systems to their core for maximum contribution to your goals and theirs, but you actually *become* the core or the DNA of human systems to more effectively achieve goal realities which reflect those cores. (More about this in the core maximization exercises.)

SYSTEMS-BASED LEADERSHIP

Which System Types do your key talents advance?

SYSTEM TYPES

- **individual system**
- **multi-individual system**
- **organizational system**
- **multi-organizational system**
- **knowledge system**
- **process system**

- you, a person, a follower, your child
- individuals *en masse*: a consumer market, a university
- a group of people: an organization or company
- a business web or community
- a science, a field, a discipline
- leadership development, business process, reengineering

18-3L   Formula 3   © 2006 Lauren Holmes

SYSTEM MAINTENANCE Single/Multi-System	SYSTEM ADVANCEMENT Single/Multi-System	SYSTEM CREATION Single/Multi-System	SYSTEM RELATIONSHIPS Multi-System
Manager: very little new creation is required	Change Leadership • Transitional • Transformational • Facilitative Frontier Leadership Flow Leadership	Creational Leadership Quantum Leap Leadership Template Leadership Emergence Leadership	System Relationships: • Co-Evolutionary Leader • Co-Adaptation Leader • Synergy

Increasing belief and information changes - Increasing impact on reality

Leadership extends Nature's systems management in the Leadering™ paradigm:
A SINGLE SYSTEMS MAXIMIZATION TOOLKIT

18-3M   Formula 3   © 2006 Lauren Holmes

System-Based Key Talent Categories

SYSTEM MAINTENANCE Single / Multi-System	SYSTEM ADVANCEMENT Single / Multi-System	SYSTEM CREATION Single / Multi-System	SYSTEM RELATIONSHIPS Each relationship creates a new system
manager: very little new creation is required. *Creativity and creation increase with each column to the right.* *Since beliefs create reality, this means that the need for belief changes increase as your move to the right.*	strategy development people development organization development multi-organization synergy process development knowledge development technology development **change leadership** • transitional • transformational • facilitative **frontier leadership** **creational leadership** **flow leadership**	**creational leadership** **frontier leadership** **quantum leap leadership** **template leadership** **emergence leadership** system creation strategy system creation implementation entrepreneur company creation intrapreneur project creation new product creation new technology creation new infrastructure creation new process creation new science creation new knowledge creation new skill creation new frontier creation creation research merger-created system acquisition-created system innovation / creativity	System relationships: • to maintain systems • to advance systems • to create systems **co-evolutionary leadership** **co-adaptation leadership** collaboration and synergy business web development CRM: customer relationship management customer development customer chain development supplier chain development network development relationship building team building market development unifying and integrating problem solving conflict resolution peace keeping negotiation mergers and acquisitions relationship strategy/vision relationship-related implementation

Increasing belief and information changes   -   Increasing impact on reality

In the Leadering™ paradigm, leadership extends nature's systems management.
This exercise demonstrates LEADERING'S SINGLE SYSTEMS MAXIMIZATION TOOLKIT

18-3N   Formula 3   © 2006 Lauren Holmes

Determine your Formula 3

COMPETENCIES targeted by traditional leadership development programs	META-COMPETENCIES and DRIVES targeted by Leadering™ Shared by leaders, entrepreneurs, innovators, & high achievers
develop and deliver value command and control planning (strategic, tactical, vision) trend analysis financial management marketing/sales management customer relationship mgt - CRM IT management operations management project management performance management knowledge management organization learning risk management decision-making problem resolution process management business process reengineering change management HR management team building relationship building / maintenance conflict resolution globalization	**Systems-Based and Core-Based Operation** systems thinking, relational thinking, big-picture thinking, conceptual skills, belief system management, model development and application, system co-evolution and adaptation, leadership (advancing human systems in opportunistic synergy)

Leadering's meta-competencies enable better assimilation and application of traditional competency development programs

Traditionally, leaders are developed bottom up skill by skill
Leadering™ uses a single paradigm shift to an integrated system of meta-competencies, drives, reflexes, and beliefs.

Traditionally, senior leaders use different meta-competencies.
Leadering™ offers a single systems maximization toolkit for use universally thus unifying organizations around a single culture and modus operandi. Leadership is distributed.

Accelerating and Continuous Development
- conditioned reflexes are installed to trigger multi-front life-long advancement and leadership development.
- Addictive drives are heightened so one is pulled to growth.
- learning to learn, mental agility, adaptivity, expanding self-expression and self-awareness, belief engineering, expanding consciousness

Improved and Improving Cognitive Capabilities
- thinking: conceptual, inductive, deductive, abstract, relational, big-picture,
- learning to learn, mental agility, pattern recognition, internally referenced, emotional intelligence, use of models, theories, and inferences

Expertise with Ambiguity and the Unknown
- **pioneering**: penetrating the unknown
- **creativity/innovation**: bringing unknown into being
systems thinking, informationless decision-making, abstract thinking, conceptual skills, pattern recognition, trend perception, change detection, environmental scanning, problem reframing, ambiguity resolution

Improved Performance
flow (our peak performance state), enhanced functionality, systems-based operation, accelerated implementation through quantum leap change management

Addictive Drives cultivated and capitalized upon by Leadering™
(the more you use them,
the more you want to use them) :
- Drives to: learning, pioneering, creativity, innovation, meaning, positive emotions, adaptivity, creativity, learning knowledge, achievement, flow, (the optimal experience), self-expression, self-knowledge, advancement, unity, growth
- Drives to using and improving your key talents - a must for operating at your full potential

Notice how most leader competencies are system-based and designed to improve the flow of systems to congruence based on the 15 leader dynamics or paradigm dynamics of Leadering™

18-3P   Formula 3   © 2006 Lauren Holmes

FORMULAS 3, 4, and 5: Advancing your personal system by creating, advancing, and maximizing other systems:

Talent-based system leadership in the flow to flow

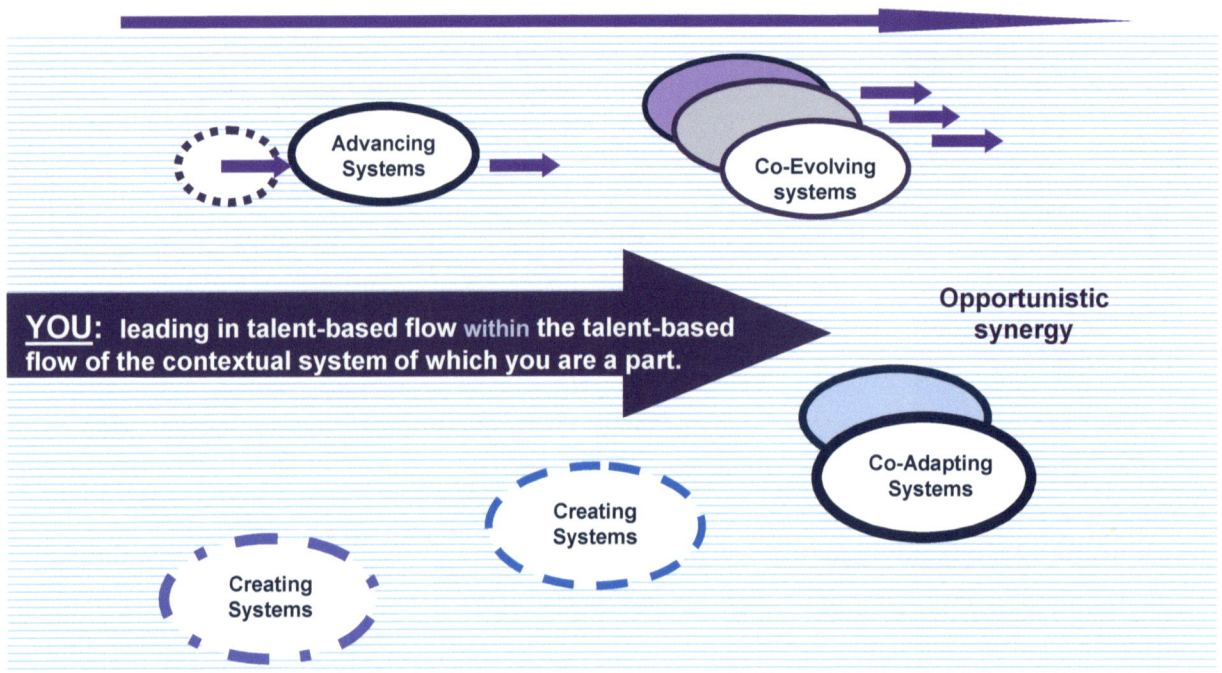

YOU: leading in talent-based flow *within* the talent-based flow of the contextual system of which you are a part.

Opportunistic synergy

Advancing your system by applying your key talents to other systems	Individual Systems	Multi-Individual Systems	Organization Systems	Multi-Organization Systems	Knowledge Systems	Process Systems

Leadering™ provides a single systems maximization toolkit for advancing your personal system or those that you choose to lead.

Formula 3

© 2006 Lauren Holmes

Leadering™ Leadership Development Directions

| | Transitional | Transformational | Creational Leader / |
Manager	Change Leader	Change Leader	Frontiering Leader
Run an existing business as is	**Linearly advance an existing business** • Incremental upgrades • Harvest	**Non-linearly advance an existing business** • Turnarounds • Explosive Growth • Merge 2 existing businesses	**Create the unknown or Penetrate the unknown** • Business startups • Pioneering / Frontiering • Re-engineering • New ventures • Innovation

LEADERING™ AMPLIFIES LEADER DRIVES

As leader drives strengthen, leader impact increases:
INCREASED DRIVES to change – creativity/creation – frontiering™
INCREASED BELIEF CHANGES MADE

| Systems maintenance | Increasing systems advancement | Systems Creation: including new systems from re-grouping existing systems |

Managers run existing systems ➡ Leaders create and advance human systems

As individuals advance along the leadership development continuum,
their ability to advance reality increases.
If there is no change in beliefs, there is no change in reality.
If there is no change on reality, leadership has not occurred.
The magnitude of change is the measure of leadership in the Leadering™ paradigm.

18-3R   Formula 3   © 1995 Lauren Holmes

THE LEADERING™ QUANTUM LEAP PROCESS

Design it!   Feel it!   Be it!

PRE-LEAP
1. Choose the right quantum leap or post-leap state
7. Define the post-leap state with clarity
3. Define the post-leap state without previous limitations or toxicity
4. Emotionally template the post-leap state
5. Add the information to fuel emergence
6. Expect the unexpected post-leap

LEAP
1. Release the linear connection to the past
2. Feel yourself 100% fluid
3. Feel the post-leap state
4. Feel who the "post-leap you" will be
5. Commit to the quantum leap
6. Make an abrupt, no-return, reincarnation
7. Trigger spontaneous self-organization by intent

POST-LEAP
1. Operate as if the quantum leap was successful
2. Walk around as the person with the post-leap reality
3. Hold this new identity until reality restructures
4. Ignore evidence of events created by the old template
5. Trigger cascading quantum leaps by intent
6. Establish quantum leaping as a way of life
7. Consolidate your new quantum leap expert beliefs

18-3S   Formula 3   © 1998 Lauren Holmes

Determine your Formula 3   196

Co-Evolution

FORMULAS 3, 4, and 5:   Advancing your personal system by creating, advancing, and maximizing other systems:

Leadering™ Leadership and Leadership Development

Continuum Start Point:
Formula 3:
talent-based leadership

Continuum End Point:
Formula 5: greatest level of talent-based leadership

Formulas 1 and 4 share a development continuum:
Formula 4 talent-based leader development continuum is a subset development stream of the Formula 1 lifetime key talent development continuum.

Lifetime development and leadership development define the same continuum in the Leadering™ paradigm:
the expansion of the innate core of your system while creating and expanding the foundational core of other systems.

18-3T   Formula 3   © 2006 Lauren Holmes

Evolution + Co-Evolution

All 5 FORMULAS: Advancing your personal system by creating, advancing, and maximizing other human systems

Flow to Flow - Flow to Congruence - Flow to fusion

Formula 1

Formulas 3,4,5:   Strategies for advancing your own system by creating and advancing other systems

Formula 3   Formula 4   Formula 5

Formula 2

Formulas 1 to 2 lifetime key talent development continuum

Projected direction of your historical talent-based life themes

18-3U   Formula 3   © 2006 Lauren Holmes

FORMULA 4

Leadering's quantum leap process only works within the Leadering™ paradigm where you drive a multi-system, multi-dynamic Leadering™ machinery personalized to how natural forces are acting on your personal system and the human systems you choose to advance or capitalize on to achieve your goals.

7 PERSONALIZING THE LEADERING™ PARADIGM

I FLOW MAXIMIZATION EXERCISES continued

Determining your 5 Formulas:

Exercises, notes, and questions are provided to assist you in determining each of your 5 formulas for maximizing yourself, other human systems, and the Leadering™ paradigm for goal achievement. The repetition of some figures is to enable you to have everything in one place for determining each formula. It is only necessary to derive your best hypothesis to test out for confirmation of each personal formula. Use as much or as little of this support material as is necessary for you to achieve this goal. Everyone's needs are different.

Formula 1: 14 figures	Formula 3: 17 figures	Formula 5: 13 figures
Formula 2: 8 figures	**Formula 4: 18 figures**	

Formula 4: Your talent-based leadership development formula
DESCRIPTION

Development

Your leadership development formula allows you a more specialized lens with which to examine and strategize your talent-based lifetime development. The continuous expansion of the intensity and impact of your key talents defines your development as both an individual and a leader. Therefore, leadership development and lifetime development form the same single continuum (F1-F2). The advancement of your key talents increases your strength, and impact as a leader.

Formulas 1 and 2 are strategies for advancing your personal system. Formulas 3, 4, and 5 support those two formulas. They address dimensions of the same continuum defined by Formulas 1 to 2.

Formulas 3, 4, and 5 provide additional strategies for advancing your personal system to achieve their prescribed growth and creation goals. They promote the use and improvement of your key talents by applying them to advance other human systems. Formulas 3, 4, and 5 advance your system by advancing other human systems. Your leadership development continuum is a subset of your lifetime development continuum which is systems-focused.

All 5 formulas are about advancing your system core in the ways of the growth built into the Leadering™ paradigm.

Your talent-based leadership development formula is a strategy for improving your ability to use your key talents and strengths to create and advance human systems to achieve your growth and creation goals. It is a strategy for growing and achieving beyond the current potential of your system by capitalizing on other human systems and natural forces. It is a strategy which will only work in the Leadering™ paradigm.

18-4A   Formula 4   © 2006 Lauren Holmes

Formula 4: Your talent-based leadership development formula
INSTRUCTIONS - 1

Determine your talent-based leadership development formula from an analysis of the results of your core determination exercises to this point, brainstorming with peers, and consulting individuals with systems thinking and conceptual skills who can see the bigger picture.

To derive your talent-based leadership development formula (formula 4) and your greatest performance goals as a leader by extension (formula 5):
overlay the paradigm-based leadership development process (formula 4) onto the lifetime development formula (formula 1) and the leadership formula (formula 3). All 5 formulas should be logically integrated since they are based on the advancement of the core of your system.

Add a systems-based dimension to the lifetime development process you have already envisioned for yourself in your formulas 1 and 2 work. Orchestrating human systems enhances growth, creation and leadership:

Growth: How will applying your key talents to the advancement of human systems break through new expanding frontiers of the capabilities of your key talents?

Creation: How much more impactful does each expanding frontier of the creative expression of your key talents and the core of you system become as you apply your key talents to advancing other human systems to achieve your goals to advance reality?

Leadership: For those wanting to become leaders, determine the ultimate capabilities and state of operating that you will achieve for formula 5 consistent with the F1-F2 continuum. Determine the development strategy that will get you to your formula 5 goal within the F1-F2 continuum. That is your Formula 4 talent-based leadership development strategy.

Outcome: A fully integrated customized foundation for greatness as a leader and an individual upon which classic leader competencies can be embedded.

The 5 formulas can be written individually or as a single cohesive strategy for the peer advisory database as long as peers and co-workers can quickly understand your core so as to interpret how the flow-to-flow is acting on it at any time for you or them to capitalize on any situation.

Formula 4: Your talent-based leadership development formula
QUESTIONS - 1

QUESTIONS to help you determine your ideal leadership development formula based on the advancement of your key talents as prescribed in the Leadering™ paradigm:

1. How would the previous 3 formulas define your personalized talent-based leadership development formula?

2. If you experienced all of the growth processes built into the Leadering™ paradigm, what would your talent-based leadership development process or continuum look like? (Review all included figures as a refresher)

3. If you mastered the use of the 15 dynamics and the single Leadering™ systems maximization toolkit, what would your leadership look like and how would it evolve over time in the Leadering™ paradigm?

4. What is the ideal leadership development strategy or strategy for developing your ability to capitalize on other human systems which will capitalize on all of the growth processes and internal and external dynamics and drives built into the Leadering™ paradigm personalized to your system?

5. In formula 1 you formulated how you might advance over your lifetime with respect to how you will impact reality with your key talents. In formula 2 you projected your highest operating capabilities if your talents advanced as prescribed in the Leadering™ paradigm and personalized according to your formula 1. How would your ability to impact and advance systems increase and change as your system of key talents and addictive drives advanced?

6. The continuous expansion of the intensity and impact of your key talents defines both your development as an individual and a leader. Therefore, leadership development (formula 4) and lifetime development (formula 1) form a single continuum. The advancement of your key talents increases your strength, impact, and creation ability as a leader. How would the advancement and use of your key talents as determined in the previous 3 formulas define your personalized talent-based leadership development formula?

7. Merge your life-time development formula based on the advancement of your key talents (formula 1) with your leadership formula (formula 3) based also on the application of those key talents to human systems to merge leadership development and lifetime development into a single continuum. How would you apply what you learned about your projected development in formula 1 to your ability to advance other systems as in formula 4 to achieve the reality advances you envisioned for your F1-F2 continuum?

Formula 4: Your talent-based leadership development formula
QUESTIONS - 2

8. If you are frontiering new territory every day around using your key talents as a result of merging with the flow-to-flow, how would those frontiers be progressing?

9. Look again at the talent-based life themes that you examined in order to develop formula 1. Merge this with what you have formulated for your leadership strategy in formula 3. How will the life themes project your capacity as a leader over time. How will your talent-based ability to advance systems evolve as you progress?

10. Look again at the systems-based key talents application exercise. How will the systems change that you are trying to advance as your historical life themes proceed into the future?

11. Who will you become if the skills associated with your system of key talents expand and intensify? How will you be able to impact human systems to advance reality?

12. How will your leadership or systems orchestration advance if you develop all of the leader competencies and drives in figure 18-3P.

13. Examine the leadership development continuum in figure 18-12 to determine to which business strategy you are currently most suited and how the strengthening of the key talents at your core will manifest as you progress to the right of the chart.

14. What do you know about the human systems you will be creating, advancing or linking into new systems? What are the most complex systems you will be impacting at the height of your leadership strength? Take each of the columns in figures 18-4H through 18-4M to figure out what kind of systems you will be advancing for formulas 3, 4 and 5 and how your key talents will develop as a result.

15. If your system was operating at its maximum every day in peak-performing and peak-advancing talent-based flow state, how will your system advance and how will the systems in reality advance as a result. Where would your capabilities be if your ability to advance reality reached a new maximum every day for 10 years?

16. If the stream of natural quantum leaps, facilitating dynamics and events, spontaneous knowledge and creativity, and plethora of coincidences inherent in the flow-to-flow were catapulting your system and its performance ahead, what is the natural development process that you are likely to undergo and how will your ability to impact reality increase?

17. What does your leadership look like based on the continuous development of your key talents as the underpinning dynamic?

Formula 4: Your talent-based leadership development formula
Quantum Leap Suggestions

CORE UPGRADE and EXPANSION QUANTUM LEAPS

1. Quantum leap to lock in everything you have learned from all 5 formulas to this point about your lifetime development as an individual and a leader. This includes using your abilities to advance systems for growth and improved goal achievement. Review all of the included figures to incorporate your highest understanding of your personal ultimate capabilities and then quantum leap to the identity of a person who has operated successfully with these capabilities for the last 5 years. All 5 formulas should be logically integrated.

2. Quantum leap to the creational leadership and frontiering leadership on the leadership development diagram in figure 18-4J.

3. Quantum leap to the maximum intensification or expansion of your key talents and associated addictive drives that you have envisioned to this point to operate at full power in talent-based leadership.

4. Quantum leap to an expert at maximizing human systems, both yours and those relevant to achieving your goals for advancing reality. Quantum leap to system-based leadership impacting the largest or most complex or most impactful systems you have envisioned applying your key strengths to. (figures 18-4H through 18-4Q)

5. Quantum leap to the greatest impact of your key talents

6. Quantum leap to merge your advancement formula around your key talents with your leadership formula based also on those key talents to merge leadership development and personal development into a single continuum. The advancement of your key talents results in an increase in your strength, impact and creativity as a leader.

REALIGNMENT QUANTUM LEAPS

1. Quantum leap to merge yourself into the single development continuum defined by your 5 personalized operating strategies. This continuum includes advancing other human systems as a tool for maximizing your growth and achievements.

2. Quantum leap to becoming an extension of nature's systems maximization process or even to becoming nature. Quantum leap to full expertise in maximizing all human systems using the 15 dynamics or leader drives that the Leadering™ paradigm machinery copies from nature. (figures 18-4R and 18-4H)

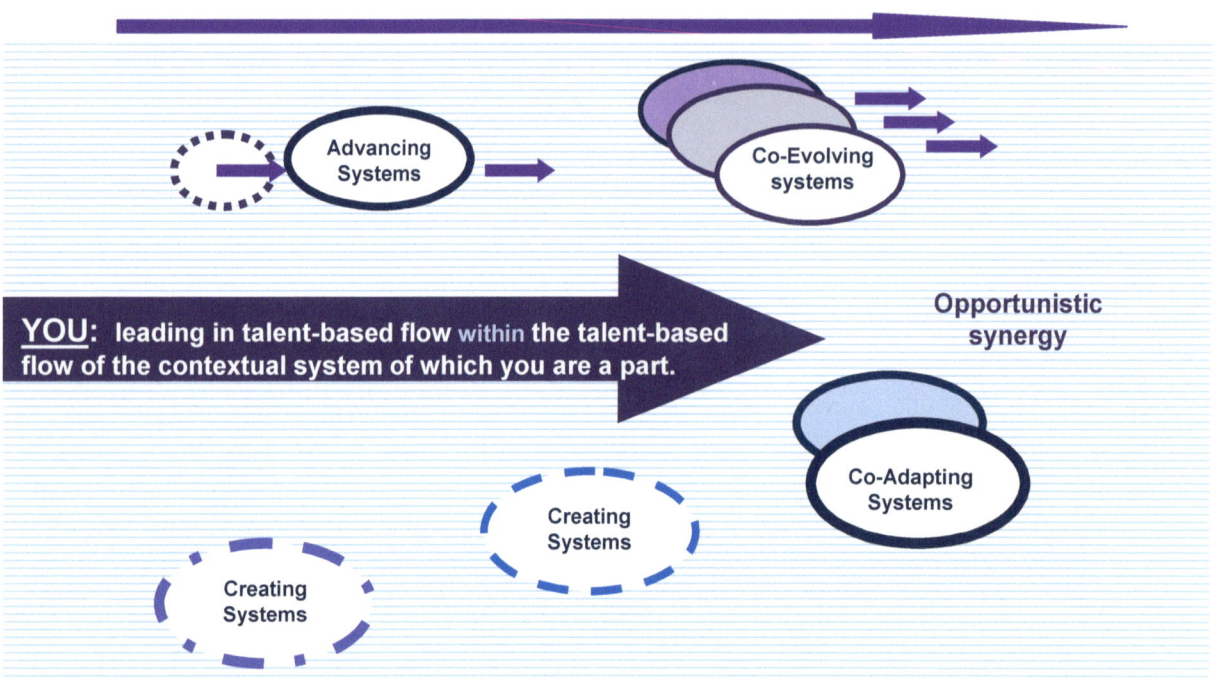

Determining your Formula 4   204

LEADERING™ LEADERSHIP / INDIVIDUAL DEVELOPMENT DIRECTIONS

LEADERING™ AMPLIFIES LEADER DRIVES

Manager	Transitional Change Leader	Transformational Change Leader	Creational Leader / Frontiering Leader
Run an existing business as is	Linearly advance an existing business • Incremental upgrades • Harvest	Non-linearly advance an existing business • Turnarounds • Explosive Growth • Merge 2 existing businesses	Create the unknown or Penetrate the unknown • Business startups • Pioneering / Frontiering • Re-engineering • New ventures • Innovation

As leader drives strengthen, leader impact increases:
INCREASED DRIVES to change – creativity/creation – frontiering™
INCREASED BELIEF CHANGES MADE

| Systems maintenance | Increasing systems advancement | | Systems Creation: including new systems from re-grouping existing systems |

Managers run existing systems ➔ Leaders create and advance human systems

As individuals advance along the leadership development continuum, their ability to advance reality increases. If there is no change in beliefs, there is no change in reality. If there is no change on reality, leadership has not occurred. The magnitude of change is the measure of leadership in the Leadering™ paradigm.

18-4G   Formula 4   © 1995 Lauren Holmes

SYSTEMS-BASED LEADERSHIP or SYSTEM MAXIMIZING FOR LEGACY GOALS

SYSTEM MAINTENANCE Single/Multi-System	SYSTEM ADVANCEMENT Single/Multi-System	SYSTEM CREATION Single/Multi-System	SYSTEM RELATIONSHIPS Multi-System
Manager: very little new creation is required	Change Leadership • Transitional • Transformational • Facilitative Frontier Leadership Flow Leadership	Creational Leadership Quantum Leap Leadership Template Leadership Emergence Leadership	System Relationships: • Co-Evolutionary Leader • Co-Adaptation Leader • Synergy

Increasing belief and information changes - Increasing impact on reality

Leadership extends Nature's systems management in the Leadering™ paradigm:
A SINGLE SYSTEMS MAXIMIZATION TOOLKIT

18-4H   Formula 4   © 2006 Lauren Holmes

System-Based Key Talent Categories

SYSTEM MAINTENANCE Single / Multi-System	SYSTEM ADVANCEMENT Single / Multi-System	SYSTEM CREATION Single / Multi-System	SYSTEM RELATIONSHIPS Each relationship creates a new system
manager: very little new creation is required. **Creativity and creation increase with each column to the right.** **Since beliefs create reality, this means that the need for belief changes increase as your move to the right.**	strategy development people development organization dev't multi-organization synergy process development knowledge development technology development **change leadership** • transitional • transformational • facilitative **frontier leadership** **creational leadership** **flow leadership**	**creational leadership** **frontier leadership** **quantum leap leadership** **template leadership** **emergence leadership** system creation strategy system creation implementation entrepreneur company creation intrapreneur project creation new product creation new technology creation new infrastructure creation new process creation new science creation new knowledge creation new skill creation new frontier creation creation research merger-created system acquisition-created system innovation / creativity	System relationships: • to maintain systems • to advance systems • to create systems **co-evolutionary leadership** **co-adaptation leadership** collaboration and synergy business web development CRM: customer relationship management customer development customer chain development supplier chain development network development relationship building team building market development unifying and integrating problem solving conflict resolution peace keeping negotiation mergers and acquisitions relationship strategy/vision relationship-related implementation

→ **Increasing belief and information changes**
Increasing impact on reality

In the Leadering™ paradigm, leadership and peak legacy protocol extends nature's systems management. This exercise demonstrates
LEADERING'S SINGLE SYSTEMS MAXIMIZATION TOOLKIT

18-4l   Formula 4   © 2006 Lauren Holmes

Systems-Based Leadership or Goal-Directed Systems Maximizing

Which System Types do your key talents advance?

SYSTEM TYPES

- **individual system**
- **multi-individual system**
- **organizational system**
- **multi-organizational system**
- **knowledge system**
- **process system**

- you, a person, a follower, your child
- individuals *en masse*: a consumer market, a university
- a group of people: an organization or company
- a business web or community
- a science, a field, a discipline
- leadership development, business process, reengineering

18-4J Formula 4

© 2006 Lauren Holmes

Nonlinear continuum directions

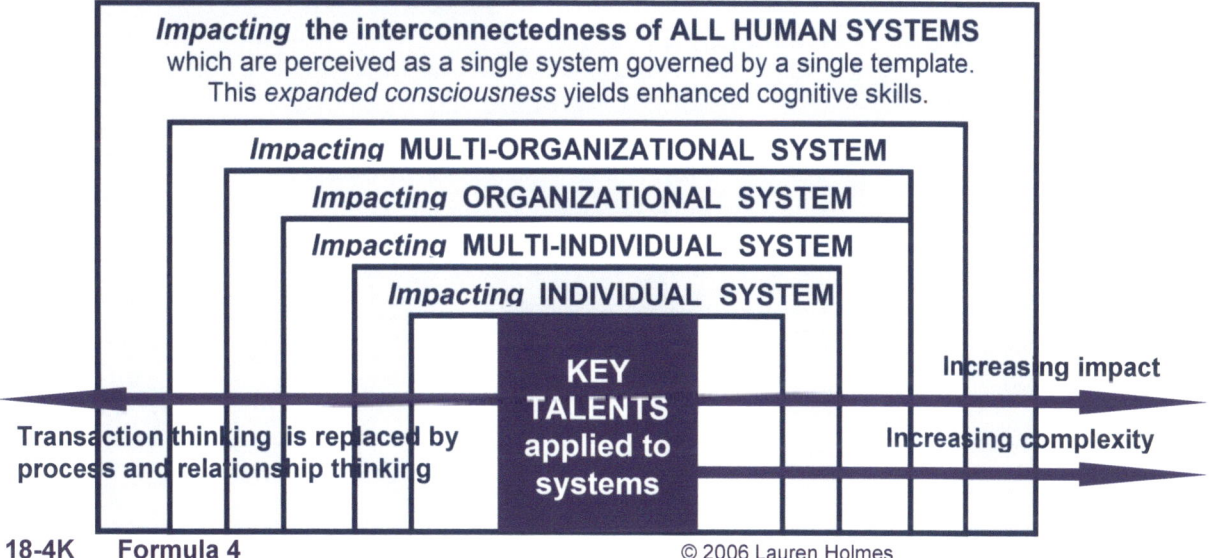

18-4K Formula 4

© 2006 Lauren Holmes

CREATING WORLD LEADERS

YOUR REALITY   ORGANIZATION   INDUSTRY   BUSINESS ECOSYSTEM   CIVILIZATION

POWER MUST INCREASE TO:

> **Imprint Beliefs** → **Unify Identities** → **Increase Creations**

18-4L   Formula 4   © 1995 Lauren Holmes

COMPETENCIES targeted by traditional leadership dev't programs	META-COMPETENCIES and DRIVES targeted by Leadering™ Shared by leaders, entrepreneurs, innovators, achievers
develop and deliver value command and control planning (strategic, tactical, vision) trend analysis financial management marketing/sales management customer relationship mgt - CRM IT management operations management project management performance management knowledge management organization learning risk management decision-making problem resolution process management business process reengineering change management HR management team building relationship building / maintenance conflict resolution globalization	**Systems-Based and Core-Based Operation** systems thinking, relational thinking, big-picture thinking, conceptual skills, belief system management, model development and application, system co-evolution and adaptation, leadership (advancing human systems in opportunistic synergy) **Accelerating and Continuous Development** • conditioned reflexes are installed to trigger multi-front life-long advancement and leadership dev't • Addictive drives are heightened so one is pulled to growth. • learning to learn, mental agility, adaptivity, expanding self-expression and self-awareness, belief engineering, expanding consciousness **Improved and Improving Cognitive Capabilities** • thinking: conceptual, inductive, deductive, abstract, relational, big-picture, • learning to learn, mental agility, pattern recognition, internally referenced, emotional intelligence, use of models, theories, and inferences **Expertise with Ambiguity and the Unknown** • **pioneering**: penetrating the unknown • **creativity/innovation**: bringing unknown into being systems thinking, informationless decision-making, abstract thinking, conceptual skills, pattern recognition, trend perception, change detection, environmental scanning, problem reframing, ambiguity resolution **Improved Performance** flow (our peak performance state), enhanced functionality, systems-based operation, accelerated implementation through quantum leap change management **Addictive Drives cultivated and capitalized upon by Leadering™** (the more you use them, the more you want to use them): • Drives to: learning, pioneering, creativity, innovation, meaning, positive emotions, adaptivity, creativity, learning knowledge, achievement, flow, (the optimal experience), self-expression, self-knowledge, advancement, unity, growth • Drives to using and improving your key talents - a must for operating at your full potential

Leadering's meta-competencies enable better assimilation and application of traditional competency development programs

Traditionally, leaders are developed bottom up skill by skill
Leadering™ uses a single paradigm shift to an integrated system of meta-competencies, drives, reflexes, and beliefs.

Traditionally, senior leaders use different meta-competencies.
Leadering™ offers a single systems maximization toolkit for use universally thus unifying organizations around a single culture and modus operandi. Leadership is distributed.

Notice how most leader competencies are system-based and designed to improve the flow of systems to congruence based on the 15 leader dynamics or paradigm dynamics of Leadering™

HOW GROWTH IS BUILT INTO LEADERING™

The Key Leadering™ Paradigm Growth Players

System Core:
System Flow engine:
- flow pursuit of the system
- key talents
- core addictive drives

System Template:
- immutable beliefs
- changeable beliefs: event-driven template upgrade process

System Meta-Competencies

Conditioned Reflexes

Leadering™ System Management Toolkit:
the 15 dynamics
or leader drives:
Systems Mindset
   systems-based dynamic
   expanding consciousness
Advancement Mechanics
   quantum leap dynamic
   templating dynamic
   self-organizing dynamic
   emergence dynamic
Advancement Directions
   knowledge-pursuit drive
   adaptation drive
   evolution drive
   co-evolution drive
   talent-based flow drive
   flow-within-flow drive
Drives for the Unknown:
   frontier-pursuit drive
   creation / creativity-pursuit drive

Five Talent-based Operating Formulas
lifetime development, greatest lifetime performance, leadership, leadership dev't, greatest leader lifetime performance

Self- or **System-Initiated Quantum Leaps**

Nature-Initiated Quantum Leaps
imbedded in the flow-to-flow
- coincidences (multi-system synergy,
- co-evolution, co-adaptation)
- spontaneous knowledge
- spontaneous creativity
- facilitating events
- flow states

for opportunistic synergy, co-evolution, co-adaptation, creative problem-solving, and flow-within-flow

**Talent-Based Themes of
your 'Life System'**
   an unpaid work theme
   a knowledge-pursuit theme
   a spontaneous knowledge theme
   a frontier-pursuit theme
   a creativity-pursuit theme
   a talent-based creative expression theme
   a meaning-pursuit theme
   the theme(s) of talent-based flow states
   a flow-to-flow theme,
   theme(s) of talent-based projects
   a naturality expansion theme
   a resonance theme
   a positive emotion theme

SAMPLE CATEGORIES OF LEADERING'S BUILT-IN GROWTH

CONTINUOUSLY IMPROVING PERFORMANCE
1. Increasing time operating in peak performance and peak advancement flow states
2. Depth of your talent-based flow states increases with each experience thus increasing performance further
3. Event-driven belief upgrade process continually improves performance through more supportive beliefs

CONTINUOUSLY INCREASING IMPACT
1. Increasing impact of creations, magnitude of advancement of reality, and reality creation precision
2. Reality creation precision
3. Increasing creativity and innovation
4. An increase in the level of complexity handled: from single system to multiple systems impact; from transactions to process; from process to quantum leaps; from linear to nonlinear; more impactful quantum leaps impacting more systems more quickly

CONTINUOUS DEVELOPMENT
Addiction to continuous development:
- the continuous increase in drives which addict you to using and improving your system of core talents
- these addictive drives cause the continuous improvement of your system of core talents becomes the founding dynamic of your life to which the other segments of your life are integrated.
- an accelerating increase in speed of development of your system of core talents
- the continuous increase in the development of drives associated with meta-competencies such as frontiering, creativity, learning to learn, and learning agility which promote continuous development
- addiction to flow states which continuously improve your key talents, functionality, and performance

CONTINUOUSLY INCREASING FUNCTIONALITY
1. Continuous increase in the specialization of your system of core talents
2. Accelerating improvement of abilities to use your core talents
3. Increasing ability to penetrate the unknown or bring the unknown into existence and a craving for both: frontiering and creativity.
4. Continuous improvement in your facility for nonlinear quantum leaps to speed advancement of your system and other systems
5. Systems-based modus operandi: single toolkit for advancing systems, continuous increase in your ability to advance systems and to create new systems
6. Continuous acquisition and improvement of meta-competencies associated with successful leaders, entrepreneurs, innovators and high achievers. (Meta-competencies improve the ability to assimilate and use competencies): continuous development, improved cognitive capabilities, improved performance. These allow you to move more quickly easily and safely into unknown territory and frontiers, increase your creativity and innovation, increase your knowledge-acquisition capabilities, and increase your ability to court coincidences and facilitating events which will improve your performance of your art.
7. Continuous improvement to cognitive skills:
    - concept formation, conceptualization of complex ideas, abstract thinking, deductive and inductive logic, problem reframing, dealing with multiple perspectives and ambiguity, skillful formulation of ends, ways, means
    - frame of reference development: systems understanding, environmental scanning, pattern recognition
    - proactive thinking using critical, creative, and reflective thinking
    - analysis of complicated events, trend perception, change detection, creative and opportunistic problem-solving
    - deployment of models, theories and inferences
    - visualization, addressing, and capitalization of complex interrelationships: see the interaction of more systems and the opportunities for synergy and co-evolution; impact more systems, impact more complex systems, impact larger systems
    - big-picture thinking and seeing more patterns to have more information for decision-making and strategic and tactical planning

THE LEADING™ CORE CONGRUENCE EXERCISES

These exercises are designed to identify the core of your system which is being acted upon by natural forces inside and outside of you so you can comply with and capitalize on them and avoid operating contrary to them.

FLOW EXPLOITATION EXERCISES
for maximum performance and advancement

Life Theme exercises
- key talent determination
- flow to flow determination

Key talent Determination exercises
- system-based key talent exercise
- various other exercises

5 Talent-Based Operating Formulas exercises
1: your lifetime development formula
2: your greatest lifetime achievement formula
3: your natural leader formula
4: your leadership development formula
5: your greatest leader performance formula

BELIEF MAXIMIZATION EXERCISES
for Core Congruence

Belief Template Analysis and Upgrade:
- beneficial belief determination:
  - ideal talent-based and flow-based beliefs
  - identity beliefs, reality creation beliefs
- problem belief determination:
  - fear beliefs, toxic beliefs, conflicting beliefs
- event-driven template upgrade process
- quantum leap template exchange process:
  - goal-packaging identities, reincarnation

Action Learning Experimentation
- proving beliefs create reality
- improving belief engineering in your own and other systems
- improving template determination / design
- quantum leap experimentation

YOUR FLOW ENGINE:

Natural forces inside and outside of you act on your core

YOUR BELIEF TEMPLATE

Your belief template governs both you and your reality as a single system

Beliefs are information storage units like genes

YOUR CORE CONSISTS OF:

1. **KEY TALENTS**

2. **ADDICTIVE DRIVES**
   pulling you to use your key talents

   *Note: Your key talents and associated drives are the immutable beliefs below. They continuously
   - create your reality and
   - are being acted upon by the flow to flow and Leadering's built-in growth continuums which amplify core impact.

3. **IMMUTABLE BELIEFS**
   (innate gene-based beliefs)
   These define the essence of your system and why it came together in the first place. These beliefs are genetically based and inherent to the built-in creative expression of your system. See *Note above.

4. **CHANGEABLE BELIEFS**
   ideally designed to support the key talents, addictive drives, and immutable beliefs to maximize your performance, development, and survival in biological terms. The goal is core congruence.

18-4Q   Formula 4   © 2006 Lauren Holmes

*im·mu·ta·ble: unchanging or unchangeable: not changing or not able to be changed

LIFE-LONG FORMULA REFINEMENT

Refinements to these 5 formulas are a life-long process based on action-learning experimentation.

Refinements are required as one continuously intensifies and expands around one's dynamic core:

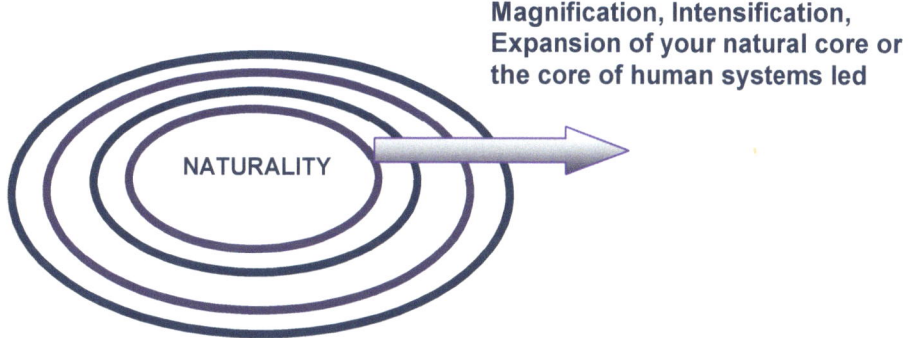

Magnification, Intensification, Expansion of your natural core or the core of human systems led

Refinements are required as one's use of one's key talents narrows to specialization.

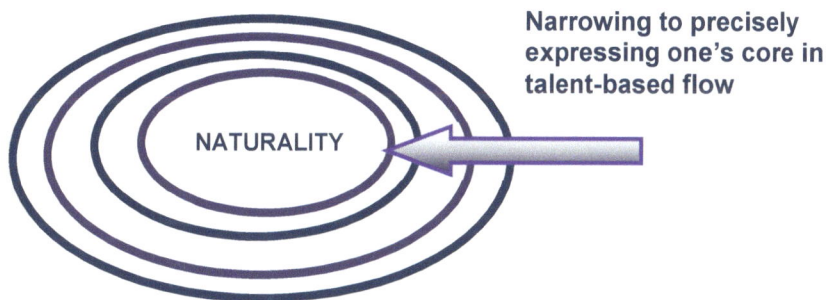

Narrowing to precisely expressing one's core in talent-based flow

Refinements will also be necessary as the flow to flow changes direction and/or brings different co-evolving systems into your context.

18-4R   Formula 4   © 2006 Lauren Holmes

THE LEADERING™ QUANTUM LEAP PROCESS

Design it!   Feel it!   Be it!

PRE-LEAP
1. Choose the right quantum leap or post-leap state:
2. Define the post-leap state with clarity:
3. Define the post-leap state without previous limitations or toxicity
4. Emotionally template the post-leap state
5. Add the information to fuel emergence
6. Expect the unexpected post-leap

LEAP
1. Release the linear connection to the past
2. Feel yourself 100% fluid
3. Feel the post-leap state
4. Feel who the "post-leap you" will be
5. Commit to the quantum leap
6. Make an abrupt, no-return, reincarnation
7. Trigger spontaneous self-organization by intent

POST-LEAP
1. Operate as if the quantum leap was successful
2. Walk around as the person with the post-leap reality
3. Hold this new identity until reality restructures
4. Ignore evidence of events created by the old template
5. Trigger cascading quantum leaps by intent
6. Establish quantum leaping as a way of life
7. Consolidate your new quantum leap expert beliefs

18-4S   Formula 4   © 1998 Lauren Holmes

FORMULAS 3, 4, and 5: Advancing your personal system by creating, advancing, and maximizing other systems:

Leadering™ Leadership and Leadership Development

Continuum Start Point:
Formula 3:
talent-based leadership

Continuum End Point:
Formula 5: greatest level of talent-based leadership

Formulas 1 and 4 share a development continuum:
Formula 4 talent-based leader development continuum is a subset development stream of the Formula 1 lifetime key talent development continuum.

Lifetime development and leadership development define the same continuum in the Leadering™ paradigm:
the expansion of the innate core of your system while creating and expanding the foundational core of other systems.

18-4T   Formula 4   © 2006 Lauren Holmes

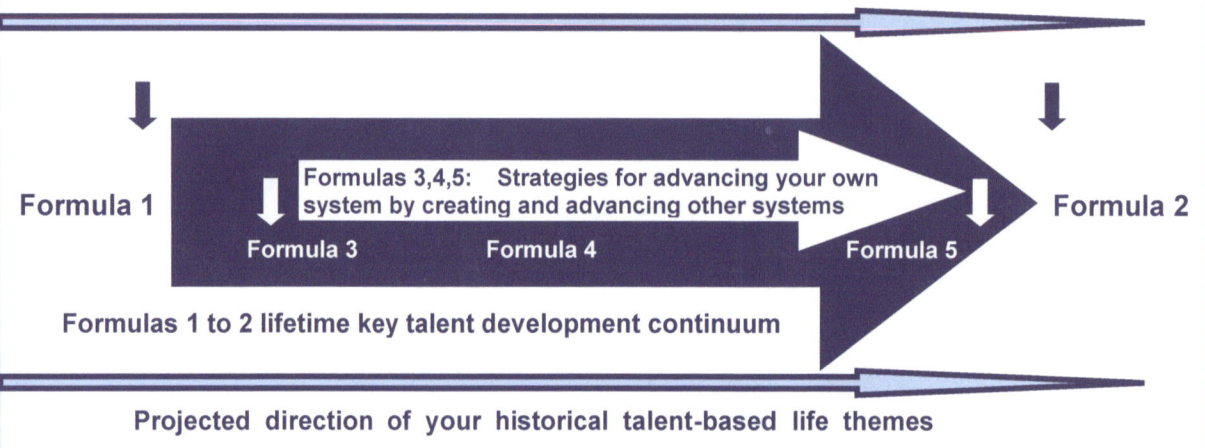

FORMULAS 1 and 2:   Advancing your personal system

Identified by Core Determination Exercises:
- Life themes exercises
- Key talent determination exercises

FORMULAS 3, 4, and 5:   Advancing your personal system by creating, advancing, and maximizing other system:

- Determined by the lifetime development continuum defined by formulas 1 and 2
- Core Determination Exercises: systems-based key-talent application exercise

FORMULA 5

Leadering™ re-structures one's life to enable one to operate at full power in talent-based "flow" states, our peak-performing, peak-growth state, the goal state-of-being promoted in the Leadering™ paradigm.

7 PERSONALIZING THE LEADERING™ PARADIGM

I FLOW MAXIMIZATION EXERCISES continued

Determining your 5 Formulas:

Exercises, notes, and questions are provided to assist you in determining each of your 5 formulas for maximizing yourself, other human systems, and the Leadering™ paradigm for goal achievement. The repetition of some figures is to enable you to have everything in one place for determining each formula. It is only necessary to derive your best hypothesis to test out for confirmation of each personal formula. Use as much or as little of this support material as is necessary for you to achieve this goal. Everyone's needs are different.

Formula 1: 14 figures
Formula 2:   8 figures
Formula 3: 17 figures
Formula 4: 18 figures
Formula 5: 13 figures

Formula 5: Your greatest talent-based operation as a leader
Maximized leader formula

DESCRIPTION
Destination

- **Formula 2 is the maximized operation of the individual.**
- **Formula 5 is the maximized operation of the leader or 'systems maximizer'.**

Relationship to other formulas:
Formula 2 is the culmination of a lifetime of amplifying the core of your system and its system of key talents. Formula 5 is this culmination expressed in systems advancement terms.

Formula 5 is Formula 2 in systems terms plus your personalized leadership modus operandi of formula 3 merged with your talent-based leadership development of formula 1 and 4

This is formula 2 maximization relating to advancing other systems.
At your maximum expansion and functionality: what is your level of operating for your maximum impact on reality by creating and advancing systems

Based on your 4 previous formulas, determine your greatest lifetime level of performance as a talent-based, system-based leader.
Determine your ultimate advancement as an individual and a leader based on
- the continuous intensification of your key talents, and
- given your formula 2 for your greatest performance as an individual

The result of the 4 previous formulas is a fully integrated customized foundation for greatness as a leader and an individual upon which classic leader competencies can be embedded.

Highest functionality and operating levels
What would be the dimensions of your ultimate performance level as a leader?
In generic terms, what will be your greatest level of capability for causing advances in reality?

The only foundation for greatness as a leader is to be at full power, peak performance and peak advancement. In other words, being in talent-based flow state while you are in a leadership role.

18-5A   Formula 5   © 2006 Lauren Holmes

Formula 5: Your greatest talent-based operation as a leader
Maximized leader formula
INSTRUCTIONS - 1

Destination

If you are operating with your key talents at their maximum as you defined in Formula 2, what will be your greatest level of operation as a talent-based, system-based leader or individual applying those same key talents to the advancement of other human systems to achieve shared goals?

Take the below into consideration to determine your greatest lifetime level of operation through your skill at capitalizing on other human systems to achieve goal realities:

1. Your formula 2 greatest performance or level of operation as an individual

2. Your formula1-formula2 lifetime development continuum based on Leadering's built-in growth continuums

3. Your formula 3 strategy for capitalizing on, co-evolving with, and adapting to other human systems in the service of shared meaningful goals

4. All of the growth continuums, mechanisms and drives built into the Leadering™ paradigm which integrate into your formula 4 talent-based leadership development operating strategy, capabilities, and modus operandi including:

5. Projecting your discovered historical life themes with respect to using and improving your key talents into the future, especially your
   - unpaid work theme
   - talent-based knowledge-pursuit or learning-pursuit theme
   - creation/creativity-pursuit themes
   - frontiering-pursuit theme

6. The highest levels of achievement and impact on reality that you have envisioned for yourself throughout the Leadering™ program: generically, what will be the greatest legacy of applying your key talents to advance reality by capitalizing on all the human systems available to you?

7. The highest levels of functionality and way of operating that you have envisioned for yourself throughout the Leadering™ program

8. Being in talent-based flow state every day for the rest of your life: to enter this state, you must be applying your key talents to do the work your system is meant to do, and which your addictive drives are pulling you to do, but extended beyond your previous capabilities. it is your peak performing and peak advancing state. Every flow state adds functionality to your system

9. Given your skills and capabilities are extended by nature's machinery and the Leadering™ paradigm machinery or system of drives and dynamics so that you can operate beyond the potential of your system

10. Sitting in the driver's seat for the Leadering™ paradigm machinery which is personalized or customized to the forces and drives acting on the core of your system from inside and outside.

Formula 5: Your greatest talent-based operation as a leader
Maximized leader formula
INSTRUCTIONS - 2

Destination

IDEAL OUTCOME:

A working hypothesis:

The result of the 4 previous formulas is a fully integrated customized foundation for greatness as a leader and an individual upon which classic leader competencies can be embedded.

The 5 formulas can be written individually or as a single cohesive strategy for the peer advisory database as long as peers and co-workers can quickly understand your core so as to interpret how the flow-to-flow is acting on it at any time for you or them to capitalize on the situation.

18-5C   Formula 5   © 2006 Lauren Holmes

Formula 5: Your greatest talent-based operation as a leader
Maximized leader formula
QUESTIONS - 1

Destination

QUESTIONS to help you determine your maximized leader formula based on the application of your key talents to the advancement of systems as prescribed for the Leadering™ paradigm:

Maximizing human systems: yours and others

1. Maximized operation is based on using one's greatest talents and strengths:
   - Formula 2 is the maximized operation of the individual
   - Formula 5 is the maximized operation of the leader or 'systems maximizer'.

   What is the ultimate level of operation that you can conceive of for yourself if you can capitalize on other human systems?

2. Formula 5 merges:
   - your formula 2 maximum level of operating with your key talents with
   - your formula 4 leadership development continuum to determine your maximum level of operation as a talent-based systems-based leader, and
   - your formula 3 talent-based leadership modus operandi or your ability to advance reality by advancing systems using your key talents

   a. What is the ultimate level of operation that you can conceive of for yourself?

   b. What kind of work will you be doing that advances reality and human systems?

   c. What is your greatest lifetime level of performance and operation as a leader based on the maximum levels of development of your key talents in the 4 previous formulas.

   d. What would be the dimensions of your ultimate operating level and functionality as a talent-based, systems-based leader?

   e. Generically describe your greatest levels of capability for causing reality to advance.

   f. If you were to become the greatest leader you could be, what work based on your key talents would you be doing? How would you be changing reality?

   g. If you are frontiering new territory every day to take your key talents to the next level as required to achieve and sustain talent-based flow state, what would you be doing at your maximum?

   h. If you experienced all of the growth processes built into the Leadering™ paradigm, what would your talent-based leadership development process or continuum look like?

   i. If you are changing reality at your greatest conceivable level by advancing other human systems using your key talents, what is the generic description of what you would be doing?

Formula 5: Your greatest talent-based operation as a leader
Maximized leader formula

QUESTIONS - 2:

Destination

QUESTIONS continued

Human systems impacted by you using and improving your key talents as a talent-based leader or system maximizer:

3. If you develop your talents to the maximum you have determined for the growth continuum defined by formula 1 and formula 2:
   - what categories of systems will you impact and advance and how?
   - what kind of systems are you applying your key talents to at the maximum possible growth of those key talents?
   - what kinds of human systems will you be creating, advancing or linking into new systems?
   - What are the most complex systems you will be impacting at the height of your leadership strength

Operating the Leadering™ Machinery

4. If you mastered the use of the 15 dynamics in the single Leadering™ systems maximization toolkit, what would your leadership look like and how would it evolve over time in the Leadering™ paradigm.
   Imagine you have all of nature's systems maximization capability, how would you advance the systems in your world to maximum impact. As nature, how would you maximize your system in order to accomplish that maximum impact?

18-5E   Formula 5   © 2006 Lauren Holmes

Formula 5: Your greatest talent-based operation as a leader
Maximized leader formula
Quantum Leap Suggestions - 1

Destination

YOUR FORMULA 5 MERGES CORE UPGRADE, EXPANSION AND REALIGNMENT QUANTUM LEAPS:

Note: The below quantum leaps will not only revise your formula 5 post-leap state of operation but the post leaps for all 5 talent-based operating formulas. Revisit the previous formulas to adjust your operating strategies and destinations for within the Leading™ paradigm to include your upgrades, expansions and realignments as informed by the below formula 5 quantum leaps.

Quantum leap to your ultimate formula 5 operating strategy and state of capability in the Leading™ paradigm.

Merge and resolve the following previously identified information to begin to define a stable, fully integrated post-leap state for formula 5:

1. Revisit your lifetime development continuum (F1-F2) to ensure you have clarity about how your system will be advancing based on the expansion and intensification of your key talents to their maximum through frontier after frontier. Be sure to revisit the below contributors to your first 4 formulas:

    - the subset formula 4 development continuum for advancing you along your F1-F2 continuum by capitalizing on human systems to achieve your growth and creation goals
      (your formula 4 leader or systems maximizer development continuum)
    - the growth mechanisms built into the Leading™ paradigm for advancing one's core system of key talents and associated drives
    - the projection into the future of your personal historical life themes indicating the addictive drives pulling you to use and improve your key talents along the flow-to-flow
    - the 15 leader dynamics of the Leading™ systems maximization toolkit (and nature's systems maximization process) and your ability to not only apply these dynamics to advance your own system but any human systems.
    - being continuously upgraded by operating in your peak-performing and peak-advancing flow states incited by using and improving your key talents.

2. Now add the following to the integrated formula 5 post-leap state your are building:

    - Quantum leap to a leader who has successfully operated for over 10 years at your formula 5 greatest level of application of your key talents routinely advancing and capitalizing on human systems to achieve goal realities. Assume you are now able to orchestrate large, complex, meaningful systems to dramatically change the world as a daily occurrence.

    - Assimilate the following identities based on your having mastered the 15 leader dynamics: an evolution leader, a co-evolution and synergy leader, a frontiering leader, a creational leader, a flow leader, a quantum leap leader, a system-based and talent-based leader, an opportunistic adaptation leader, a system creator, a human systems maximizer, a reality creation expert, a leader with expansive consciousness, and the like.

Formula 5: Your greatest talent-based operation as a leader
Maximized leader formula
Quantum Leap Suggestions - 2

Destination

- Assimilate nature's expertise for creating, integrating, and orchestrating thousands of human systems simultaneously for synergy and co-evolution in the achievement of shared goals. Assume you can combine the ideal parts from many systems to bring new goal realities into existence.

- Assume that you are now effortlessly merged within the flow of all human systems (figure 18-5J) and routinely extend your own capabilities by merging with or assimilating elements of other human systems relevant to your growth and creation goals.

- Assume you have now achieved expanded consciousness and can both see and capitalize on the interconnectedness of all human systems. You have moved beyond capitalizing on individuals, beyond orchestrating human systems, to capitalizing on systems within systems - systems of infrastructures - which underpin the operation of the human race. You are now able to drive the machinery underlying the human race. You are now able to step into nature's catalytic role in the dance of creativity of human systems as they ping off of each other: adapting, co-evolving and creating new footprints in reality. Your span of influence moves into each new unknown territory as your goals dictate.

- Assume you are now so integrated into the pulse of humanity that you are able to successfully channel the ongoing flow of human systems to offload nature's process of evolution to achieve conscious evolution in the direction that maximizes the most human systems - especially in the territory of the next frontiers of applying your key talents as you proceed along your F1-F2 lifetime development continuum which is at the foundation of everything you do and every goal you set.

- Assume you have merged with the pulsating process of creating endless new systems from existing systems - bringing them together temporarily or permanently to achieve new goal realities. These new systems form the trail you leave behind your as your advance the iterations of growth and creation, growth and creation, as you experience the endless expansion s of your key talents at the core of your being.

3. Make your Formula 5 quantum leap into the plethora of systems pulsating at the heart of the machinery of the Leading™ paradigm.

18-5G   Formula 5   © 2006 Lauren Holmes

HOW GROWTH IS BUILT INTO LEADERING™

The Key Leadering™ Paradigm Growth Players

System Core:
System Flow engine:
- flow pursuit of the system
- key talents
- core addictive drives

System Template:
- immutable beliefs
- changeable beliefs: event-driven template upgrade process

System Meta-Competencies

Conditioned Reflexes

Leadering™ System Management Toolkit: the 15 dynamics or leader drives:
Systems Mindset
- systems-based dynamic
- expanding consciousness

Advancement Mechanics
- quantum leap dynamic
- templating dynamic
- self-organizing dynamic
- emergence dynamic

Advancement Directions
- knowledge-pursuit drive
- adaptation drive
- evolution drive
- co-evolution drive
- talent-based flow drive
- flow-within-flow drive

Drives for the Unknown:
- frontier-pursuit drive
- creation / creativity-pursuit drive

Five Talent-based Operating Formulas
lifetime development, greatest lifetime performance, leadership, leadership development, greatest leader lifetime performance

Self- or System-Initiated Quantum Leaps

Nature-Initiated Quantum Leaps imbedded in the flow-to-flow
- coincidences (multi-system synergy, co-evolution, co-adaptation)
- spontaneous knowledge
- spontaneous creativity
- facilitating events
- flow states

for opportunistic synergy, co-evolution, co-adaptation, creative problem-solving, and flow-within-flow

Talent-Based Themes of your 'Life System'
- an unpaid work theme
- a knowledge-pursuit theme
- a spontaneous knowledge theme
- a frontier-pursuit theme
- a creativity-pursuit theme
- a talent-based creative expression theme
- a meaning-pursuit theme
- the theme(s) of talent-based flow states
- a flow-to-flow theme,
- theme(s) of talent-based projects
- a naturality expansion theme
- a resonance theme
- a positive emotion theme

© 2006 Lauren Holmes

Determining your Formula 5 226

FORMULAS 3, 4, and 5: Advancing your system by creating, maximizing, and capitalizing on other human systems

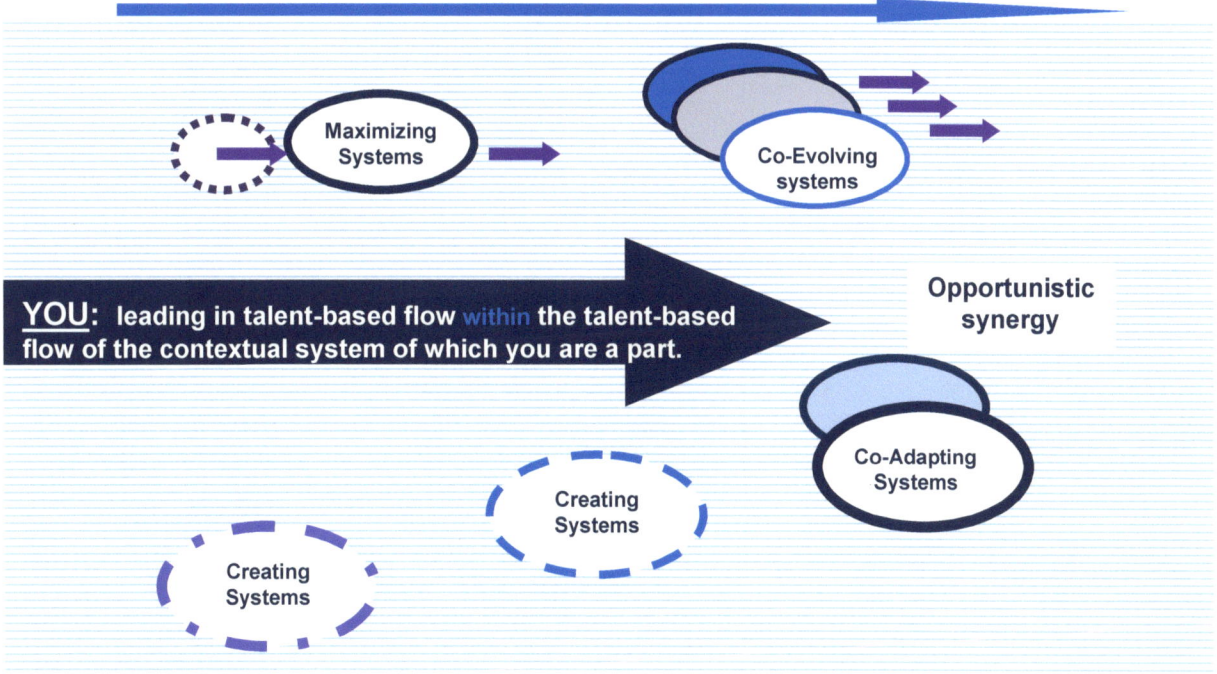

Talent-based system leadership in the flow to flow

YOU: leading in talent-based flow *within* the talent-based flow of the contextual system of which you are a part.

Opportunistic synergy

Advancing your system by applying your key talents to other systems	Individual Systems	Multi-Individual Systems	Organization Systems	Multi-Organization Systems	Knowledge Systems	Process Systems

Leadering™ provides a single systems maximization toolkit for advancing your personal system or those that you choose to lead for *peak legacy*.

18-5J   Formula 5   © 2006 Lauren Holmes

COMPETENCIES targeted by traditional leadership development programs	META-COMPETENCIES and DRIVES targeted by Leadering™ Shared by leaders, entrepreneurs, innovators, achievers
develop and deliver value command and control planning (strategic, tactical, vision) trend analysis financial management marketing/sales management customer relationship mgt - CRM IT management operations management project management performance management knowledge management organization learning risk management decision-making problem resolution process management business process reengineering change management HR management team building relationship building / maintenance conflict resolution globalization	**Systems-Based and Core-Based Operation** systems thinking, relational thinking, big-picture thinking, conceptual skills, belief system management, model development and application, system co-evolution and adaptation, leadership (advancing human systems in opportunistic synergy) **Accelerating and Continuous Development** • conditioned reflexes are installed to trigger multi-front life-long advancement and leadership development. • Addictive drives are heightened so one is pulled to growth. • learning to learn, mental agility, adaptivity, expanding self-expression and self-awareness, belief engineering, expanding consciousness **Improved and Improving Cognitive Capabilities** • thinking: conceptual, inductive, deductive, abstract, relational, big-picture, • learning to learn, mental agility, pattern recognition, internally referenced, emotional intelligence, use of models, theories, and inferences **Expertise with Ambiguity and the Unknown** • **pioneering**: penetrating the unknown • **creativity/innovation**: bringing unknown into being systems thinking, informationless decision-making, abstract thinking, conceptual skills, pattern recognition, trend perception, change detection, environmental scanning, problem reframing, ambiguity resolution **Improved Performance** flow (our peak performance state), enhanced functionality, systems-based operation, accelerated implementation through quantum leap change management **Addictive Drives cultivated and capitalized upon by Leadering**™ (the more you use them, the more you want to use them) : • Drives to: learning, pioneering, creativity, innovation, meaning, positive emotions, adaptivity, creativity, learning knowledge, achievement, flow, (the optimal experience), self-expression, self-knowledge, advancement, unity, growth • Drives to using and improving your key talents - a must for operating at your full potential

Leadering's meta-competencies enable better assimilation and application of traditional competency development programs

Traditionally, leaders are developed bottom up skill by skill
Leadering uses a single paradigm shift to an integrated system of meta-competencies, drives, reflexes, and beliefs.

Traditionally, senior leaders use different meta-competencies.
Leadering™ offers a single systems maximization toolkit for use universally thus unifying organizations around a single culture and modus operandi. Leadership is distributed.

Notice how most leader competencies are system-based and designed to improve the flow of systems to congruence based on the 15 leader dynamics or paradigm dynamics of Leadering™

THE LEADERING™ QUANTUM LEAP PROCESS

Design it!   Feel it!   Be it!

PRE-LEAP
1. Choose the right quantum leap or post-leap state:
2. Define the post-leap state with clarity:
3. Define the post-leap state without previous limitations or toxicity
4. Emotionally template the post-leap state
5. Add the information to fuel emergence
6. Expect the unexpected post-leap

LEAP
1. Release the linear connection to the past
2. Feel yourself 100% fluid
3. Feel the post-leap state
4. Feel who the "post-leap you" will be
5. Commit to the quantum leap
6. Make an abrupt, no-return, reincarnation
7. Trigger spontaneous self-organization by intent

POST-LEAP
1. Operate as if the quantum leap was successful
2. Walk around as the person with the post-leap reality
3. Hold this new identity until reality restructures
4. Ignore evidence of events created by the old template
5. Trigger cascading quantum leaps by intent
6. Establish quantum leaping as a way of life
7. Consolidate your new quantum leap expert beliefs

18-5L   Formula 5   © 1998 Lauren Holmes

Co-Evolution

FORMULAS 3, 4, and 5: Advancing your personal system by creating, advancing, and maximizing other systems:

Leadering™ Leadership and Leadership Development

Continuum Start Point:
Formula 3:
talent-based leadership

Continuum End Point:
Formula 5: greatest level of talent-based leadership

Formulas 1 and 4 share a development continuum:
Formula 4 talent-based leader development continuum is a subset development stream of the Formula 1 lifetime key talent development continuum.

Lifetime development and leadership development define the same continuum in the Leadering™ paradigm:
the expansion of the innate core of your system while creating and expanding the foundational core of other systems.

18-5M   Formula 5   © 2006 Lauren Holmes

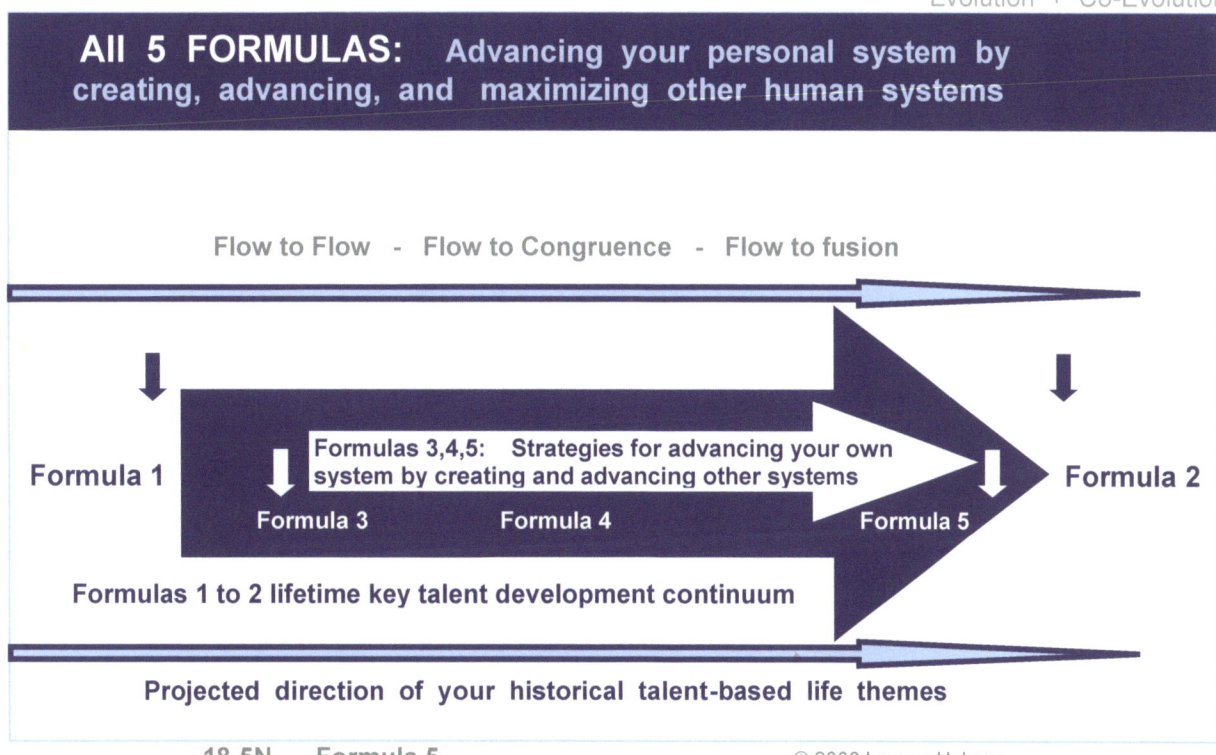

FORMULAS 1 and 2: Advancing your personal system

Identified by Core Determination Exercises:
- Life themes exercises
- Key talent determination exercises

FORMULAS 3, 4, and 5: Advancing your personal system by creating, advancing, and maximizing other system:

- Determined by the lifetime development continuum defined by formulas 1 and 2
- Core Determination Exercises: systems-based key-talent application exercise

The Development of the Leadering Paradigm Shift Program

Unprecedented transformation for unparalleled legacy

Harness the capabilities of other systems
to advance our world beyond your potential

A Childhood Vision
Leadering™ began as a vision for the future of humanity which Lauren Holmes formulated for a high school project.

Experimenting with Leadership
Lauren developed her expertise for organizational and industry change leadership as a top-rated employee in some of the world's largest multinationals (IBM and global financial institutions).

Mid-1980s to Early 1990s:
Learning from Top Global Change Leaders
To broaden her knowledge of leadership and industry and organizational change, Lauren headed an executive search firm dedicated exclusively to the recruitment of change leaders at the board, CEO, and senior executive levels. Lauren interviewed hundreds of top leaders from major global companies, both for requisitioned searches and in partnership with the large relocation counseling firms dealing with the massive release of executives during the recession of the early 90s.

Lauren Holmes
Leadering's Creator,
Developer and Proponent

1990-1993: Formulating the first iteration of Leadering™
Back-to-back interviews with so many executives enabled Lauren to realize that leaders are not operating the way most leadership development theories have specified. As an evolutionary anthropologist and primatologist trained in objective observation, Lauren came to understand leadership differently. She then found science to confirm her observations in such fields as quantum physics, chaos theory, catastrophe theory, the biological sciences, systems biology, systems theory, emergence theory, and evolutionary theory. These are the scientific foundations underpinning Leadering™ which are transparent to practitioners. No scientific discoveries to date disprove Leadering™. In fact, Leadering™ identifies plausible directions in which many scientific fields will eventually advance and how to speed that advance.

With the dearth of jobs due to fear-driven downsizing rather than smart frontiering™ and creation, so much excellent talent was discarded by society. Sadly, the leaders and change facilitators who could have rescued so many were the first to go. Both societal and individual systems were traumatized. **Leadering's mission was born.** With new ways of operating, new functionality, and especially with frontiering™ capability, individual and societal systems could adapt, advance, co-create, synergize, and co-evolve more quickly to avoid damage and suffering. If successful, a maximized individual working within his/her *field of fascination* to achieve *peak legacy* - one's greatest contribution to society - could become an achievable new human right. It would also be the smartest strategy for maximizing global human resources in the service of the world we all share.

1990-2006:   Advancing the Leading™ technology, toolkit, products, services:
Many different corporate identities were required to test out every element of the integrated Leading™ paradigm as it stands today at Leading.com (education) and Frontiering.com (legacy implementation). Action-learning experimentation conforming to scientific method was used.

1990-1991:   First Action-Learning Experimentation: Frontiering™
The first test of the foundational multi-system elements of Leading™ related to its methodology for enabling the penetration of new territory safely and expeditiously - the underpinning system of meta-competencies and drives shared by adept leaders, entrepreneurs, innovators, or high achievers.   This test was achieved by establishing an unprecedented global recycled plastics distribution company for which Lauren Holmes had no credentials or background. Frontiering™ would therefore be required. As the company became successful and globally known within that community, the frontiering™ experiment was terminated. Leading™ had passed its first test.

1991-1995:   Business Professionals: One-on-one
After the first experiment, Lauren determined it would be faster to support others in their application of Leading™ to their own goals than for her to continue to set up her own experiments. Rather than risk her connections and standing in the corporate world, Lauren found safe testing grounds managing the careers of business professionals. She used Leading™ techniques to identify the right client at the right time for each aspect of Leading™ to be tested.

1995-2003:   Corporate Executives: One-on-one
Leading™ services were applied to the careers of corporate executives locally and then internationally through the corporate identities of Teamlink Canada and TeamLink International.

Experimentation was predominantly with executives of multinationals because they usually had well-developed cognitive skills and other capabilities allowing Lauren to experiment at the upper end of the meta-competencies that Leading™ is designed to instill in practitioners. Multi-national clients included: Royal Bank, AT&T, IBM, RIM, Bell, BBDO, Young & Rubicam, Canadian Imperial Bank of Commerce and Bank of Montreal. Experimentation also included creating concentrations of individuals using Leading™ in order to learn about the Leading™ culture of an organization operating in the Leading™ paradigm.

2001 to 2005:   Non-Corporate Individuals *en masse:* One-to-many
Lauren needed a safe territory outside of corporations to test out a number of aspects of Leading™ and Leading™ distribution. Accordingly, she wrote a book entitled *Peak Evolution, Beyond Peak Performance and Peak Experience* (2001) around which a global community could form. *Peak Evolution* presents the 1992 iteration of Leading™ in non-corporate terms that would not be intimidating to the general public. Naturality.Net, LLC was the corporate identity used to create this community and it was advertised in the book. There were 4000 people on the global mailing list within the first 4 months and it was an Amazon.com bestseller.

Areas examined through the Naturality.Net community included:
- to develop/test the means to impact more people more quickly with Leading™ methodologies and technologies.
- to develop/test one-to-many techniques where, unlike in corporations, participants were strangers
- to develop/test ways in which Leading™ could impact larger groups of individuals to enable it to be used as a tool for leaders and achievers to maximize and advance organizations to achieve goals.

- to test Leadering-based group processes on many fronts
- to determine how to press natural levers to trigger group change in the way done to this point for individuals
- to experiment with community tools such as chat rooms, discussion and bulletin boards, and other group communication and work tools.
- to experiment with using Leadering™ for community-building inside and outside of corporations
- to market-test Leadering™
- to determine what the competing technologies, theories, and cultural norms were in the market place and how they caused confusion for understanding Leadering™,
- to find ways to circumvent market-related issues: competing technologies, theories, modes of operation, cultural norms, and existing infrastructures. The goal was to ensure that Leadering™ did not conflict with culture, religion, science, and society so that everyone could operate in the Leadering paradigm.
- to test new mass delivery mechanisms: teleclinics, telecalls, weekly and periodic programs, audios, videos, support systems and the best structures for achieving and operationalizing the Leadering™ paradigm shift. These were international to determine the effects of cultural differences
- to develop Lauren's own expertise in a number of areas: the speed and magnitude of group or community transformation, working with non-executives to complement her career-long focus on executives, creating and sustaining a global community, the application of Leadering™ technology to group programs and processes, and the ability to transform groups *en masse* with Leadering™ without the opportunity to use the personal goals and events of each individual's life she had had access to in her Leadering™ work to this point.
- to develop the exercises and techniques that could personalize the Leadering™ paradigm and paradigm shift to each person to empower the generic paradigm shift offered in the audio program (re last item in previous point)
- to test whether the Leadering™ paradigm shift could better be accomplished through audios and visuals. Lauren experimented with audio recordings as the means to raise people's frequencies and thus the breadth of information and the amount of interconnectedness they are able to perceive and assimilate.
Expanded consciousness is key to Leadering's ability to raise functionality
- to create/develop various programs to experiment with how each of the meta-competencies shared by leaders, entrepreneurs, innovators, and top performers could best be instilled.
- to experiment with harnessing the co-evolution of human systems for peak legacy, a key function of leaders and achievers who want to extend their capabilities with those of other systems to achieve beyond their potential.

2002-2007 Corporate Individuals and Groups
One-to-one and One-to-many Programs
Organizational Development Services

What was learned about Leadering™ at Naturality.net, LLC was taken back to the corporate world through Lauren's next corporate identities: Frontiering Leadership Group and ReCareering™. This corporate-based experimentation identified the need for the Leadering™ paradigm shift audio program now offered. Natural leaders feel that the Leadering™ paradigm perfectly defines how they operate. Therefore, many of them requested a tool which allows them to quickly upgrade their organizations to operate as they do. Putting all key people through the Leadering™ paradigm shift program accomplished this.

2005-2007   Leadering™ audio program development

2007   Leadering™ audio program release to individual executive clients
In 2007, the audio-based Leadering™ Paradigm Shift Program replaced *Peak Evolution*. The initial target market was individual corporate executives.

2008-2009   6-week subscriptions to Leadering™ sold to the public and corporations through Leadering.com
Peak Evolution was temporarily taken out of print to facilitate the transition and minimize confusion since Leadering has no overlap with the approach used in *Peak Evolution* even though their paradigms are consistent. However, a second edition and eBook version will be re-released in 2010. The experimentation with Leadering™ continued, especially with an eye to what kind of support people, services and products would be required for a public rollout globally.

2010   Leadering™ program sold to the public through Amazon.com
Educational support for those trying to master Leadering will still be offered through Leadering.com.
Support services include
- identifying client strategies for peak legacy and peak growth
- promoting the re-centering of the individual to the strength of their natural core
- facilitating the paradigm shift and providing support for the Leadering™ exercises
- integrating the paradigm shift into the life of the organization or individual
- empowering sustained operation and accelerated growth within the paradigm, and
- promoting action-learning experimentation associated with the paradigm shift and ongoing operation.

At Frontiering.com, a diversity of Leadering™ service providers supports those wanting to apply Leadering™. Leadering™ is used to design, launch, and accelerate companies, philanthropic organizations, fields of study or invention, and careers customized to an individual's or company's peak legacy, their peak contribution to advancing the world. The foundations are provided for clients to use Leadering™ to break through new frontiers in precisely the territory that fascinates them and to be rewarded for it. Alternatively, we can support you in launching your own structure(s) through which to achieve your peak legacy.

Leadering™ is now positioned to address its mission for creating value, meaning, and progress - maximizing the lives of individuals while maximizing their contribution to advancing our world.

Unprecedented transformation

Peak legacy.

Impact beyond your potential.

LEADERING VISUALS TWO
Paradigm Shift to Peak Legacy

LEADERING SUPPORT
info@leadering.com

EDUCATION: **Leadering.com**   Leadering™ Expertise Development

Educational support for such things as speeding and integrating the paradigm shift, Leadering's paradigm personalization exercises, identifying client strategies for peak legacy, growth, and re-centring to core strength, action-learning experimentation, and breaking through frontiering and adaptivity challenges.

APPLICATION: **Frontiering.com**   Leadering Legacy-Making Services and Products

On your behalf, multi-disciplinary experts will design, launch, and accelerate companies, philanthropic organizations, careers, and fields of study or invention personalized in Leadering terms for your peak legacy until you feel you comfortable taking over. Alternatively, we can support you in launching your own structure(s) through which to achieve your peak legacy.

RECRUITMENT: **Become a Leadering Support Services Provider**

If you wish to provide products and services through either Leadering.com or Frontiering.com you are invited to email the following to info@leadering.com: your proposed offerings, your credentials, and a brief summary of your personal peak legacy findings from Leadering's flow maximization exercises (*Leadering Visuals Two*, recordings 10-18).

www.ingramcontent.com/pod-product-compliance
Lightning Source LLC
Chambersburg PA
CBHW042129010526
44111CB00031B/40